Postcard History Series

Edwardsville

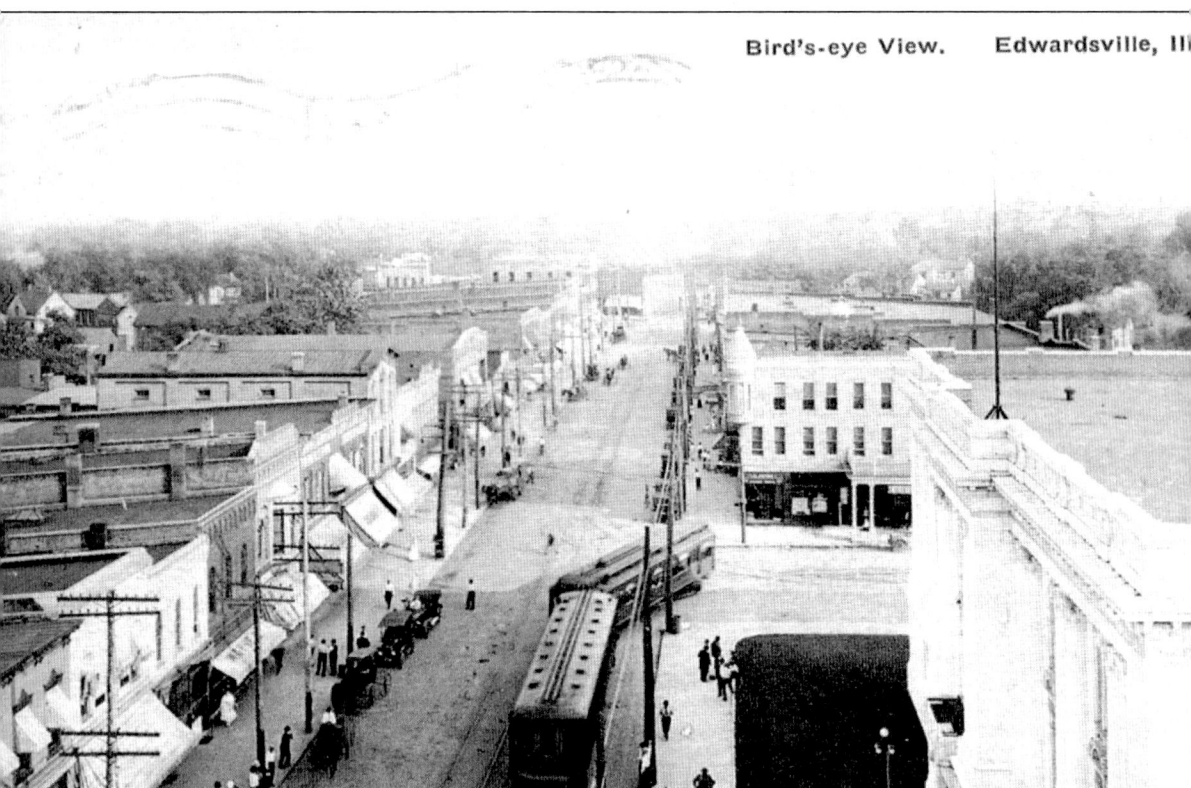

In this photograph, taken around 1917 from the top of the Bank of Edwardsville's new building, one has a bird's-eye view of North Main Street. The Illinois Traction System cars round the corner from North Main Street onto St. Louis Street. At that corner is the Leland Hotel with its distinctive corner turret, and in the foreground on the right is the new Madison County Courthouse, completed in 1915. (Courtesy of SJ Morrison.)

On the front cover: In 1912, Edwardsville and Madison County celebrated a century of history with a weeklong celebration, the Madison County centennial. Many special events were held, and thousands of people attended. Local architect M. B. Kane designed a magnificent plaster of paris arch, which was constructed in front of the Madison County Courthouse. (Courtesy of Neal Strebel.)

On the back cover: Numerous parades were held during the week of the Madison County centennial. During this parade, the members of the 4th Regiment Band pause for a photograph near the intersection of North Main and St. Louis Streets. The city's main streets were adorned with bunting and flags for the week's festivities. (Courtesy of Neal Strebel.)

Postcard History Series

Edwardsville

Cheryl Eichar Jett

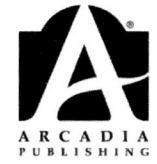

ARCADIA
PUBLISHING

Copyright © 2009 by Cheryl Eichar Jett
ISBN 978-0-7385-6018-2

Published by Arcadia Publishing
Charleston, South Carolina

Printed in the United States of America

Library of Congress Catalog Control Number: 2009926205

For all general information contact Arcadia Publishing at:
Telephone 843-853-2070
Fax 843-853-0044
E-mail sales@arcadiapublishing.com
For customer service and orders:
Toll-Free 1-888-313-2665

Visit us on the Internet at www.arcadiapublishing.com

For Jim

Contents

Acknowledgments 6

Introduction 7

1. Main Street 9
2. Body and Spirit 21
3. Courthouses and Public Buildings 37
4. Going to School 51
5. Residential Streets 63
6. Banks, Business, and Industry 73
7. N. O. Nelson and Leclaire Village 89
8. Getting There 97
9. Living the Social Life 109
10. Parks, Monuments, and the Madison County Centennial 117

Bibliography 127

Acknowledgments

I wish to thank SJ Morrison, June Nealy, Michael A. Sporrer, Neal Strebel, and Madison County Historical Society for sharing their wonderful postcard collections; Dale Jenkins of Illinois Traction Society and SJ Morrison of Madison County Transit for answering my railroad questions; Ethan Firestone, James Lask, Karen Mateyka, and Cindy Reinhardt for reading drafts; Edwardsville Historic Preservation Commission and Madison County Historical Society for assistance, encouragement, and wise counsel; and my editor, Jeff Ruetsche, for his patience and encouragement.

There are many people who have paved the way for this book through their research, writing, and dedication to preserving local history. I am especially grateful for the work done by past and current members of the Edwardsville Historic Preservation Commission, Friends of Leclaire, Madison County Historical Society, and the authors of *Edwardsville: An Illustrated History*, Ellen Nore and Dick Norrish.

Special thanks are due to Cindy Reinhardt for the idea for the book, contacts, suggestions, and general support. And, as always, thank you to my family for your patience, understanding, love, and support throughout this project.

INTRODUCTION

Vintage postcard images of Edwardsville freeze in time the people, places, and events of a century ago. When it is hard to access even recent memory of what building formerly stood where a newly built one now exists, one realizes how elusive and fragile is the past of a century or more ago. Yet the citizens of Edwardsville left glimpses of their lives in postcard messages and letters, newspaper articles and books, and photographs and drawings. Edwardsville's Main Street facade and its other streets have evolved over nearly 200 years of history, but, since its very beginnings, it has stood as the seat of government and a center of banking and trade in Madison County.

Edwardsville began life as a frontier fort and a gateway to settlers in the area. In 1805, early settler Thomas Kirkpatrick acquired title to 100 acres above and to the east of Cahokia Creek. He built one or more cabins in the area of what is now known as O Street, not far from North Main Street. Kirkpatrick's friend Ninian Edwards, appointed territorial governor of Illinois in 1809, designated Kirkpatrick's cabin as the county seat of Madison County. Kirkpatrick honored his friend by naming the new town Edwardsville. A military blockhouse, Fort Russell, was established northwest of Edwardsville in 1811.

By 1820, Kirkpatrick had platted the town; Abraham Prickett, Benjamin Stephenson, and the Pogue brothers had established stores; a U.S. Land Grant Office and an Indian agency had been opened; and Edwardsville boasted a hotel and a bank. A public square was marked off along North Main and Liberty Streets, and upon it was built a log jail. Soon a courthouse and a small county office building were also constructed there. Also by 1820, Benjamin Stephenson and Ninian Edwards had each built a fine two-story brick home—Stephenson's on Buchanan Street still stands today, while Edward's at Buchanan and Vandalia Streets was lost to fire just a few years after its construction.

Soon after Edwardsville was established, pioneer publisher Hooper Warren began the town's first newspaper, the *Spectator*, which was published until 1826, when Warren, a strong believer in the abolition of slavery, left for Cincinnati and sold out to Lippincott and Abbott. Since then, there has always been at least one active newspaper in Edwardsville to record its events. In 1866, James T. Hair in the *Gazetteer of Madison County* noted that "this venerable County Seat has been the local habitation of at least sixteen periodical publications." The *Intelligencer* has been published since 1862.

Another early arrival in Edwardsville was Edward Coles, a Virginian who had inherited slaves but wished to free them. Believing that the ordinance of the Northwest Territory specifically forbade slavery within its territory, he had formulated a plan to emigrate to Illinois and bring with him his slaves in order to free them. Coles had served as secretary to Pres. James Madison and maneuvered to get the appointment as registrar for the land office in Edwardsville. During their journey down the Ohio River, Coles informed his slaves of his plan to issue them freedom papers and to purchase land for them. As Coles ran for governor in Illinois, the question of slavery hung heavy on voters' minds. Missouri to the south was a slave state. Much of early Illinois was settled by people from southern states. In 1822, Coles was elected as the second governor of Illinois, and he led the opposition against strong efforts to call a constitutional convention to legalize slavery in Illinois. In 1824, Coles's political opponents sued him in the courthouse at North Main and Liberty Streets for illegally freeing his slaves. Two monuments to this principled man can be seen in Edwardsville—one at North Main and Liberty Streets on the site where he was sued for freeing his slaves, and one at the northeast corner of Valley View Cemetery on Illinois Route 157.

In the 1830s, Edwardsville's trade was rapidly disappearing, first to St. Louis and then to Alton. Altonians began a movement to have the county seat moved to their city, which at that time was growing at a fast pace due to its location along the river. Only a move by Edwardsville's Edward M. West, who drafted an article of the 1848 Constitution requiring a majority vote to change the location of the county seat, saved Edwardsville's status as the seat of law. Soon farming and trade began to flourish and, after the Civil War, railroad connections came to the city. Several coal mines and small industries were established. N. O. Nelson founded Leclaire Village, a company town, for his new manufacturing complex. Edwardsville was in an upswing. Modern farm machinery, industry, Edward M. West, and N. O. Nelson turned the corner for the city. N. O. Nelson Company workers, contented with profit sharing, fair wages, and the opportunity to own their own homes, constructed cottages along the winding streets of Leclaire. More and more fine homes of entrepreneurs and professional men filled the lots sold on the north side of St. Louis Street, the city's fashionable avenue.

By the time of the 1912 Madison County centennial, Edwardsville had much to celebrate. The city was firmly cemented as the seat of law and government in the county and as a center of banking and trade. A new public library and other public buildings had been constructed. Streets were being paved. Children were attending school and more of them were graduating. The population (including Leclaire) had reached about 5,000 at the dawn of the 20th century. Thousands attended the centennial festivities, and the electric lines and the new motor cars regularly brought visitors back and forth to Edwardsville. Mr. and Mrs. Louis Rieg wrote on the back of a postcard to a friend in Teutopolis that they "arrived safe and all OK at Edwardsville at 8 pm. All we do is loaf. Just came home from the band concert." A woman who signed her name as simply "Edna" wrote a postcard message to a St. Louis friend, "arrived here Friday evening and have been having a fine time ever since. I don't know just when we will be back."

One

MAIN STREET

Edwardsville's first town square, first hotel, first and second courthouses, and first stores were all on North Main Street in an area that came to be known as Lower Town. The first two stores were opened in 1815 and 1816 by Abraham Prickett, who came from Kentucky, and Benjamin Stephenson, who was a Virginian. John Lusk opened the first hotel in 1816 at Main and Union Streets. Edwardsville's status as the county seat and the home of the area land grant office spurred its growth.

However, in the 1830s, nearby St. Louis and then Alton with its tremendous economic growth as a river city during the steamboat age began to pull trade away from Edwardsville. Edwardsville's population and economic strength began a decline. This trend gained momentum as some Altonians strengthened their call to move the county seat to Alton. The shrewd Edward M. West, a store owner and later banker, kept the county seat in Edwardsville. He drafted an article of the 1848 Constitution requiring a majority of voters to approve a change in location for a county seat. Edwardsville's central location in the county won out.

The first big change in Edwardsville's Main Street occurred in the 1850s, when the third courthouse was constructed about a mile farther east on North Main Street, and the town moved along with it to Upper Town. As the new courthouse was being constructed in Upper Town, the U.S. Land Grant Office was closing out in Lower Town, signaling the end of an era. Public lands had been bought up, the land grant office was no longer needed, the population had increased, and a new Main Street was evolving.

Local agriculture was beginning to flourish due to steel plows and other farm machinery, and Edwardsville became a market and milling center. Plank roads enabled farmers to reach town, and the new bridge on the Springfield Road across Cahokia Creek improved travel. In 1964, attorney Leland Buckley remembered that, "When farmers came to town on Saturdays, they'd line the horses up along the courthouse and it was a big day in Edwardsville."

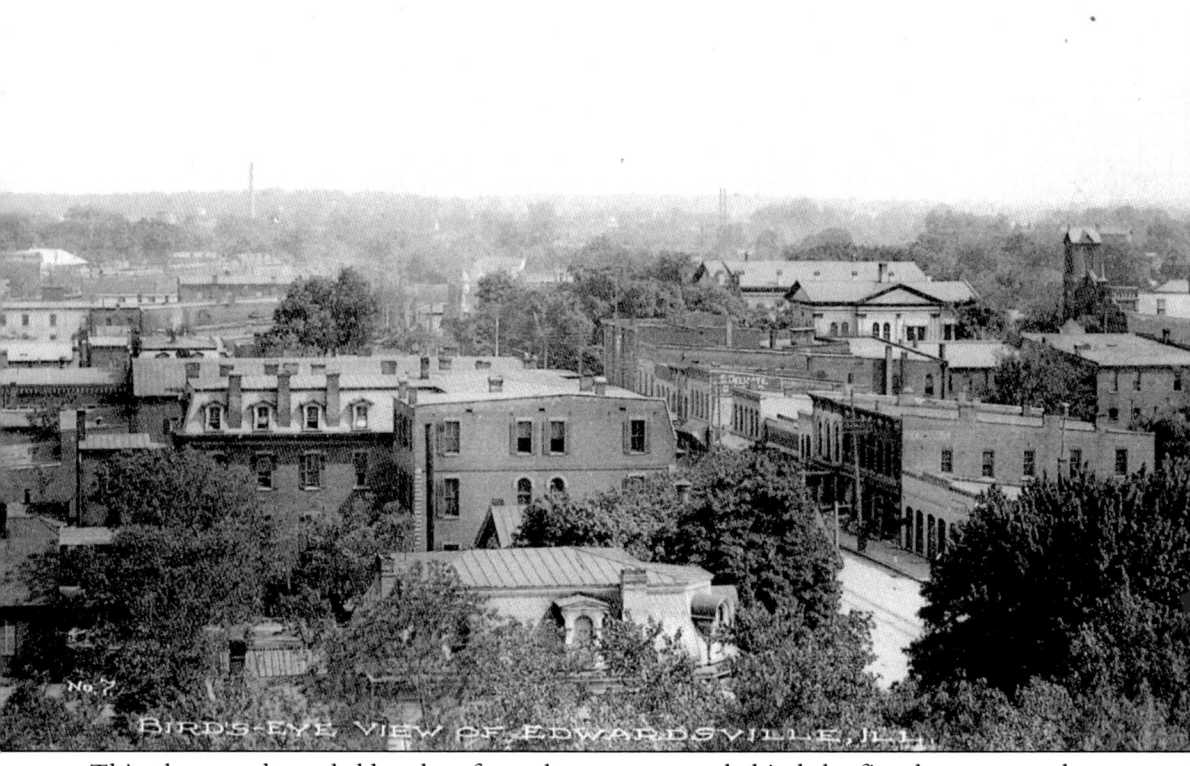
This photograph, probably taken from the water tower behind the fire department, shows Edwardsville's Main Street. In the foreground, the building with the mansard roof is the Dr. Edward William Fiegenbaum home. Behind it is the St. James Hotel. Farther back on the right, one can see the roof and arched windows of the courthouse, and behind it the bell tower of the Methodist Episcopal church. (Courtesy of June Nealy.)

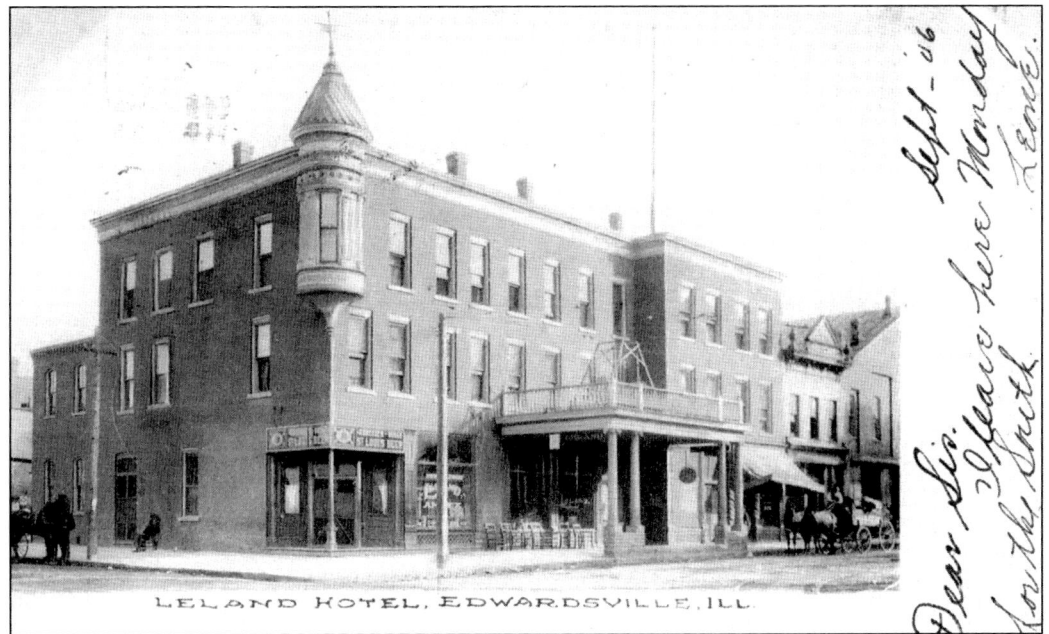

The Leland Hotel, with its recognizable corner turret, graced the corner of Main and St. Louis Streets for many years until most of it was razed in 1923, to be replaced by the Edwardsville National Bank. The hotel housed the Leland Café and the Leland Barber Shop; the portion of the building housing the barbershop remained for another half century. (Courtesy of June Nealy.)

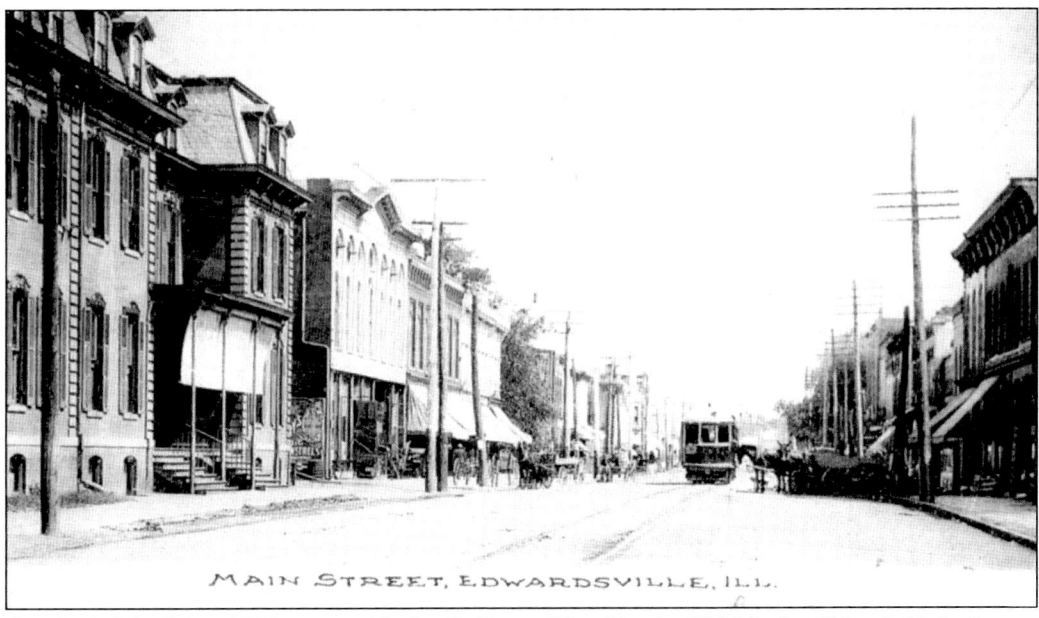

On the left in this c. 1907 postcard is the St. James Hotel in the 200 block of North Main Street, an elegant three-story hotel with a mansard roof and a columned front porch. A second-floor walkway connected the hotel with an 800-seat theater next door, making it a popular place for touring performers to stay. (Courtesy of June Nealy.)

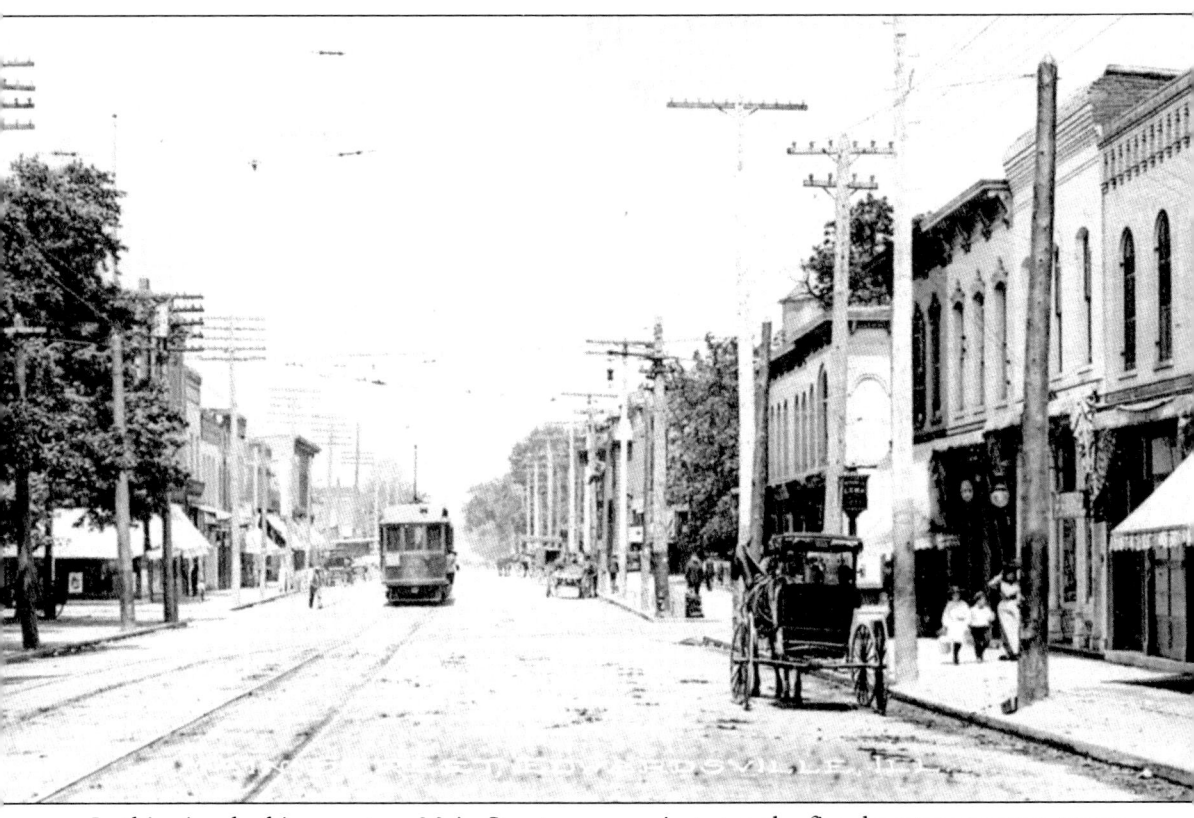

In this view looking west on Main Street, one can just spot the fire department water tower down the street on the right. The mother and two children on the sidewalk at the right are, from left to right, Freda Steiner (who married into the Bayer family), Arnold W. Steiner, and Pauline B. Schwarzkopf Steiner. (Courtesy of June Nealy.)

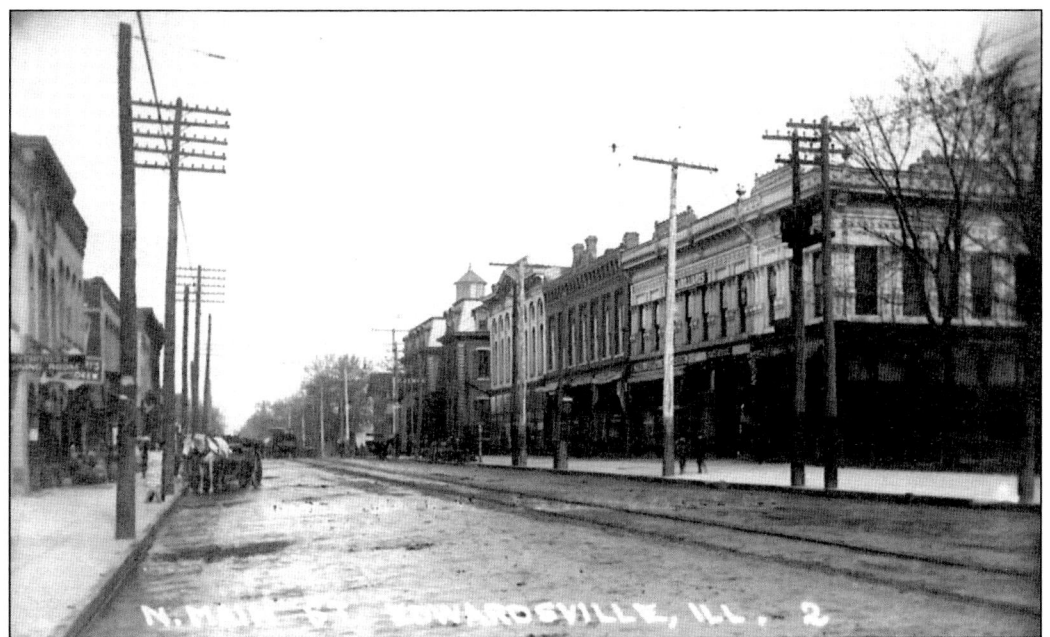

In another c. 1909 photograph looking west on Main Street, the water tower behind the fire department can be seen farther down the street, with the St. James Hotel before it. The Gerber building, which later housed Woolworth's, is on the corner on the right. (Courtesy of June Nealy.)

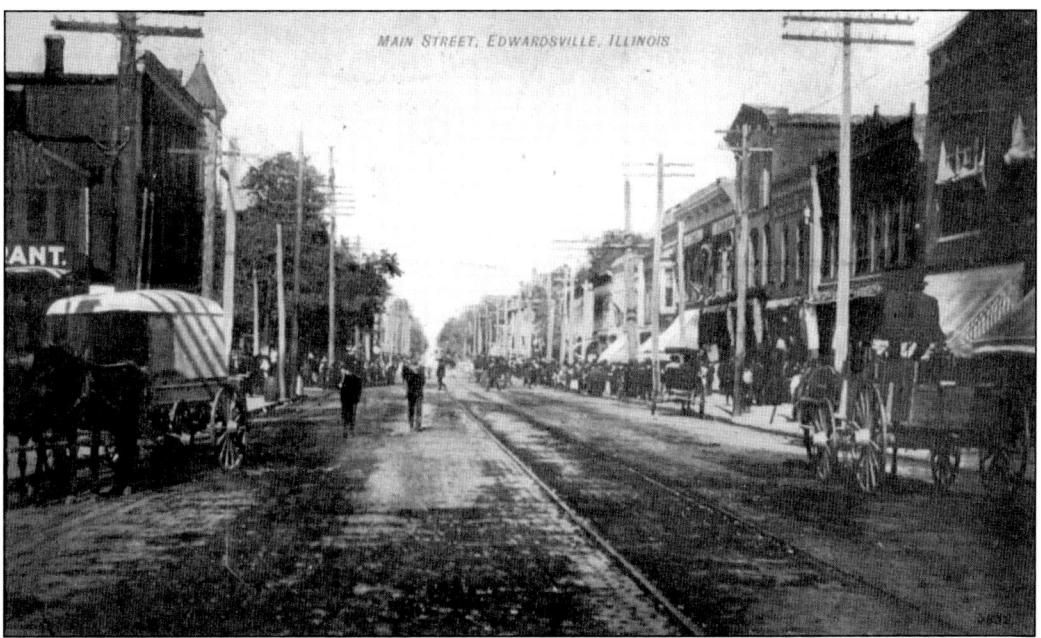

This photograph looks west along Main Street around 1909. Behind the delivery wagon at the left is the Leland Hotel with its distinctive turret visible. Beyond that on the left the large trees are at the front of the courthouse lawn. Note the trolley tracks down the center of the street. (Courtesy of June Nealy.)

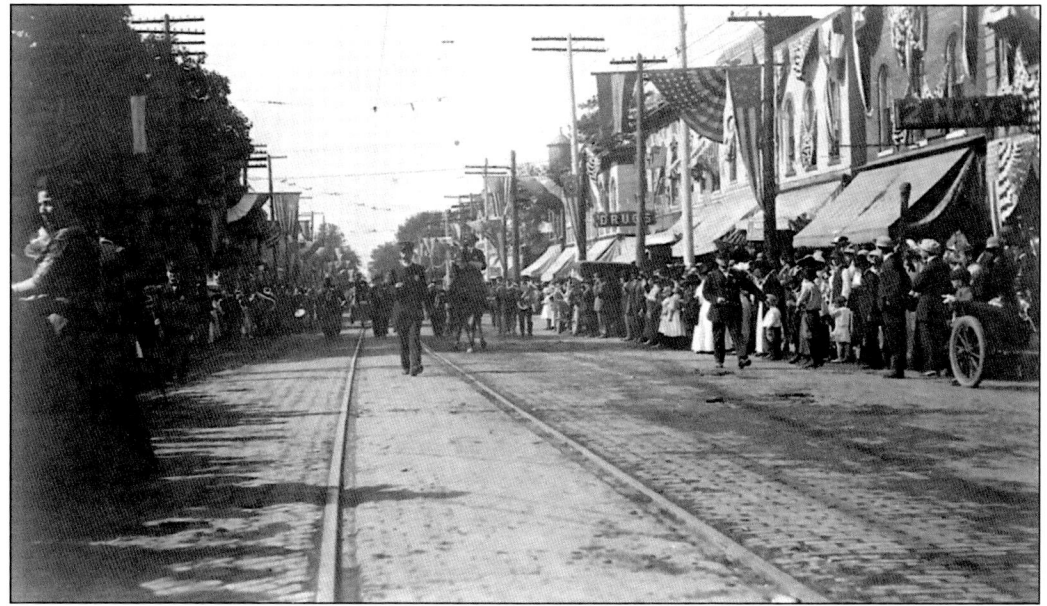

A large crowd is gathered, and Main Street is decorated for an unidentified parade. The Mays store and the Harnist Drugstore are on the right in the 100 block of North Main Street. This photograph is looking west. Courthouse square is to the left behind the large trees. (Courtesy of June Nealy.)

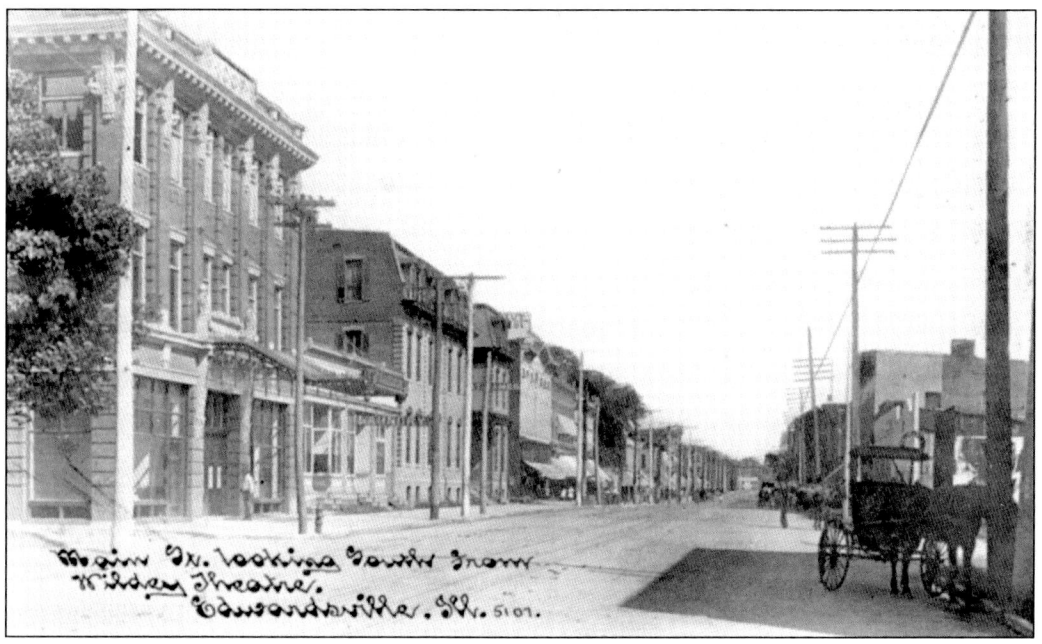

The Wildey Theatre is at the left, followed by, from left to right, a laundry, the St. James Hotel, and the Trares Building. Two retail establishments that occupied the Trares Building were the Walter Brothers and Yeager and Hotz. (Courtesy of June Nealy.)

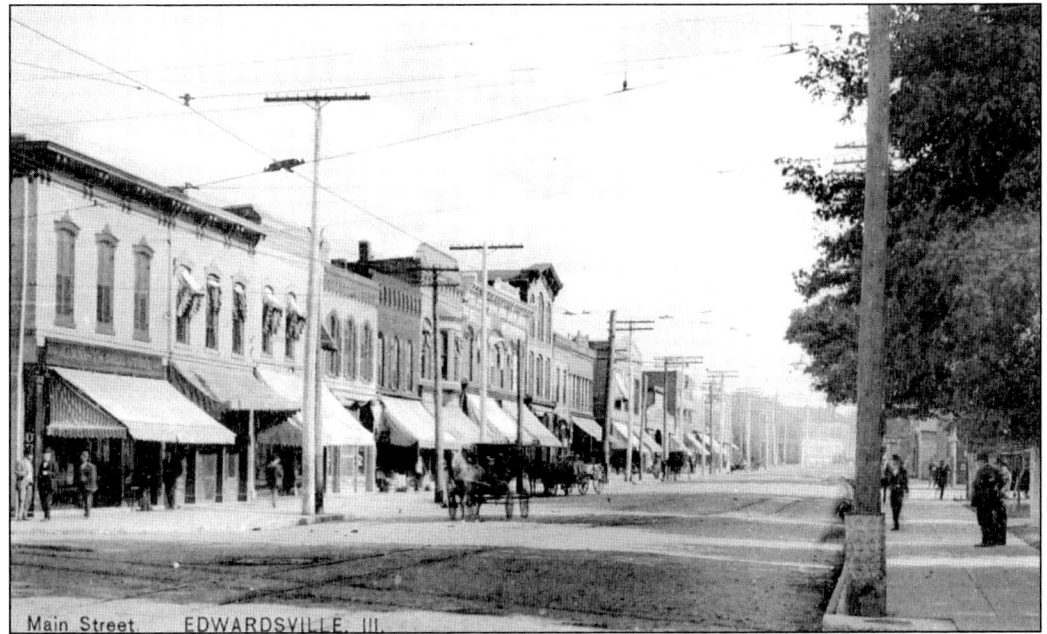

The courthouse square with its parklike front lawn is to the right. At the far left is the Harnist Drugstore. Farther along on the left behind the second utility pole is the J. E. Tunnell Building. (Courtesy of June Nealy.)

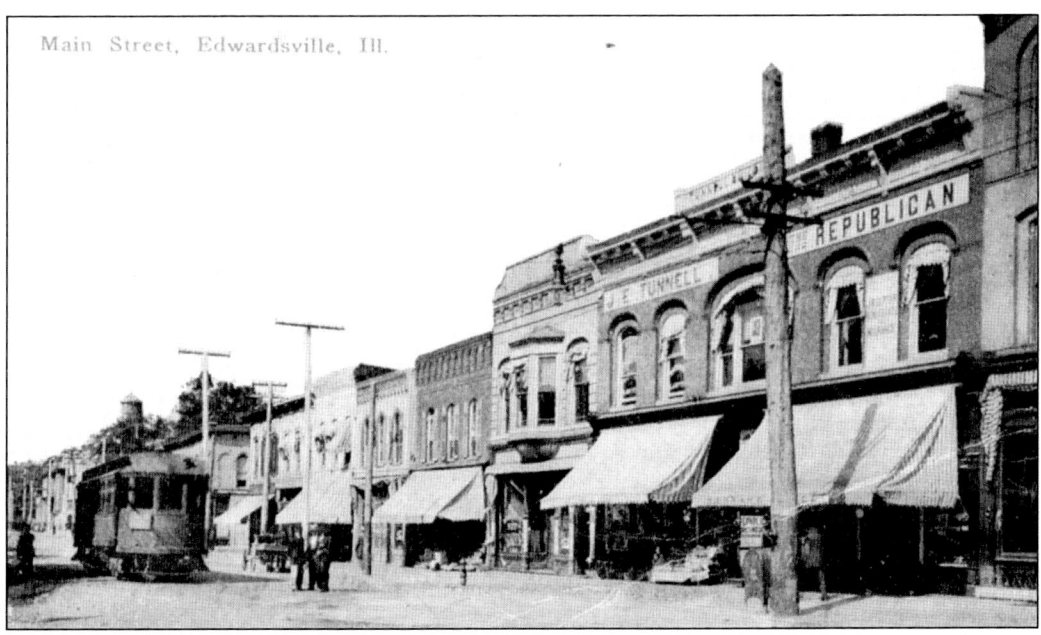

The J. E. Tunnell Building housed the Tunnell Brothers Grocers, a landmark along North Main Street. R. F. and J. E. Tunnell purchased the business in 1880 and continued to operate it at the same location. This building faces the St. Louis Street intersection and is still standing and in use today. (Courtesy of June Nealy.)

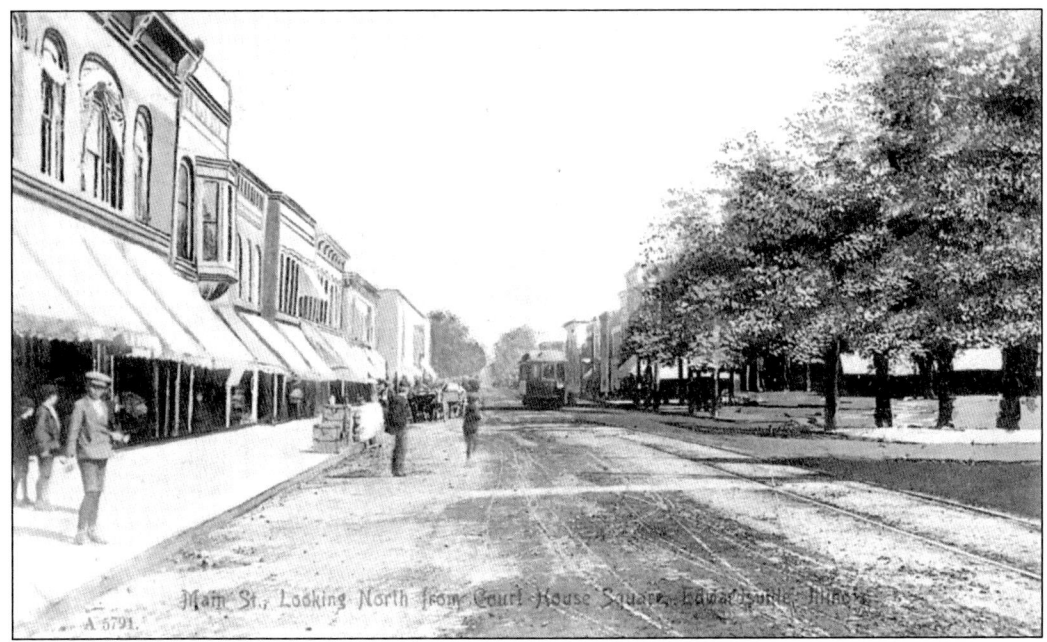

It looks like this young boy is about to step out into the street in front of the Harnist Drug Store at the corner of North Main Street and Hillsboro Road. Farther down on the left is the Tunnell Building. At the right is the courthouse square. (Courtesy of June Nealy.)

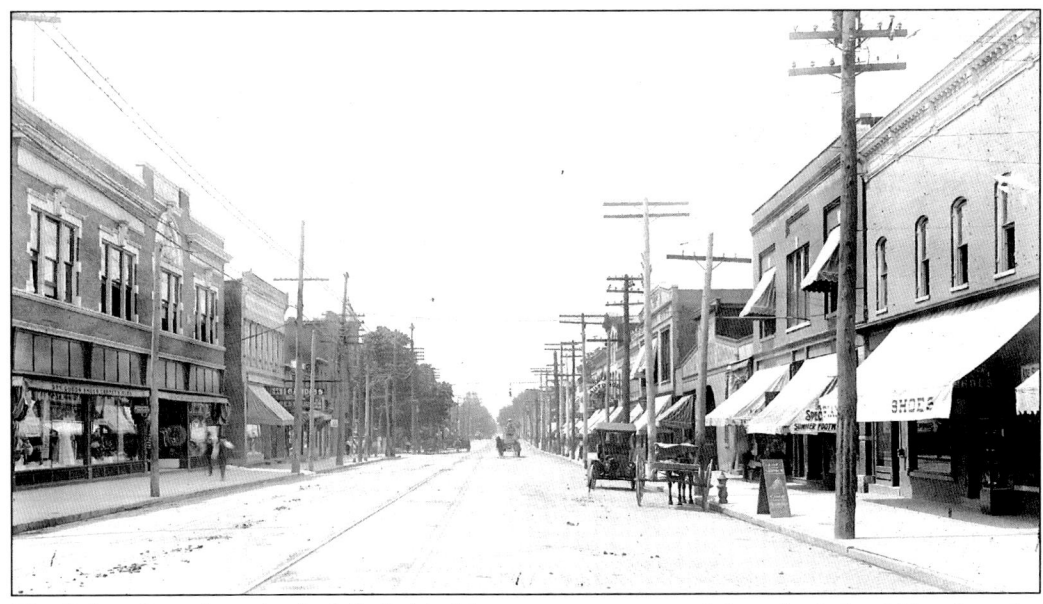

The Palace Store is at the far left. Behind it are a restaurant and then the Leland Hotel on the corner of North Main and St. Louis Streets. The trees on the left indicate the front lawn of the courthouse square. This *c.* 1915 view is looking west along the wide expanse of North Main Street. (Courtesy of June Nealy.)

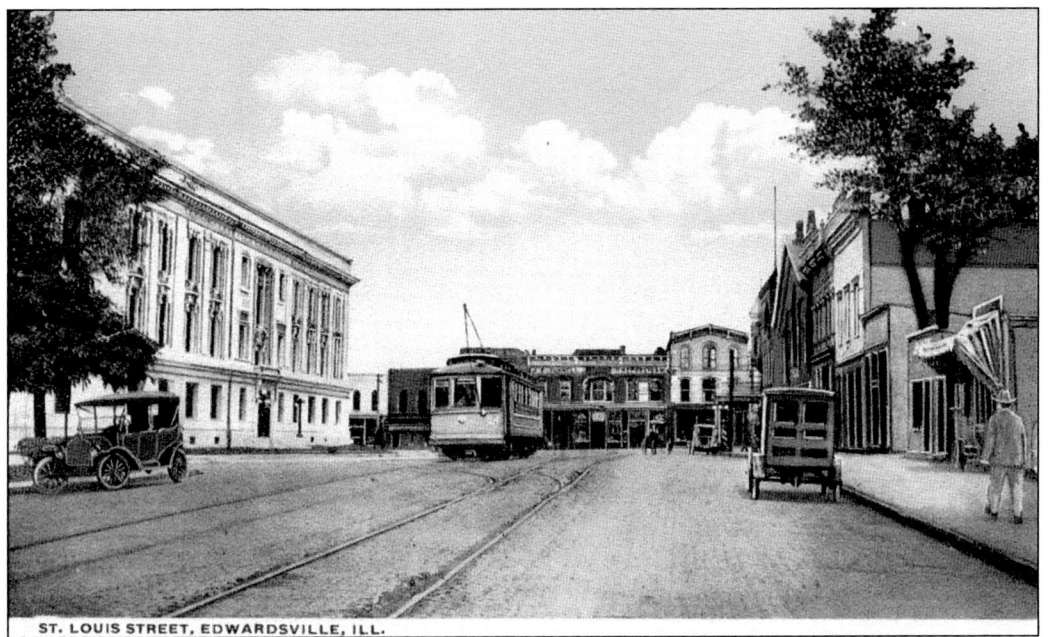

In this photograph taken after 1915, one can see the J. E. Tunnell Building and other Main Street buildings in a view from St. Louis Street. The east side of the new courthouse is on the left, and the Leland Hotel corner is toward the right. (Courtesy of June Nealy.)

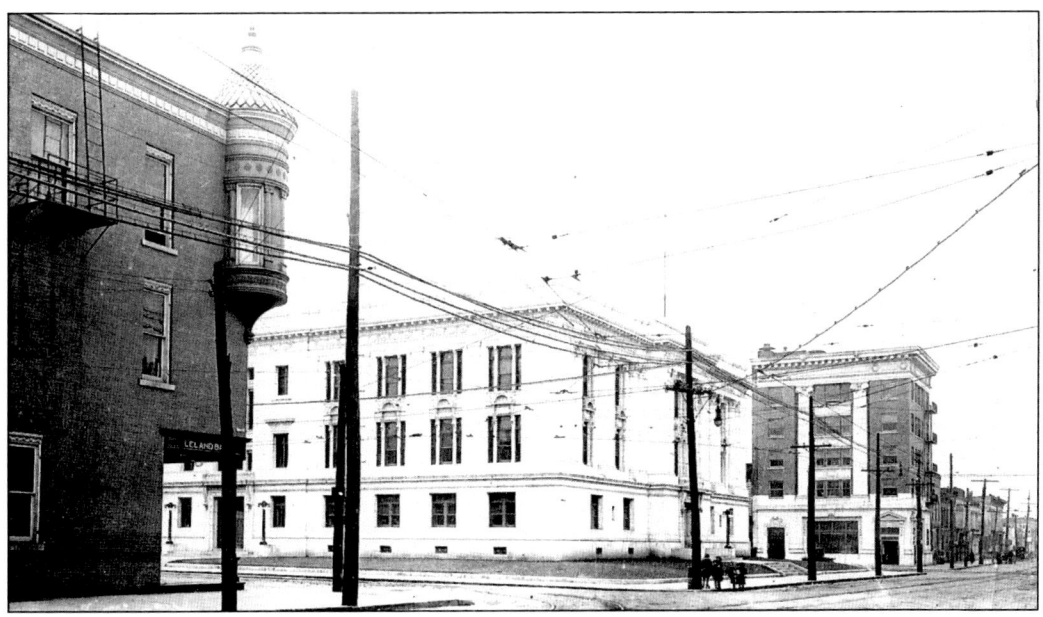

This view from the time period between 1917 and 1923 shows the buildings in the previous photograph, but from another direction, looking west. At far left is the Leland Hotel corner, then the new courthouse, and then the Bank of Edwardsville's modern five-story building. (Courtesy of Neal Strebel.)

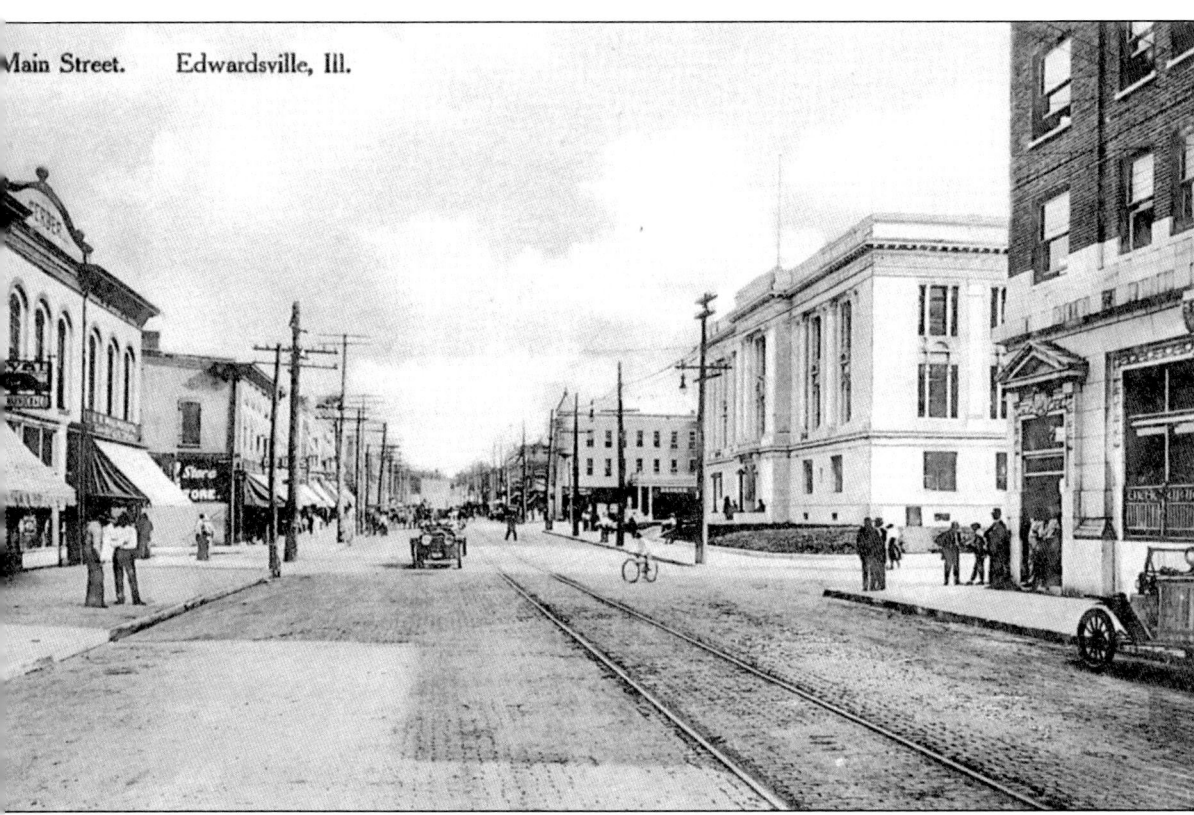

The new five-story Bank of Edwardsville building, built in 1917, is at the far right, changing the appearance of Main Street with the addition of the first "skyscraper." At center right is the new courthouse completed in 1915. Beyond the courthouse at center right is the Leland Hotel, which would be razed in 1923. (Courtesy of June Nealy.)

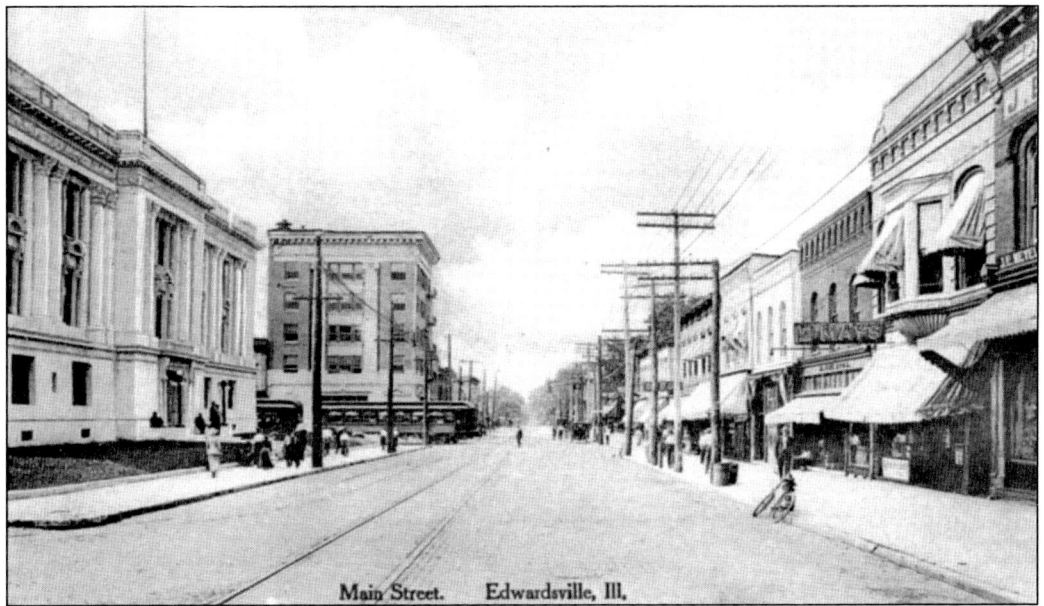

The courthouse and the Bank of Edwardsville are at the left in this postcard view taken between 1917 and 1923. At the right is the Mays Store and farther along the street behind it, the Harnist Drugstore. (Courtesy of June Nealy.)

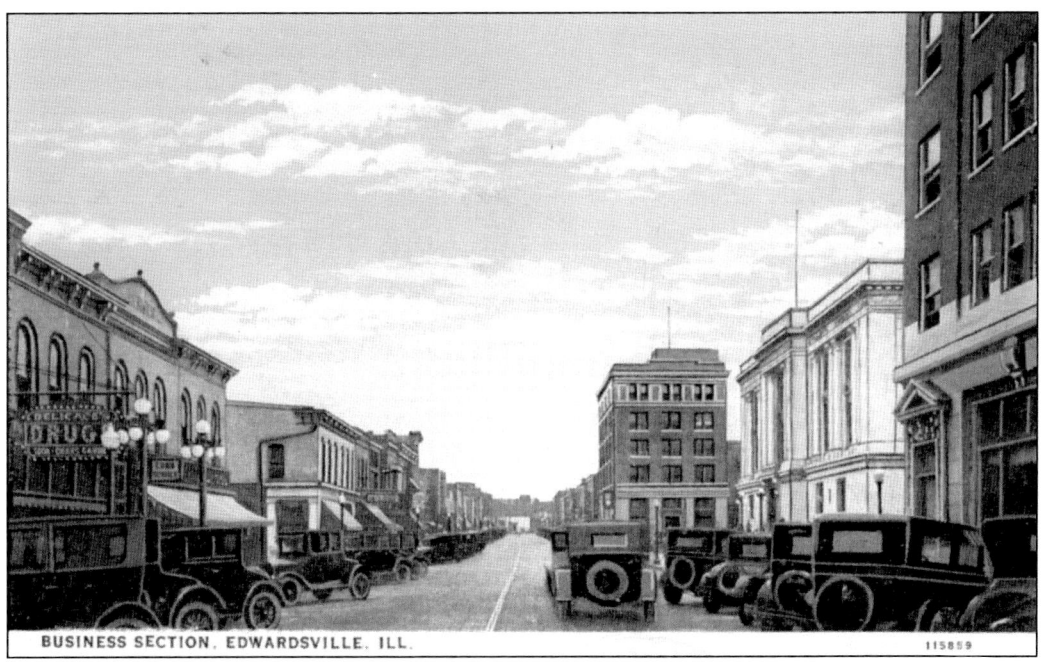

In 1923, another five-story bank building was constructed along North Main Street. The Edwardsville National Bank was built on the former Leland Hotel corner at the intersection of North Main and St. Louis Streets. On the right, the Edwardsville National Bank and the Bank of Edwardsville can be seen flanking the 1915 courthouse. (Courtesy of June Nealy.)

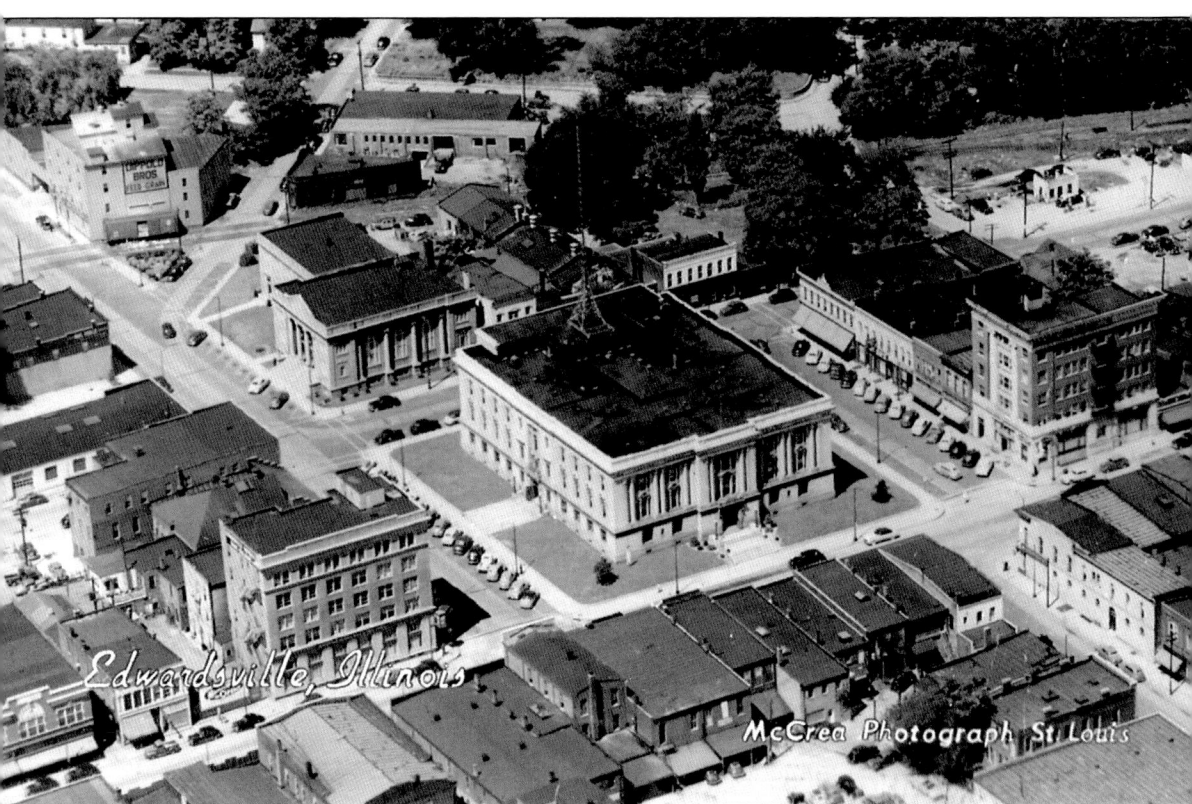

An aerial view of downtown Edwardsville, believed to be taken during the 1930s, gives a clear view of the 1915 courthouse in the center, the Edwardsville National Bank on the left, and the Bank of Edwardsville on the right. Extending from left to right in front of them is North Main Street. (Courtesy of June Nealy.)

Two

Body and Spirit

James T. Hair wrote in his 1866 *Gazetteer of Madison County* of the early Edwardsville settlement that "Sickness was more prevalent then than now, owing, doubtless, to the great vegetable decomposition, and exposure of the people from the want of comfortable habitations and clothing. The Country has become much drier than it was in early days, and consequently less productive of fever and ague and other bilious complaints."

Nevertheless, medical challenges affected Edwardsville along with the rest of the country—the cholera outbreaks in the 1800s, the 1918 influenza epidemic, and tuberculosis. Johannah Hentz, an employee of the *Intelligencer*, remembered the influenza epidemic as follows: "Flu hit the whole town and all the businesses were operating with little help. . . . Mayor Hotz issued a proclamation closing the schools and Sunday church services stopped."

Some notable doctors who served the Edwardsville community were Dr. John Weir; Dr. Joseph Pogue, who had attended Pennsylvania Medical College; Dr. J. A. Hirsch, who served as pallbearer for Dr. Pogue; Dr. Adam Hale Oliver; and Dr. Edward William Fiegenbaum, who attended McKendree College, St. Louis Medical College, and graduated from the Bellevue Hospital Medical College of New York in 1876. That year he began his practice in Edwardsville, serving the community for 50 years.

Early in Edwardsville's settlement, groups began to gather for prayer or Bible study in each others' homes. Methodist gatherings are recorded as being held early in the 1800s about two miles west of Edwardsville at a meetinghouse and campground known as Ebenezer. Two ministers officiating there were John Dew and Samuel H. Thompson.

The Mount Joy Baptist Church, an African American church, was built on Olive Street in 1871 but later burned. Another church building replaced it, which lasted until the 1990s, when a new edifice was again constructed. The Wesley Chapel African Methodist Episcopal Church was constructed in 1881 on Aldrup Street and, although modernized since then, continues to serve its congregation. St. Andrew's Episcopal Church at 406 Hillsboro Avenue was constructed in simplified Gothic design in 1916 and resembled its first building, which was on the same site.

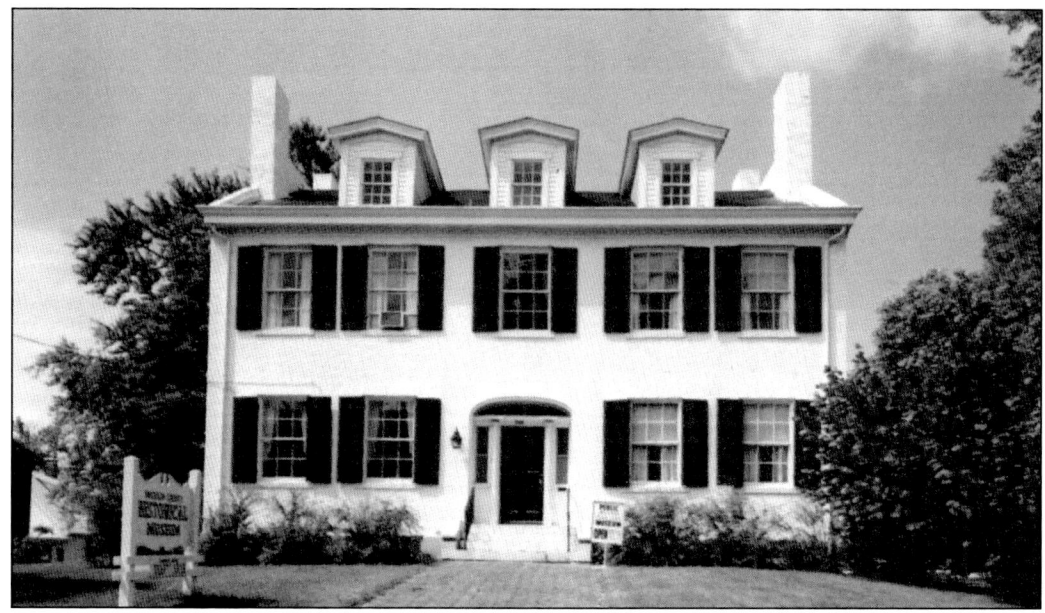

Dr. John Weir had this Federal-style brick home constructed in 1836 at 715 North Main Street. Situated on a corner lot, the side street provided access to a side door into his medical office. The house was built according to Philadelphia row house plans that Weir brought with him to Edwardsville. This house served three generations of the Weir family before it was sold to the Madison County Historical Society in 1963 for use as a museum. (Courtesy of June Nealy.)

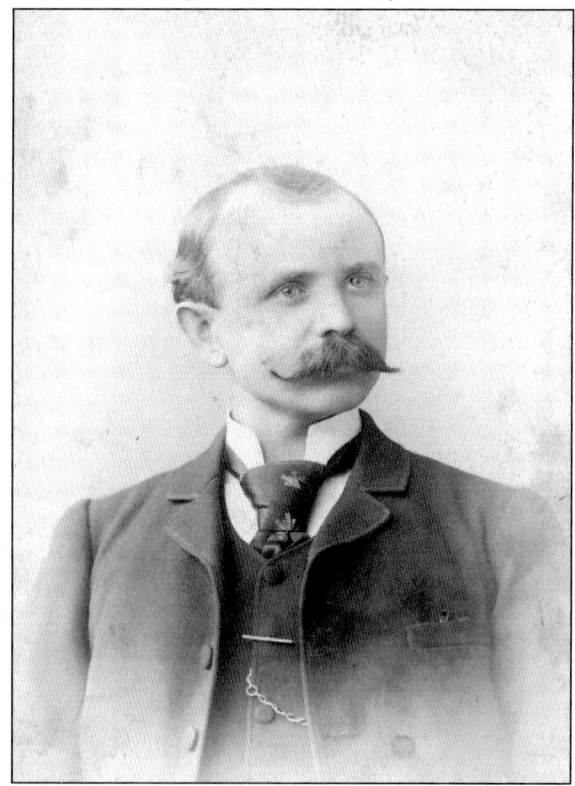

Dr. Adam Hale Oliver was born in Pennsylvania and moved as a boy with his parents to Altamont, where he received a public school education. He attended Washington University School of Medicine in St. Louis, graduating in 1893. He declined an internship at St. Louis City Hospital in order to begin private practice right away in Glen Carbon, Edwardsville's neighboring community. In 1906, he moved his practice to Edwardsville. (Courtesy of Madison County Historical Society.)

In 1896, Dr. Oliver married Effie E. Yates, the 25-year-old daughter of Michael Delves Yates, a farmer who had been born in Staffordshire, England, and Eve Wolf Yates, who was from Friedrichstadt, Prussia, Germany. Effie outlived her husband by 17 years; Dr. Oliver died in 1939, and Effie passed away in 1956. (Courtesy of Madison County Historical Society.)

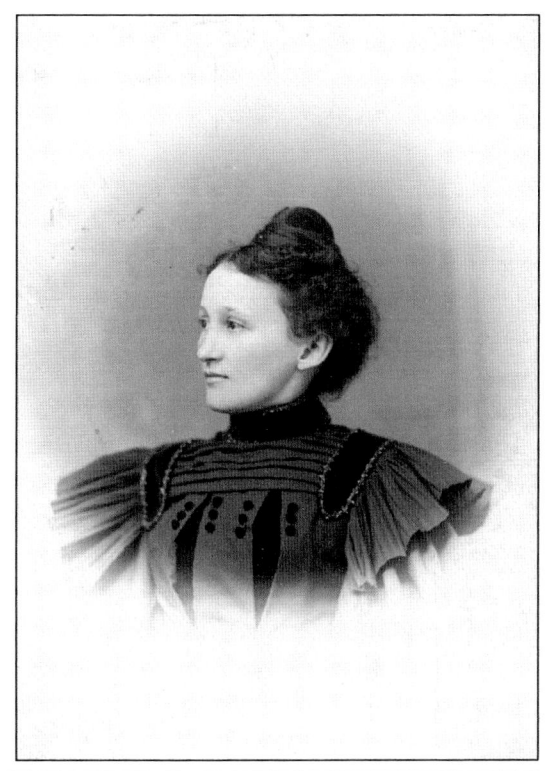

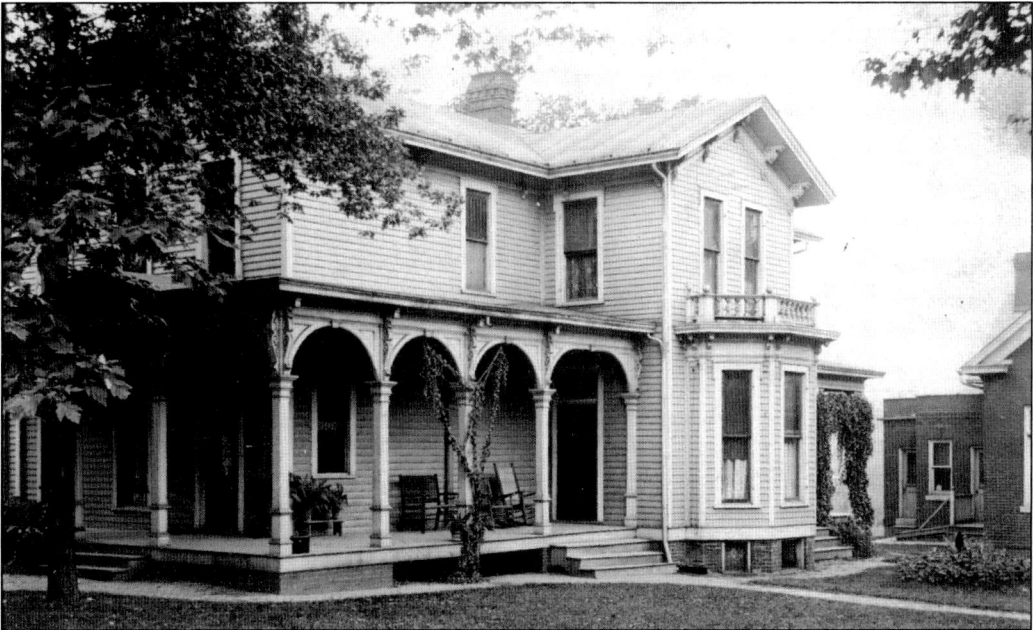

This was the Oliver residence at 121 East Vandalia Street. In his spare time, Dr. Oliver enjoyed reading, particularly Civil War history. He considered himself a Republican in political views, and he attended the Methodist Episcopal church. Dr. Oliver was a member of the Madison County Medical Society, the Illinois State Medical Association, and the American Medical Association until his death. (Courtesy of Madison County Historical Society.)

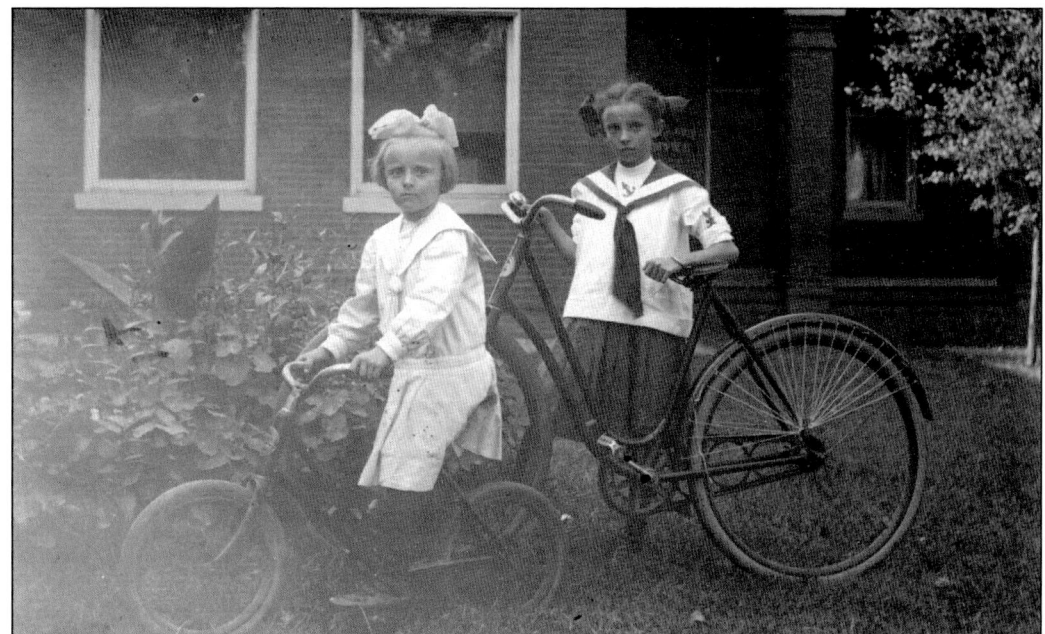

These charming images of Ila and Olga Oliver, daughters of Dr. Adam Hale Oliver and Effie Yates Oliver, are from their childhood. The photograph with their bicycles was taken in front of their father's medical office at 109 North Kansas Street. The photograph of the girls in the family car was taken at their residence at 121 East Vandalia Street. (Courtesy of Madison County Historical Society.)

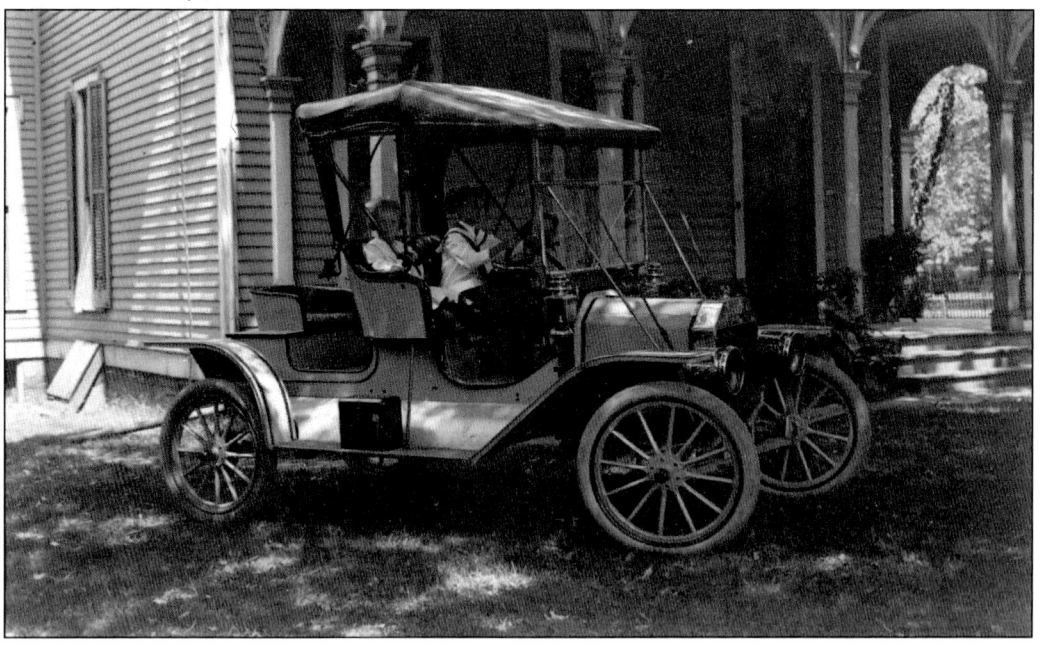

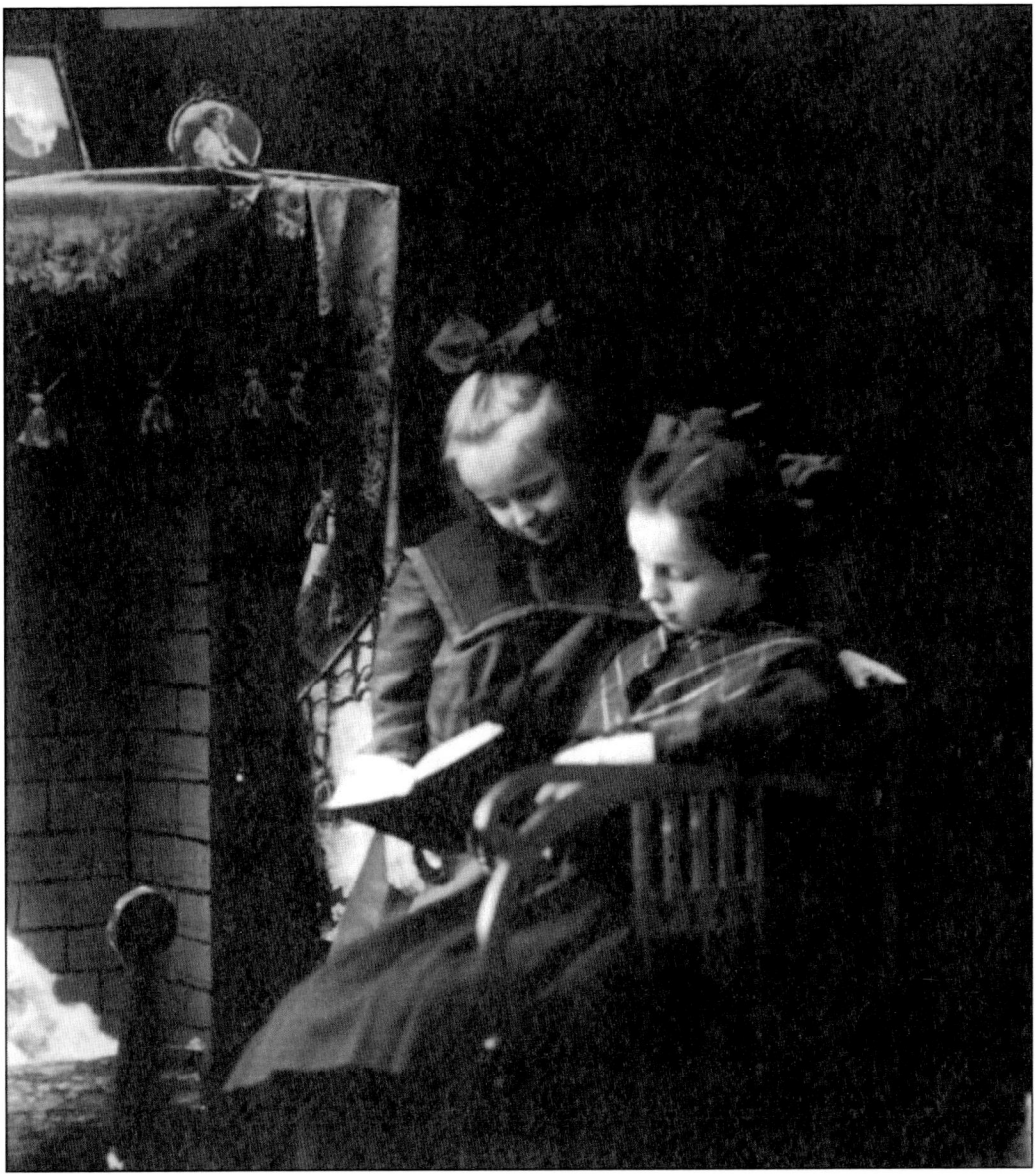

Their father's love of reading and history and his apparent satisfaction with his Washington University in St. Louis education evidently influenced Dr. Oliver's daughters. The girls are posed with a book in this photograph inside the family home. Both Ila and Olga attended Washington University in St. Louis, Ila graduating in 1922 with a bachelor of arts degree, and Olga graduating in 1925, also with a bachelor of arts degree. (Courtesy of Madison County Historical Society.)

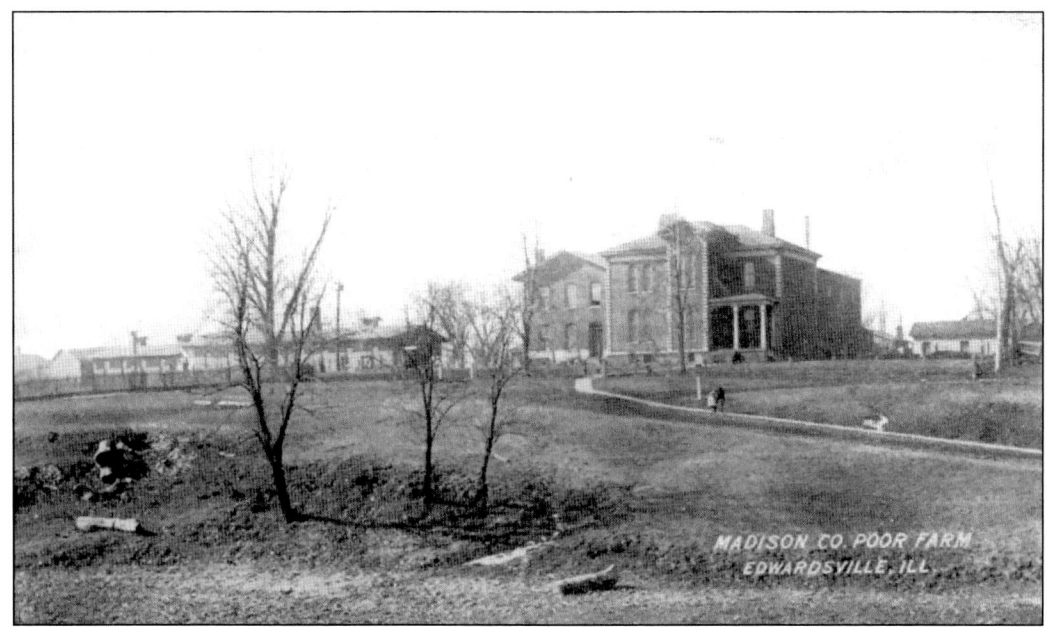

The Madison County Poor Farm was established in 1844 when a home was designated to house the county's indigent persons. It did not become a true poor farm until the 1860s, when additional land was added. A salaried county agent looked after the residents and billed the county for expenses. (Courtesy of June Nealy.)

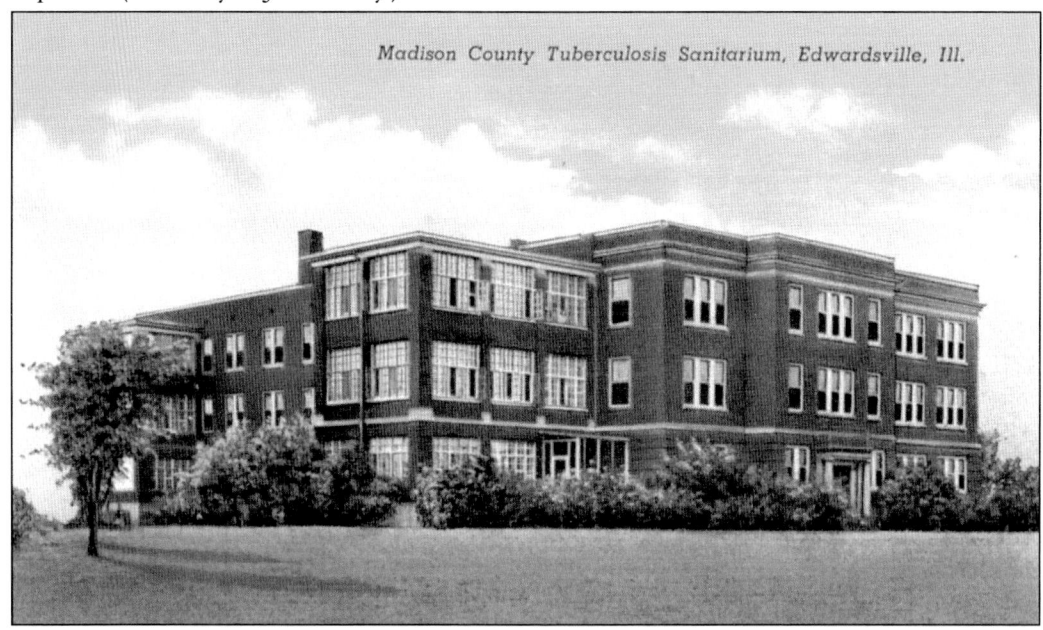

In 1908, during Charles Deneen's term as Illinois governor, legislation enabled cities and counties to build sanitariums to treat and contain tuberculosis. The Madison County Tuberculosis Sanitarium opened in Edwardsville in 1926 on Troy Road. The architect was Lucas Pfeiffenberger and Sons of Alton. Not all the patients who died there did so from tuberculosis. In 1934, a Silas B. Wilson "leaped or fell from a second story window," according to his obituary. (Courtesy of June Nealy.)

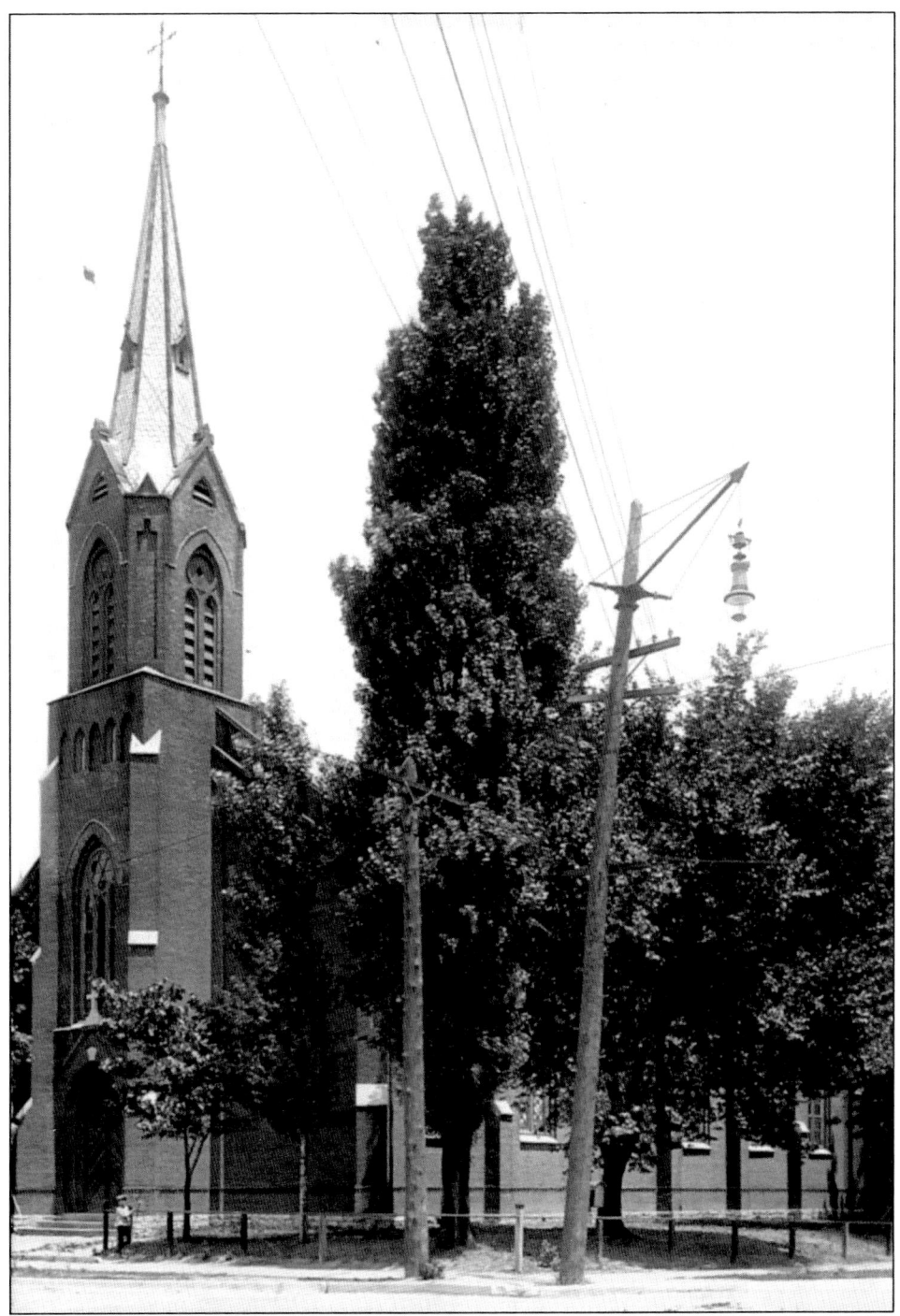

St. Boniface Catholic Church was built in 1869 at the corner of Buchanan and Vandalia Streets by H. Melcher's construction company of St. Louis, from a plan submitted by A. Druiding, also of St. Louis. Rev. William Kuchenbuch had purchased 20 lots on that corner a few years earlier. The church was constructed on the site of the former home of Ninian Edwards, Illinois territorial governor and Edwardsville's namesake. (Courtesy of Neal Strebel.)

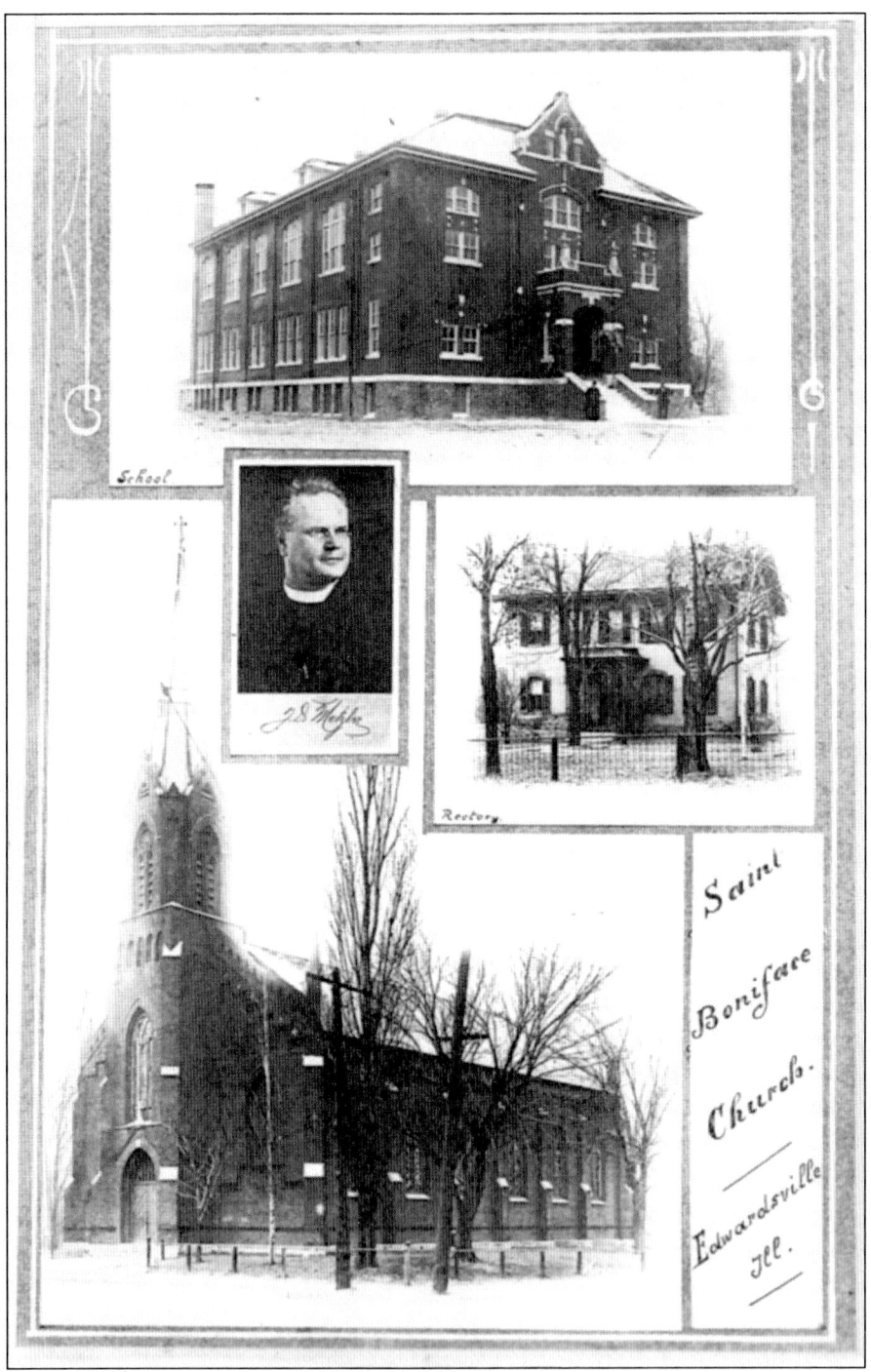

This multiview card shows St. Boniface Church, school and hall, rectory, and its eighth pastor, Rev. Joseph D. Metzler, who served from 1896 to 1911. The brick rectory was completed in 1871 at a cost of $2,531.50. The second floor served as the pastor's home while the first floor was utilized as Edwardsville's first Catholic grade school. A school building was constructed in 1882 and later converted to a convent. (Courtesy of Neal Strebel.)

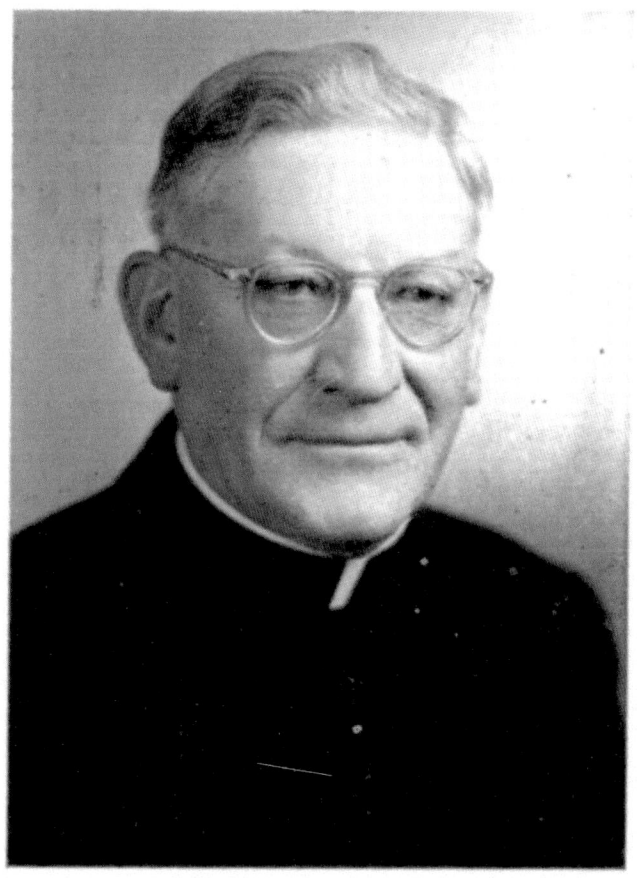

In Pious Memory of

Rev. Ernest J. Eckhard
Pastor St. Boniface Church
Edwardsville, Illinois
1919 - 1954
Born November 9, 1880
Ordained June 6, 1906
Died January 17, 1954

Rev. Ernest J. Eckhard was the longest-serving priest at St. Boniface and the only priest buried in St. Boniface Cemetery. He was called in 1919 and served until his death in 1954. During his tenure, extensive renovations were made to the interior of the church under the direction of a German artist, Max Autenrieb. Reverend Eckhard also led the formation of a school band and laid plans for a school gymnasium. (Courtesy of June Nealy.)

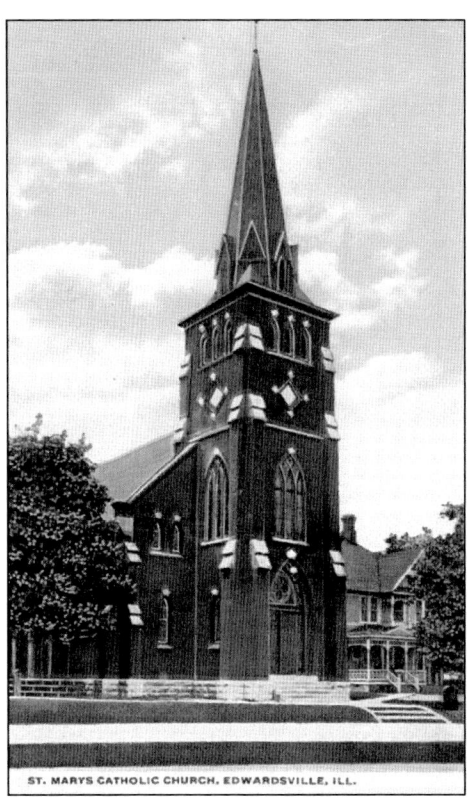

St. Mary's parish began in 1835 with a small group of Catholics who first worshipped in homes and then in 1843 built a small church just off Main Street near the Wildey Theater. In the 1860s, the German-speaking members, with Rev. William Kuckenbuch's leadership, purchased land for St. Boniface and left St. Mary's. The little St. Mary's Church eventually became too small, and the church shown here was completed in 1889 on Park Street. (Courtesy of June Nealy.)

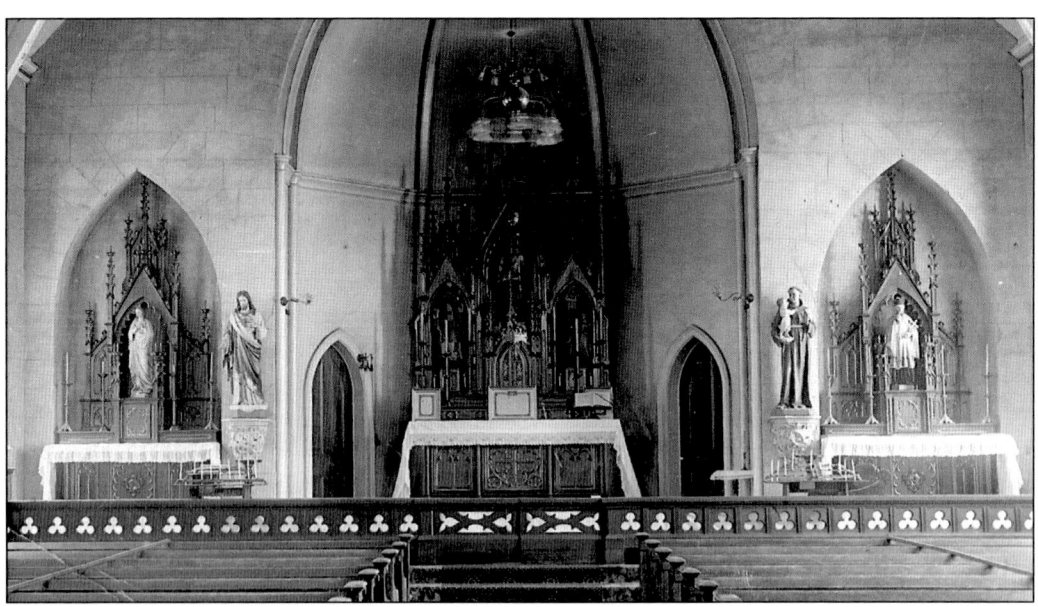

This view shows the interior of St. Mary's Church, constructed in 1889. After the German Catholics left St. Mary's to establish St. Boniface, St. Mary's congregation consisted mainly of Italian, Irish, and Czech families. A third congregation eventually grew from the original St. Mary's Church when St. Cecilia's was established in the neighboring community of Glen Carbon. (Courtesy of June Nealy.)

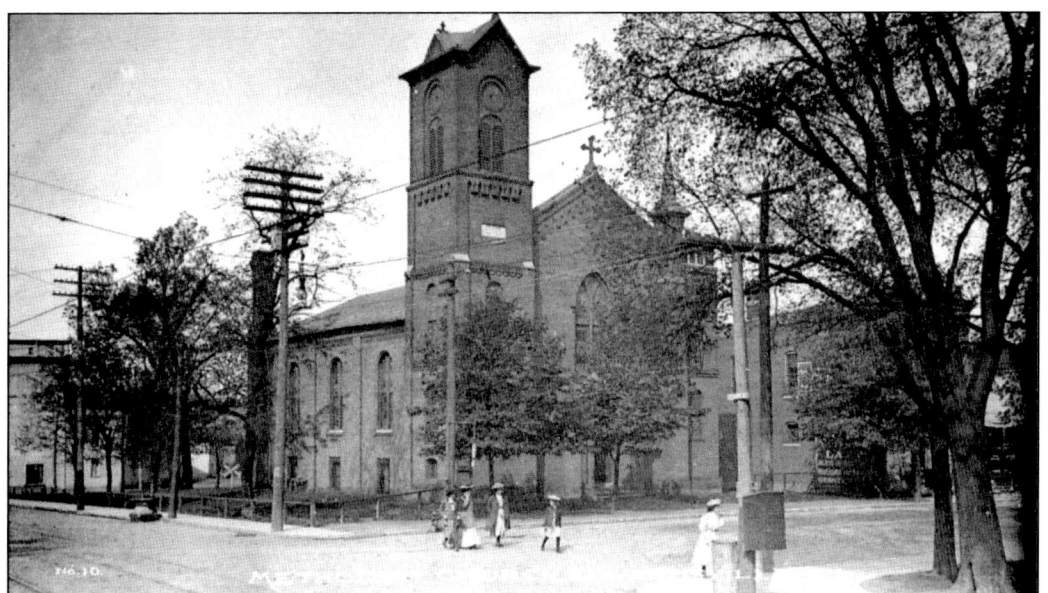

This St. John's Methodist Church was built in 1884 facing Second Street at the intersection of Second and St. Louis Streets. Two previous chapels had also been located on the site. Previous to 1828, Edwardsville Methodists had met in various public buildings. A Methodist church known as Bethel Chapel had been built in 1805 in Glen Carbon. A marker today identifies that site as the first Methodist church in Illinois. (Courtesy of June Nealy.)

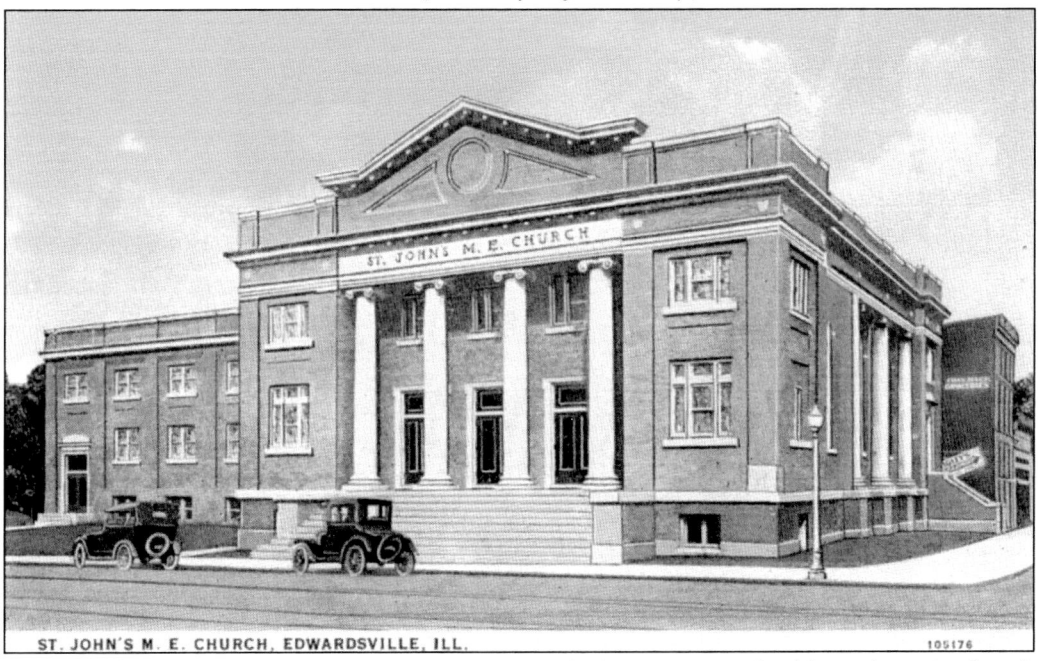

By the 1920s, the St. John's Methodist congregation had outgrown its building, the 1884 church shown in the upper picture. Constructed on the same site, this building faced St. Louis Street and was home to St. John's from 1924 until 2006, when a new facility was completed on 25 acres on Marine Road. The classical-style structure was built just a decade after the new courthouse across the street. (Courtesy of June Nealy.)

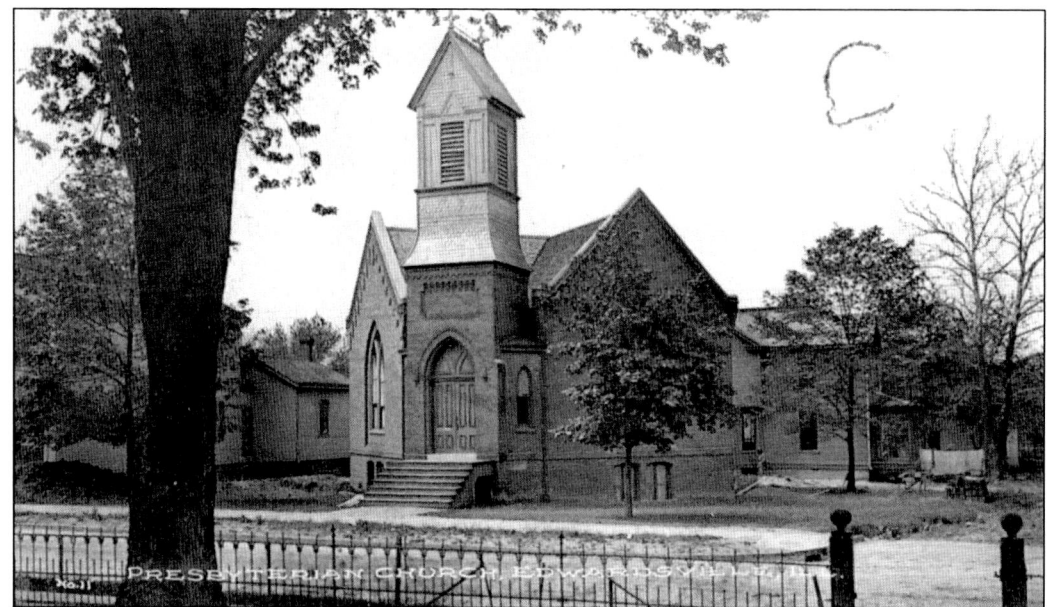

First Presbyterian Church was established in Edwardsville in 1819, the first church organized in the city. This is its second building, constructed in 1885. The church is one of 99 congregations in the Giddings-Lovejoy Presbytery, with ties to both presbytery namesakes. Rev. Salmon Giddings first formed the Edwardsville congregation. Elijah Lovejoy, an abolitionist newspaper publisher and preacher, was killed by an angry mob in Alton in 1837. (Courtesy of June Nealy.)

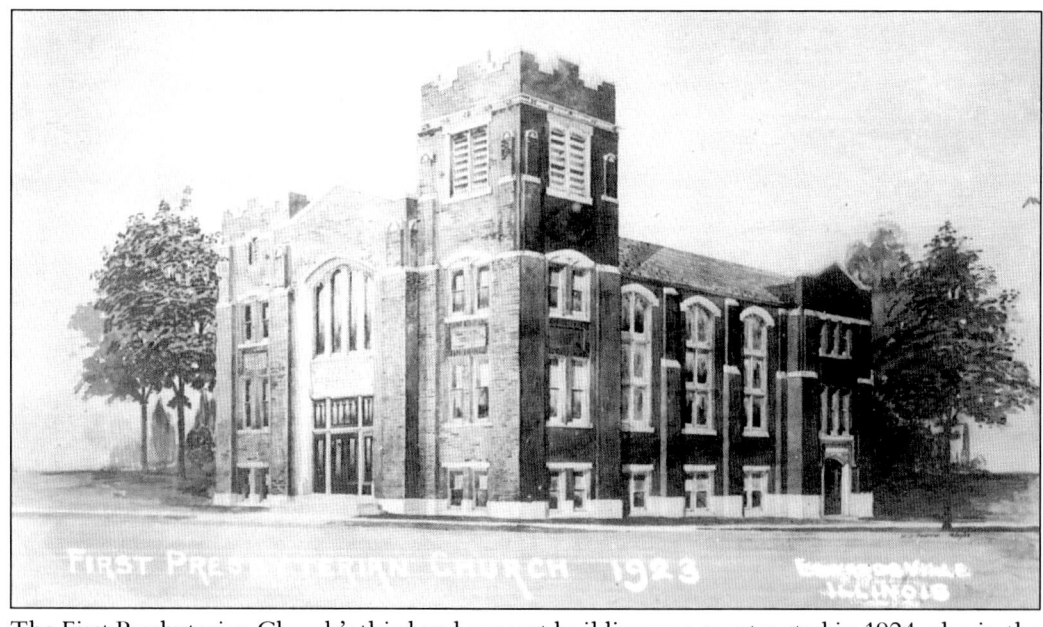

The First Presbyterian Church's third and current building was constructed in 1924, also in the 200 block of Kansas Street. In 1960, a Christian school annex was added. In 1994, in conjunction with the church's 175th anniversary, an elevator and a covered courtyard called the Inner Room were added. The beautiful faceted windows in this building were created by Emil Frei Associates of St. Louis; they were dedicated in 1983. (Courtesy of Neal Strebel.)

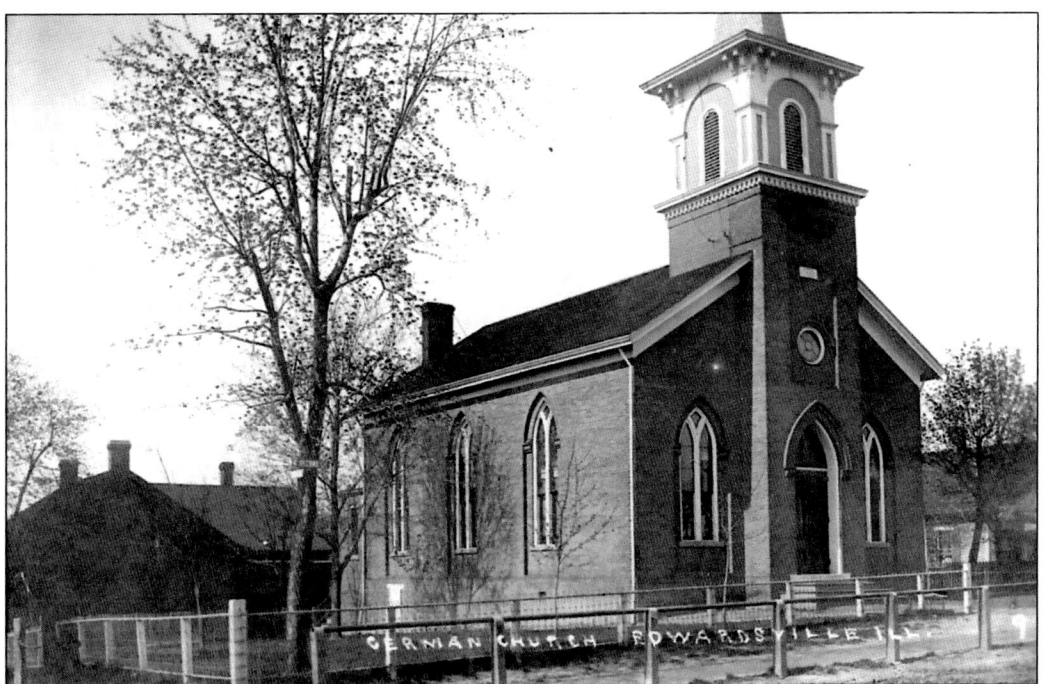

The first Eden Church was built in 1869 on Second Street, an excellent example of simple Gothic architecture. Before 1869, the small German-speaking congregation had met in a Baptist church that had stood on the site of the present city hall. (Courtesy of SJ Morrison.)

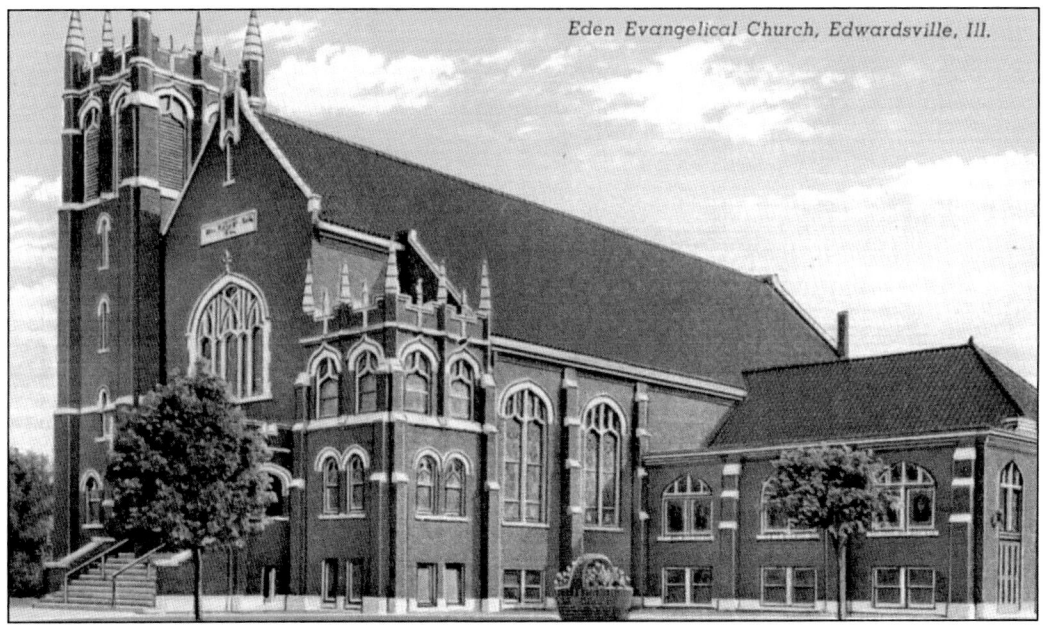

This massive Gothic-style Eden Evangelical Church was built in 1927 between Second and Fourth Streets on the site of its previous church, which had served the congregation from 1869 to 1926. In 1941, a fire caused extensive damage. During the rebuilding, the massive rose stained-glass window was added and the choir loft and organ chamber were redesigned. (Courtesy of June Nealy.)

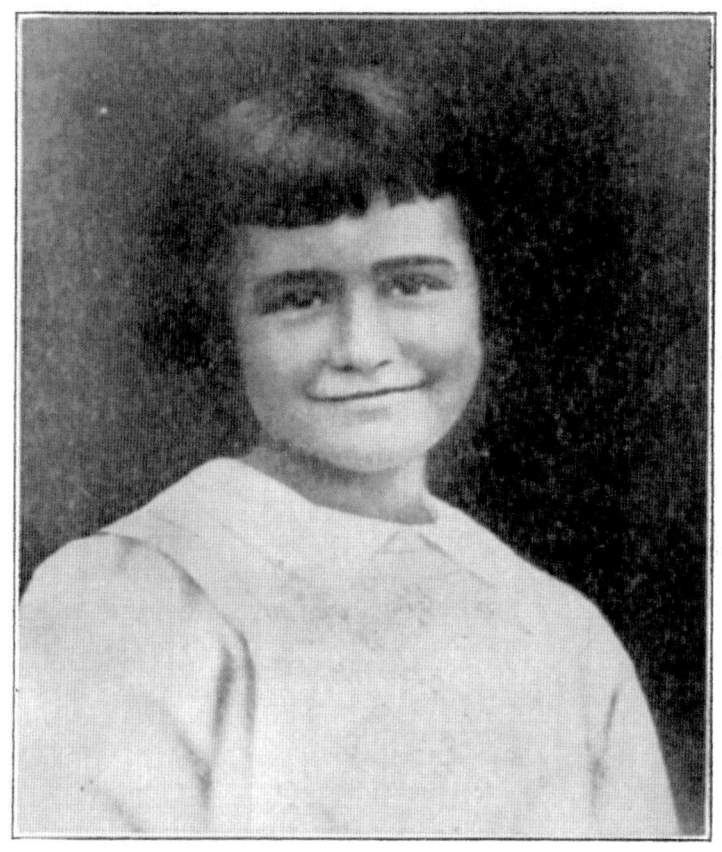

BORN JAN. 2, 1905 EDNA RAHN DIED MAY 6, 1917

1918 MOTTO

Der Engel des Herrn lagert sich um die her, so Ihn fuerchten und hilft ihnen aus.

The angel of the Lord encampeth 'round about them that fear him and delivereth them.—*Ps. 34. 7.*

Sincere wishes from

H. RAHN, Pastor
MRS. EMMA RAHN

"EDEN," EDWARDSVILLE, ILL.

Edna Rahn, daughter of Pastor Herman Ulrich Rahn of Eden Church and Emma Rahn, died in 1917 at the age of only 12. Their other five children lived to adulthood. Pastor Rahn was the fifth generation of his family to serve in the ministry over a period of 233 years, earlier generations serving in Switzerland. He studied at Elmhurst College in Elmhurst and then Eden Theological Seminary in Webster Groves, Missouri. (Courtesy of June Nealy.)

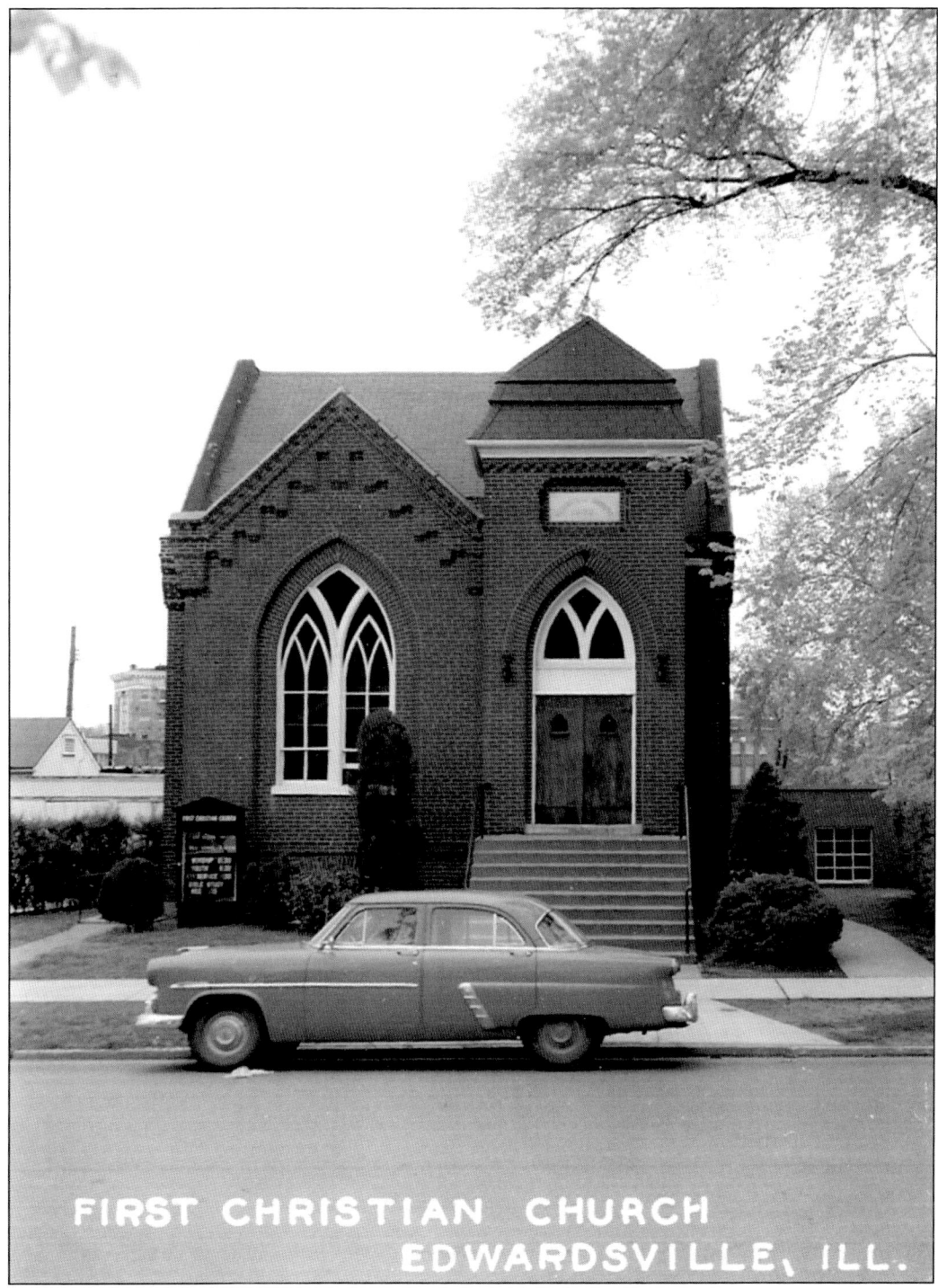

The First Christian Church was first established in a building on Silver Creek in 1830. This small but elegant Gothic building was constructed in 1888 at 211 North Kansas Street and was used by the congregation until 1989. The first pastor in this building is believed to be Rev. James H. Garrison, editor of the *Christian Evangelist*. (Courtesy of Michael A. Sporrer.)

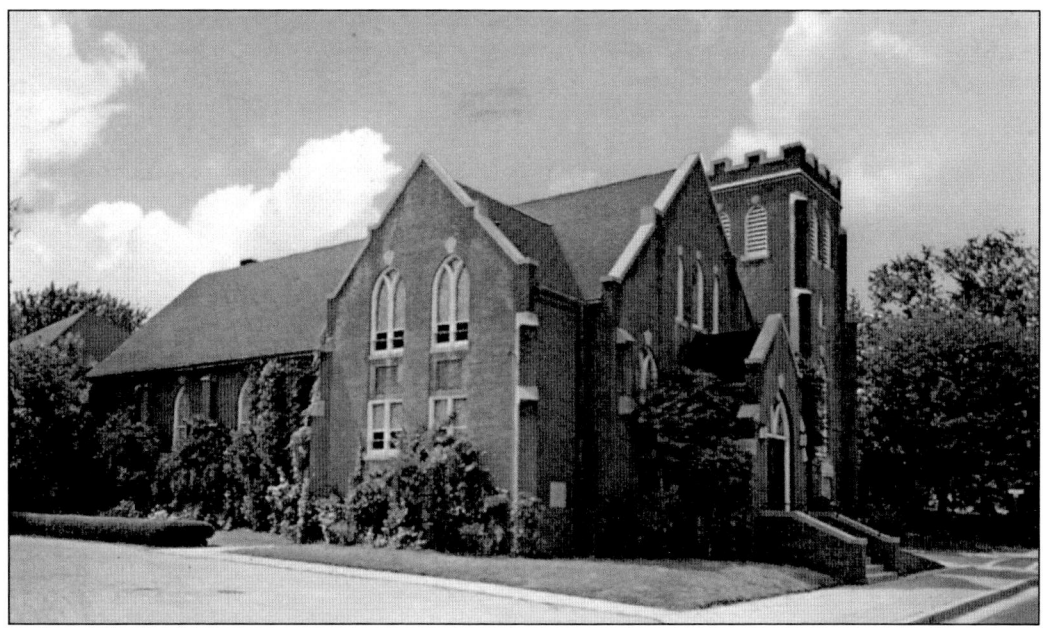

The Evangelical Lutheran Church was founded in 1901, and the first building was completed in 1906 at the corner of Fillmore and Chapman Streets. In the 1920s, a large addition was built onto the Fillmore Street side. Edwardsville architect M. B. Kane worked with the congregation's request to include a balcony and space for a pipe organ. Dedication day on March 18, 1928, included services in both English and German. (Courtesy of SJ Morrison.)

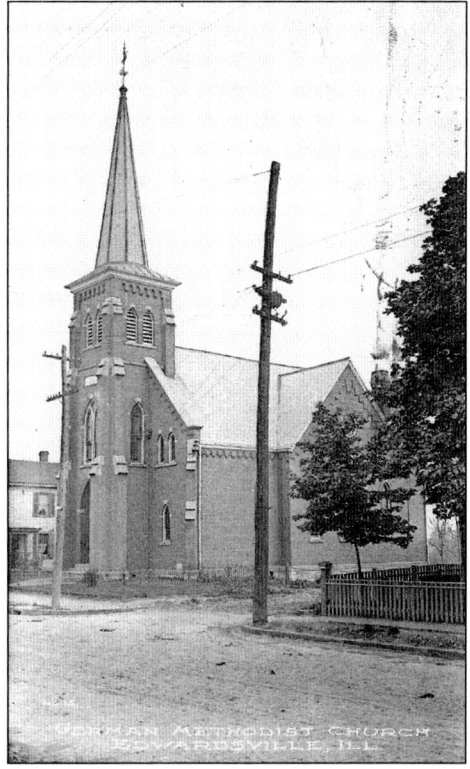

This postcard shows the German Methodist Church at 800 North Main Street. One of its pastors, Rev. William Fiegenbaum, who served from 1870 until 1875, emigrated to America at the age of 10. Reverend Fiegenbaum's three brothers were also ministers, and his two sisters were married to ministers. (Courtesy of June Nealy.)

Three

Courthouses and Public Buildings

Edwardsville's first seat of government was a log cabin near Cahokia Creek. Beginning in 1812, the cabin of settler Thomas Kirkpatrick served as the first county building. That year, territorial governor Ninian Edwards and Pres. James Madison announced the formation of Madison County and designated Kirkpatrick's site as the location of the county seat. Several years later, Kirkpatrick surveyed the emerging town on his land and named it Edwardsville for his political patron.

In 1816, the U.S. Land Grant Office opened on North Main Street, with Benjamin Stephenson appointed receiver of public money to manage it. Edwardsville became the largest land-selling office in the United States. Stephenson also was appointed subagent of Indian Affairs for the Illinois Territory. Stephenson's success with land revenue and Edwardsville's designation as county seat for the then-huge Madison County combined to make the town an early center of political and economic importance. Prominent leaders, including Ninian Edwards, Benjamin Stephenson, Edward Coles, and Auguste Chouteau, lived or spent time in Edwardsville.

In 1822, David Prickett was appointed as the first postmaster of Edwardsville. His office was a brick building on North Main Street across from the intersection of the Springfield Road, near the public square.

In 1826, the need for a larger courthouse was evident, but the city coffers were not up to the challenge. Several of the wealthier citizens provided some of the materials, hence the nickname "donation courthouse." This courthouse was constructed of brick on a plot of ground several blocks southeast of Kirkpatrick's cabin, on what came to be recognized as Edwardsville's public square. An undated plat shows a courthouse building, a jail, and a clerk's office building, the latter of which would become Edwardsville's school for black children in years to come. This area was bound by North Main Street on the southwest side and Springfield Road on the northeast side. Although the donation courthouse was constructed of brick, the walls, floors, and furnishings remained unfinished until the 1830s, when money was borrowed from the school fund to pay for improvements.

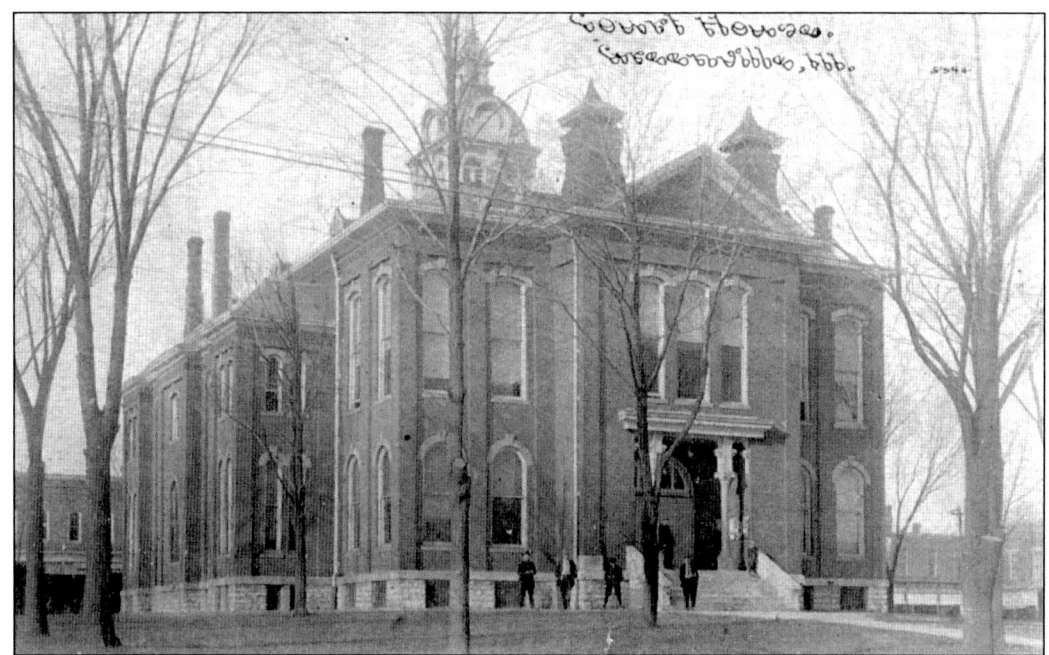

By the 1850s, the Illinois public lands had been sold and the U.S. Land Grant Office, no longer needed, was closed out by its last registrar, Michael G. Dale. Edwardsville's population had grown, and a new and larger courthouse was planned approximately a mile southeast of the donation courthouse public square. This elegant neoclassical-style building was constructed between 1853 and 1857 on the 100 block of North Main Street. (Courtesy of June Nealy.)

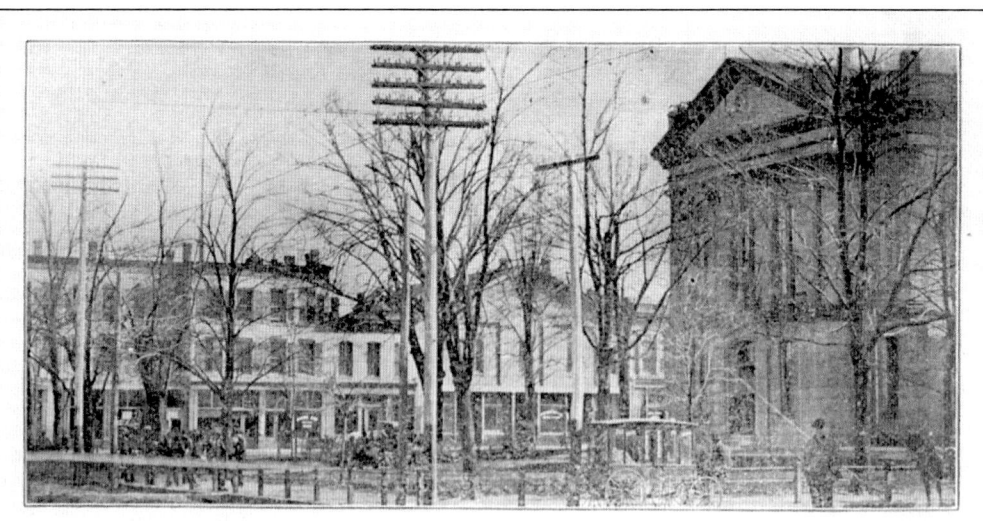

Court Square in Edwardsville, County Seat of Madison County, Illinois

As the new courthouse was constructed, businesses moved from Lower Town to the new Upper Town area and the center of town shifted. Soon commercial enterprises lined the streets surrounding the courthouse block—North Main, St. Louis, Second, and Purcell Streets. (Courtesy of June Nealy.)

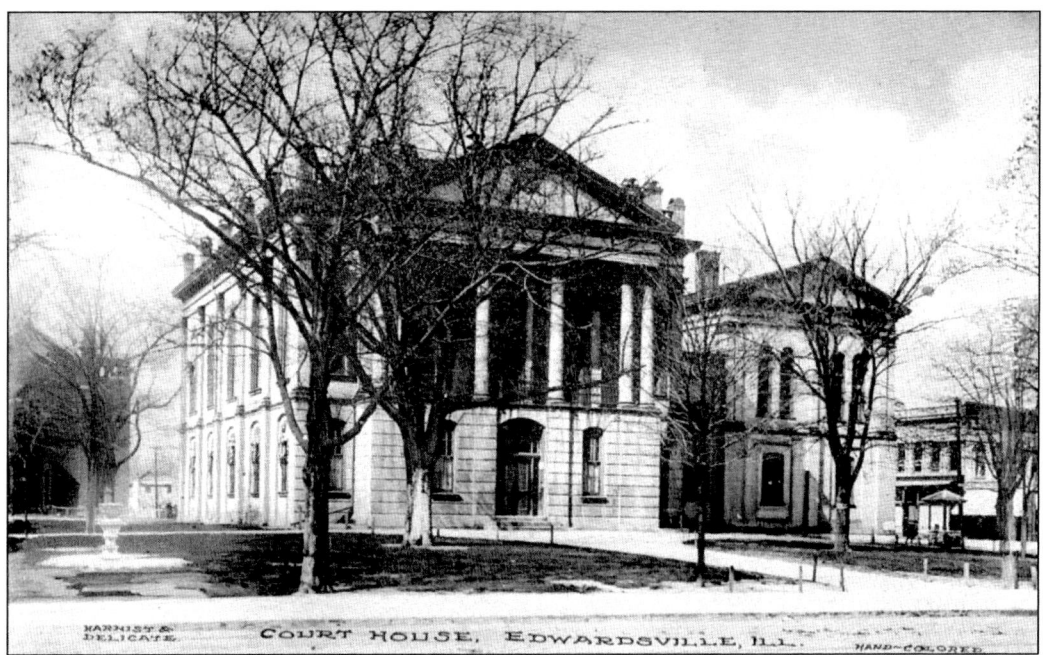

In 1890, with county government outgrowing its space, an addition to the courthouse was built on the north side toward Purcell Street. The new wing was designed in a similar style to the courthouse but constructed of brick with less adornment. Business buildings on Purcell Street can be seen on the right. (Courtesy of June Nealy.)

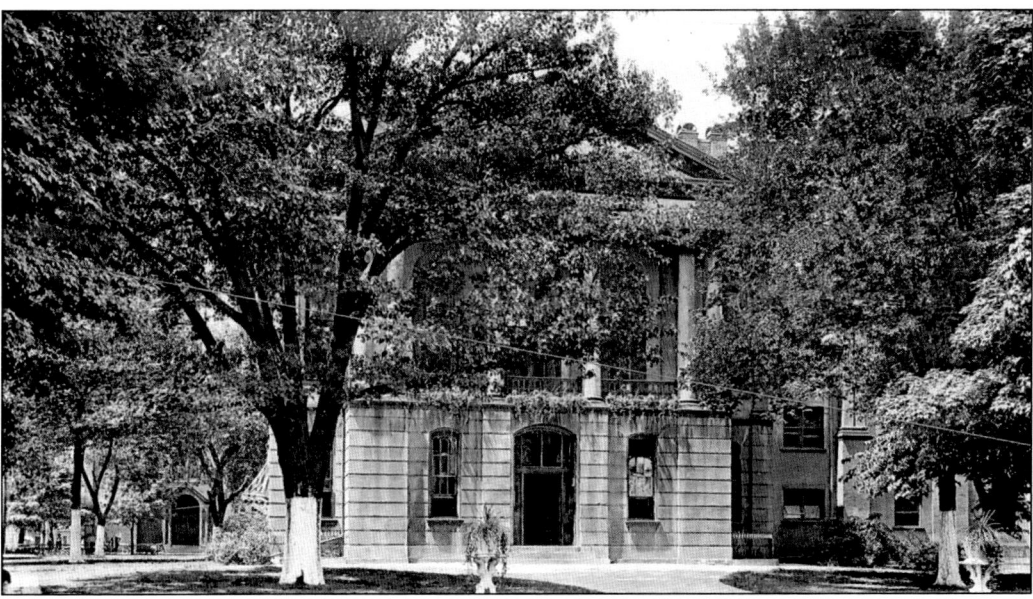

The land on which this courthouse and its successor in 1915 were built originally belonged to Thomas Kirkpatrick, Edwardsville's first settler, who later sold it to James Mason. It is believed that Mason donated the land for the purpose of constructing the county courthouse on it. (Courtesy of June Nealy.)

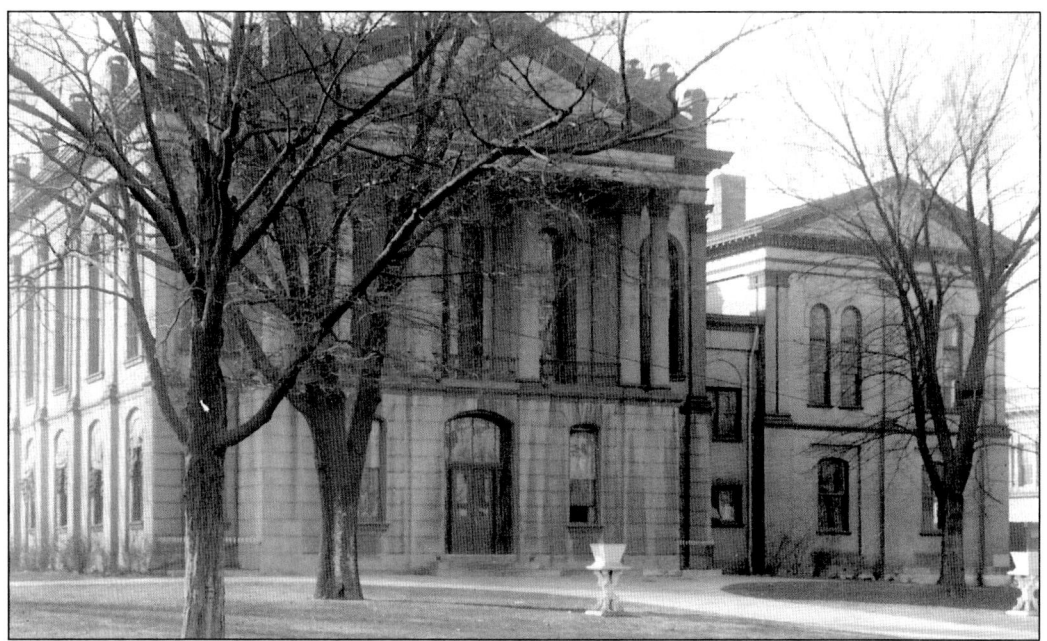

The courthouse square was bordered by Purcell Street on the northwest, North Main Street on the northeast, St. Louis Street on the southeast, and Second Street on the southwest. This image shows the courthouse in winter with bare trees. (Courtesy of June Nealy.)

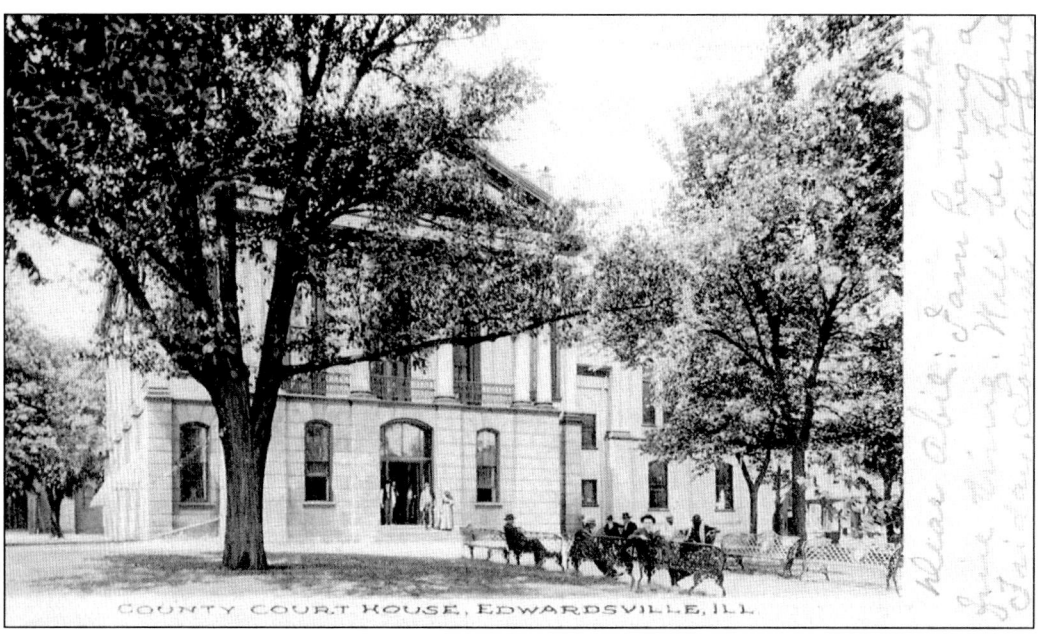

The county courthouse with its welcoming benches in front was a natural gathering place as the town moved south into what was then known as Upper Town. In 1912, the Madison County centennial arch was constructed from plaster of paris on the courthouse lawn. Within three years, the centennial arch and the 1850s courthouse and its addition would all be gone. (Courtesy of June Nealy.)

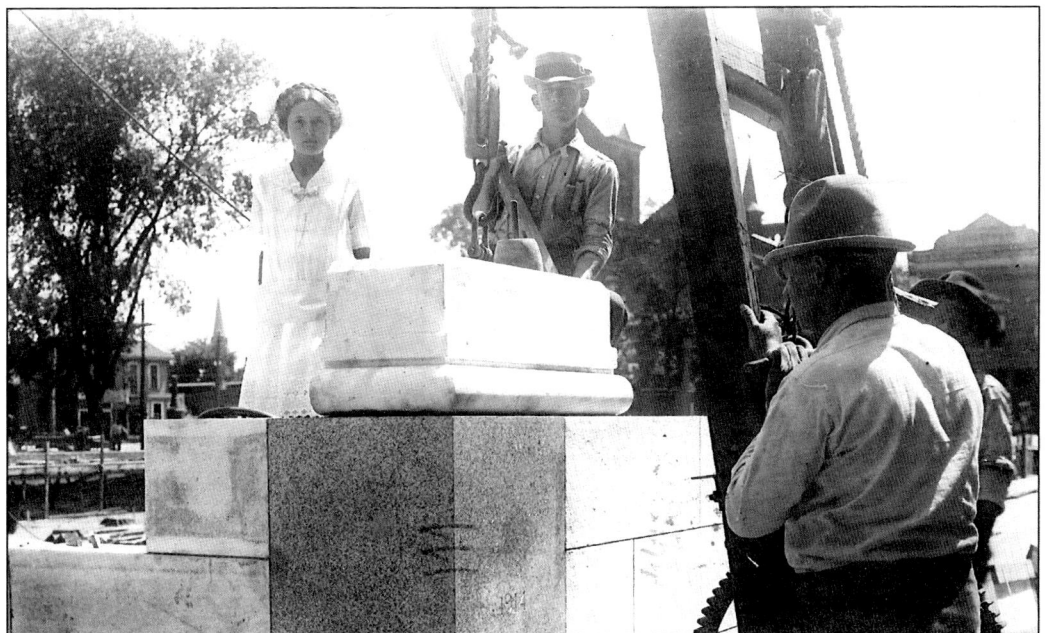

In 1914, construction began on the fourth and present Madison County Courthouse. In this photograph, Lee Little, daughter of Sheriff and Mrs. George E. Little, assists with setting the first courthouse stone. The cornerstone, containing documents and photographs in a metal box, was set in place on the previous day. (Courtesy of Neal Strebel.)

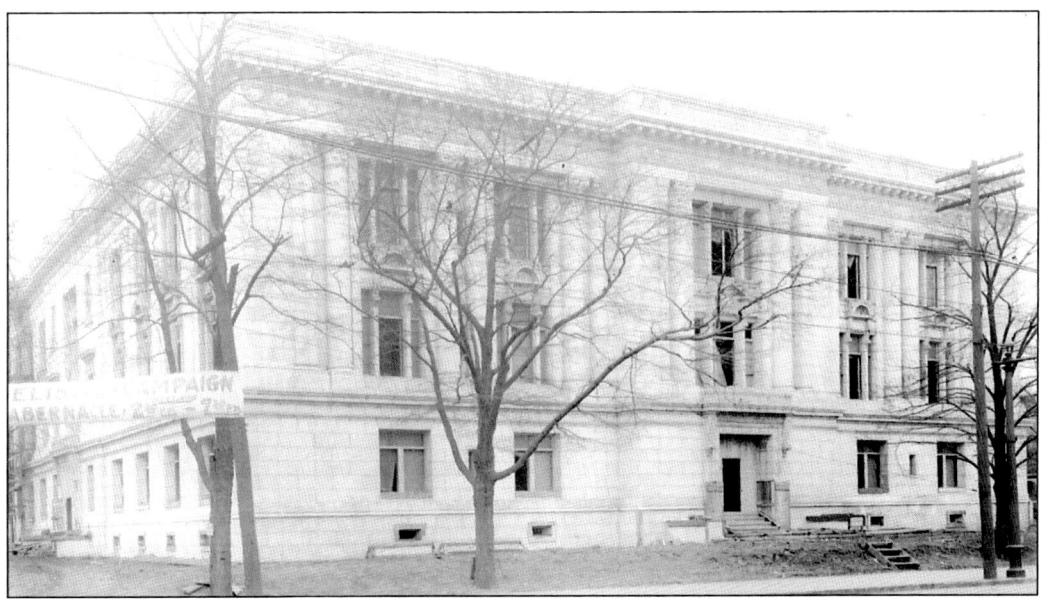

This photograph taken in late 1914 or early 1915 shows the new courthouse with its exterior of unpolished Georgian white marble largely completed. The architectural style of the structure has been debated and has been variously described as neoclassical, Greek Revival, French Renaissance, and classic revival. The building covers almost an entire city block. (Courtesy of June Nealy.)

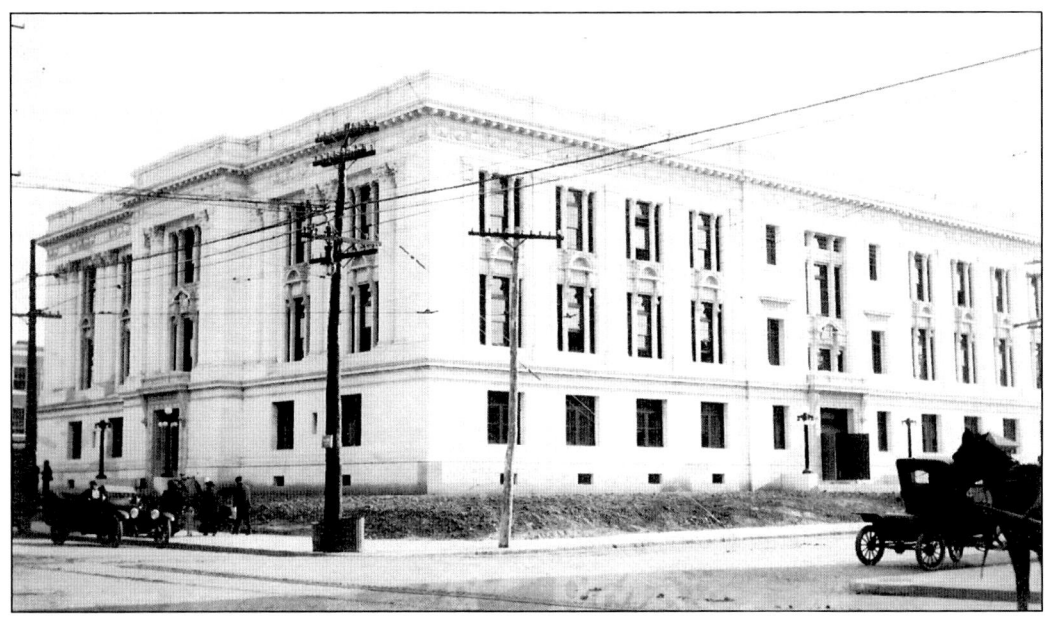

Architectural adornments of the new courthouse included inset Grecian columns, pedimented windows, and a floral garland frieze. Terra-cotta ornament was used in the window, doorway, and cornice trim and accents and in the figures that surround the scales of justice at the entrances. The architect was Robert G. Kirsch of St. Louis, who also designed the Miners' Theatre in nearby Collinsville. (Courtesy of Neal Strebel.)

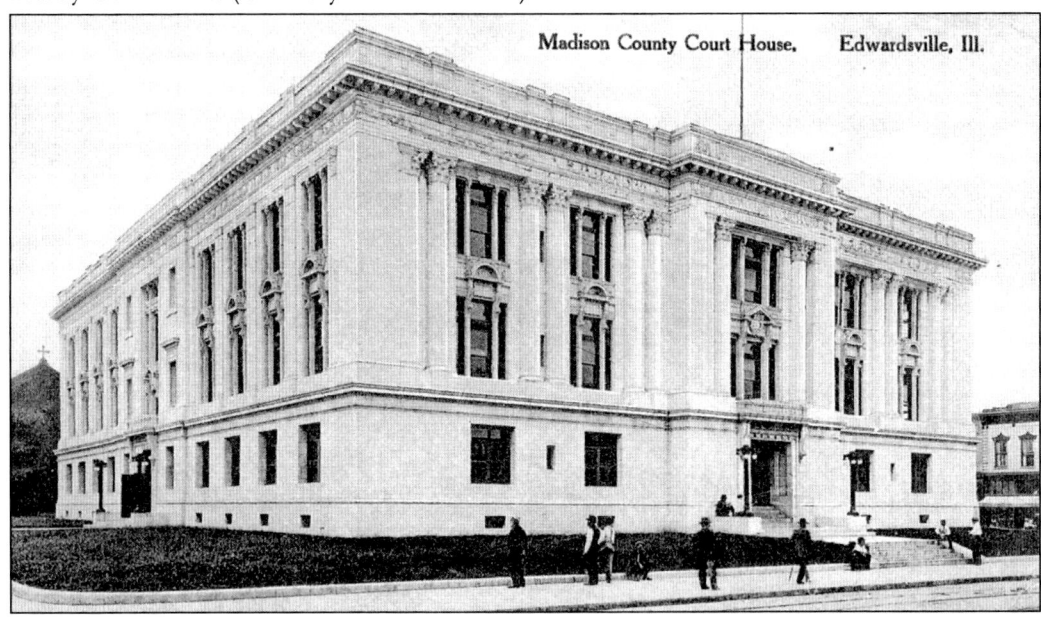

During the new courthouse's construction, county government had carried out its day-to-day business in temporary quarters hastily erected at Vandalia and Johnson Streets. The move to the new courthouse began on October 11, 1915. A week later, on Monday, October 18, the county celebrated the dedication of the new building with speeches by dignitaries, including former speaker of the U.S. House of Representatives "Uncle Joe" Cannon of Danville. (Courtesy of June Nealy.)

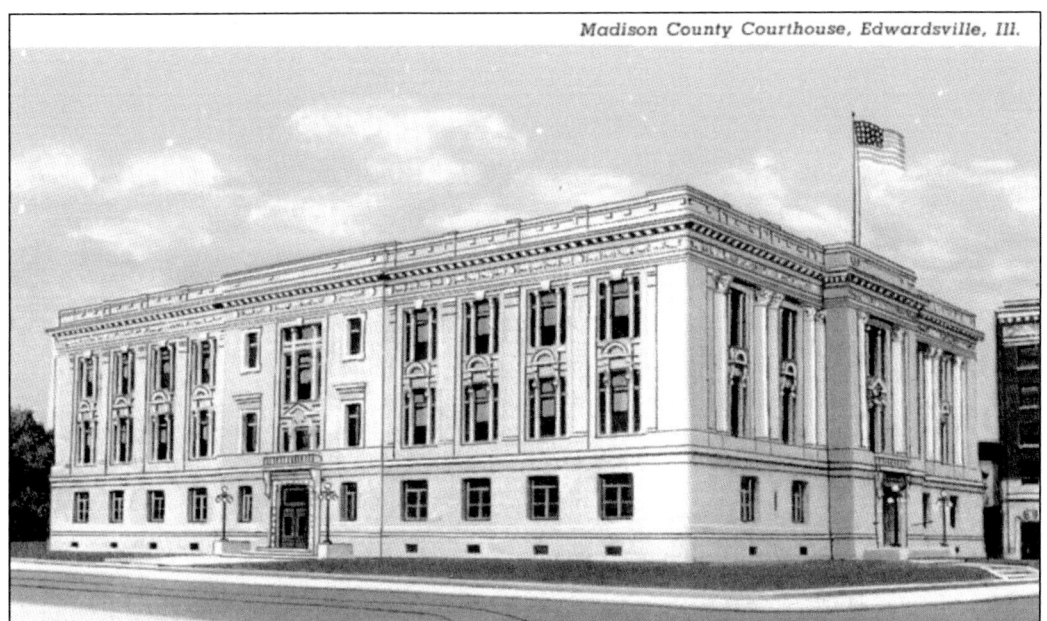

The dedication of the new courthouse on October 18, 1915, drew a huge crowd. Although this later image does not show a soul in sight, one can imagine the throngs of people who came out that day. On one of these postcards, the message on the back from a woman living in Highland reported to a friend, "Fred and I were at Edwardsville last Monday at the dedication of this building, and surely was some crowd there." (Courtesy of June Nealy.)

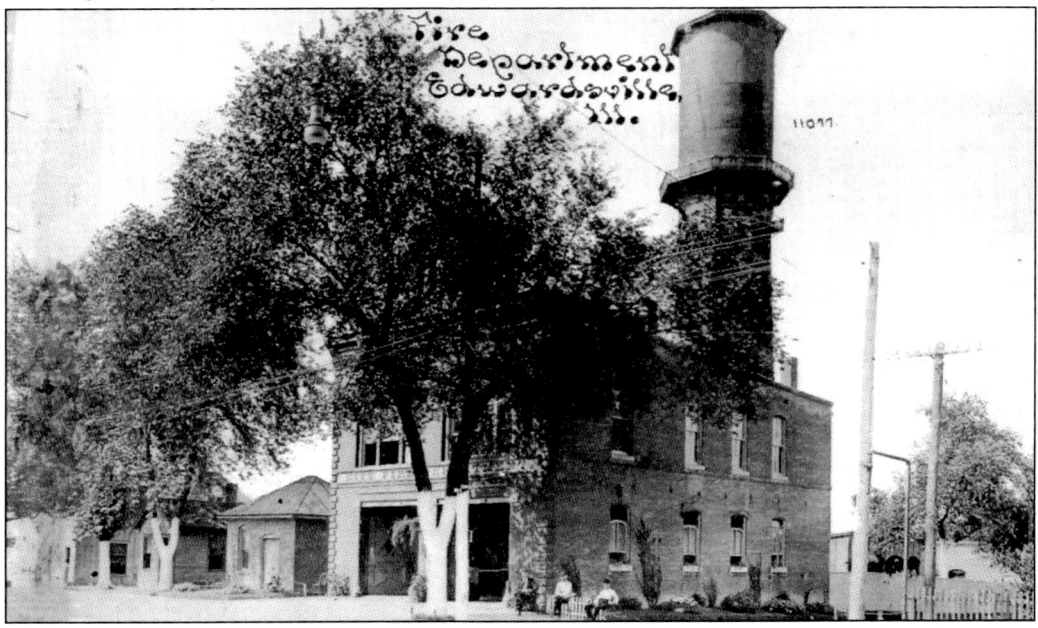

This Edwardsville City Hall and Fire Department was built in 1892 at 400 North Main Street. There was no city fire department until 1874, when Edwardsville Volunteer Fire Company No. 1 was organized with 33 charter members. The firemen pulled a hand-drawn wagon with ladders and buckets to fires. The city council authorized the purchase of a fire bell and uniforms in 1875. The fire chief during the 1890s was Dennis Hentz. (Courtesy of June Nealy.)

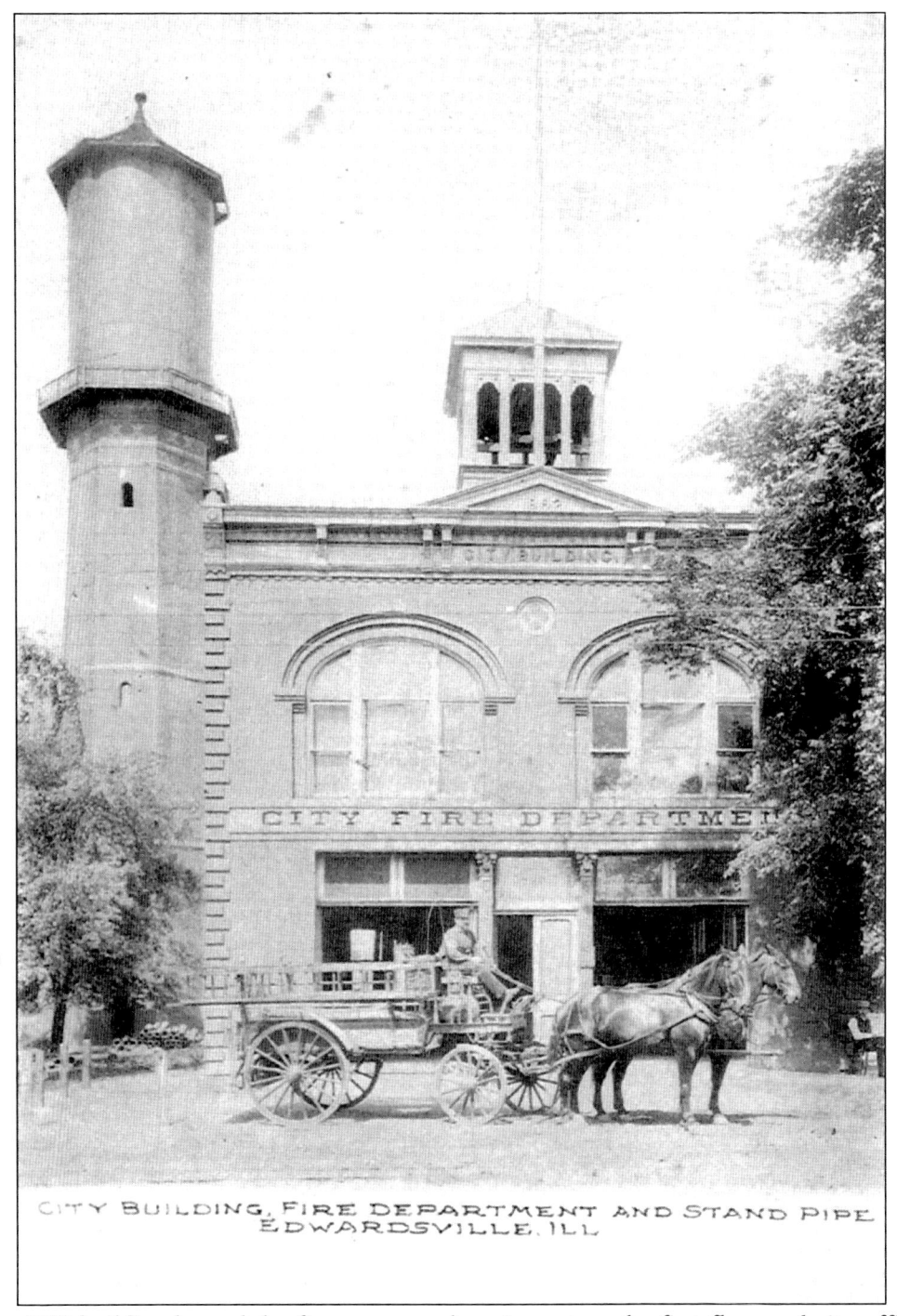

CITY BUILDING, FIRE DEPARTMENT AND STAND PIPE
EDWARDSVILLE, ILL.

The 1892 building housed the fire wagon and equipment on the first floor and city offices on the second floor. As stated in *Edwardsville: An Illustrated History*, the city outfitted its fire department with "an almost new combination hose, chemical wagon and ladder truck and a team of beautiful black horses that had been part of the 1904 St. Louis World's Fair equipment." (Courtesy of June Nealy.)

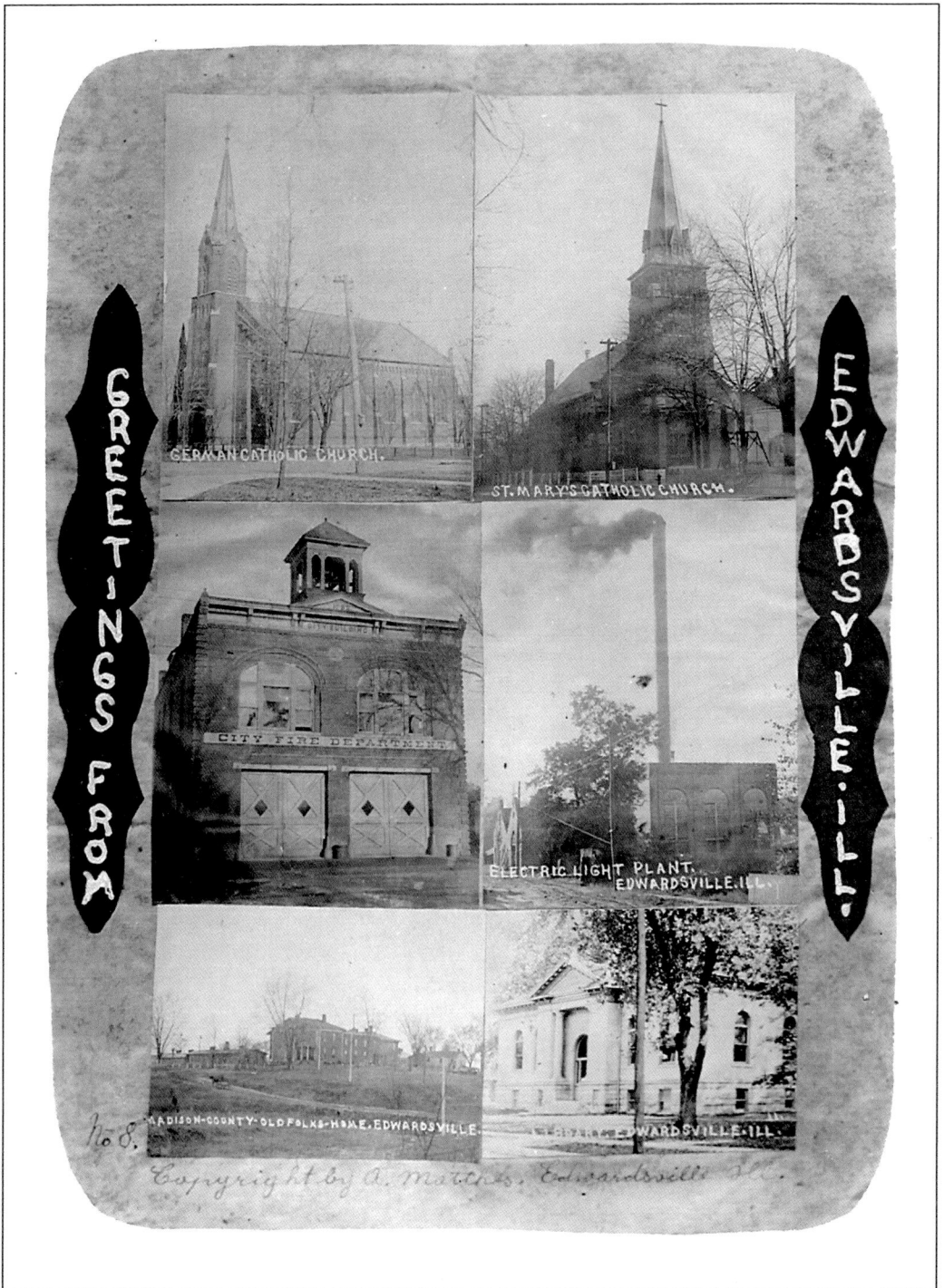

This multiview card shows, in the center row, the fire department on the left and the Electric Light Plant on the right. Edwardsville was one of the first cities in Illinois to get electric streetlights. This plant on Second Street provided Edwardsville's electric power until 1927, when the city began to acquire electrical power from a plant in Cahokia. (Courtesy of June Nealy.)

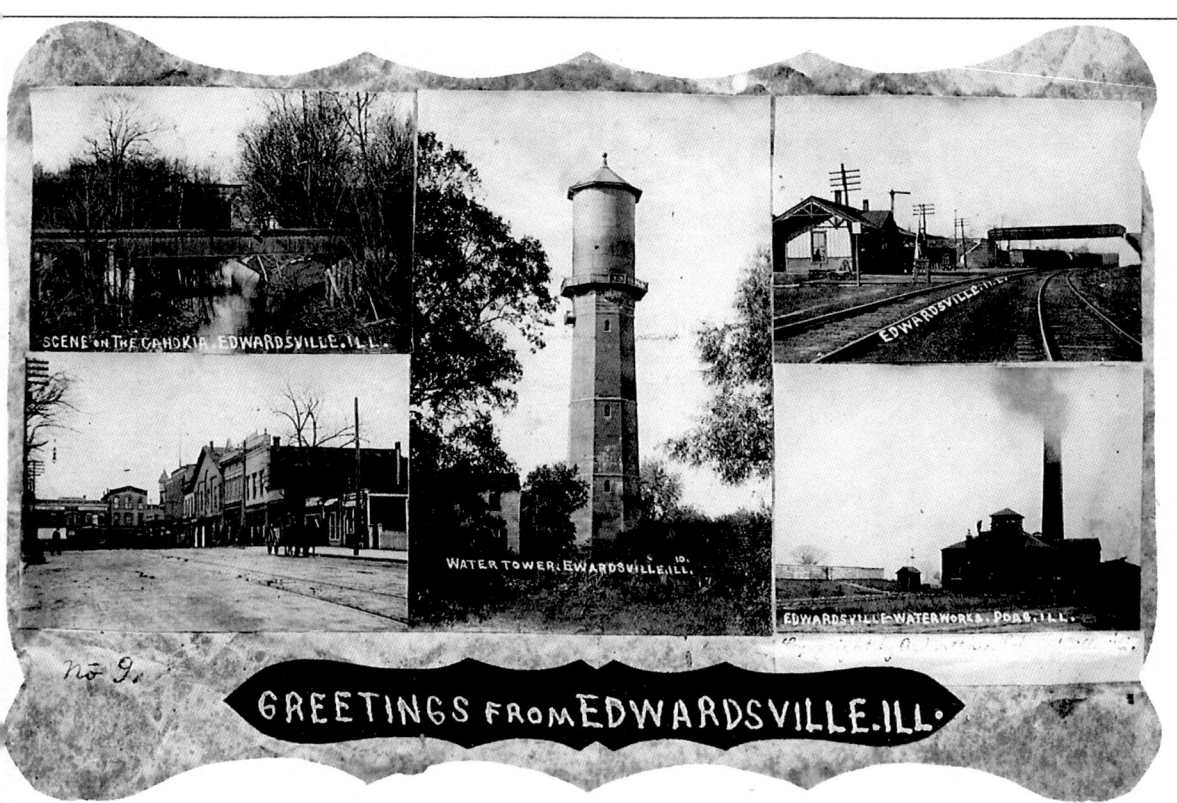

This multiview card shows views of the water tower (center) and the Edwardsville Water Company (lower right). The original water tower was located behind the city hall and fire department on North Main Street, built by Tuxhorn Brothers Contractors. The Edwardsville Water Company was located four and a half miles west of town at Poag and was incorporated by local businessmen and encouraged by Mayor Charles Boeschenstein. (Courtesy of Neal Strebel.)

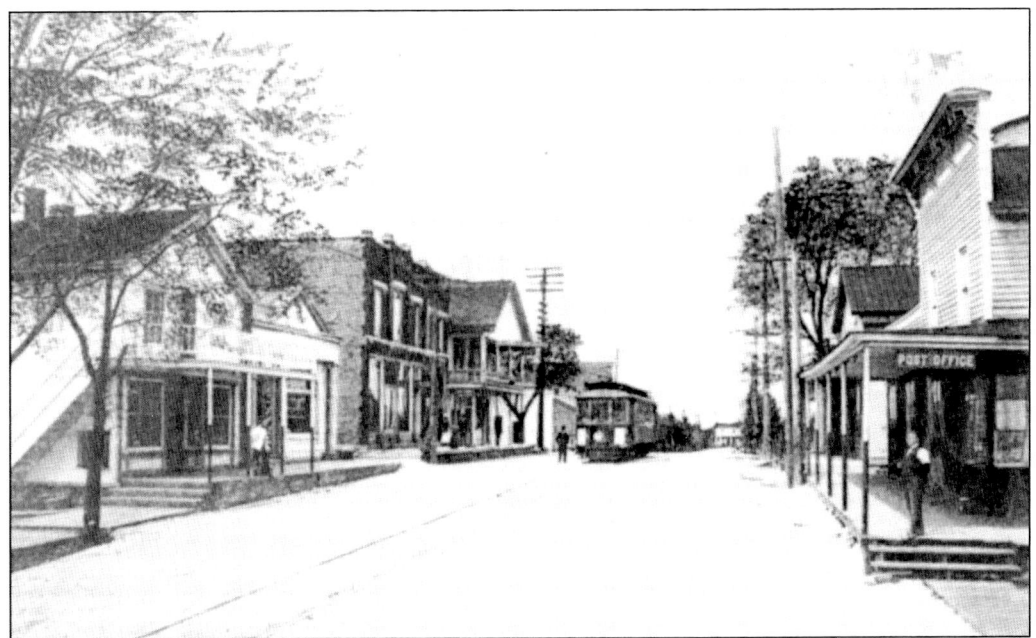

In most small American communities, the location of the town post office changed with each new postmaster until a federal post office building was constructed in the community. Early Edwardsville post offices include this one in an unidentified building and one in the Prickett Building at 109 Purcell Street prior to 1905. (Courtesy of Michael A. Sporrer.)

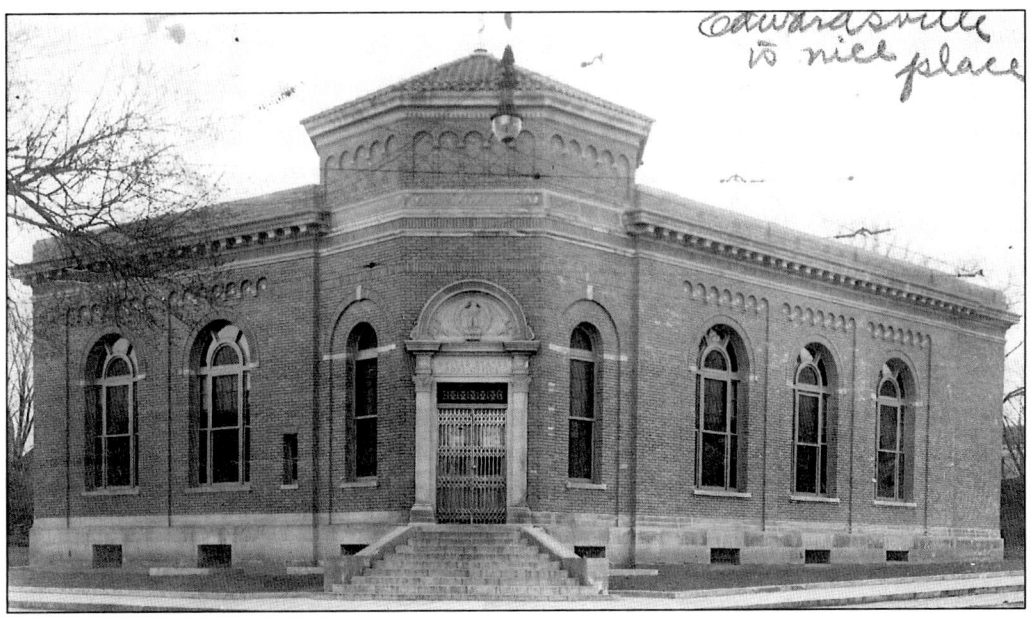

The United States post office building, with its octagonal tower entrance at the intersection of Hillsboro and Commercial Streets, opened in 1915 with T. M. Crossman as postmaster and W. M. Crossman Sr. as assistant postmaster. The annual salary of the postmaster at that time was around $2,500; in 1912, he directed a staff of 15 clerks and carriers. (Courtesy of Neal Strebel.)

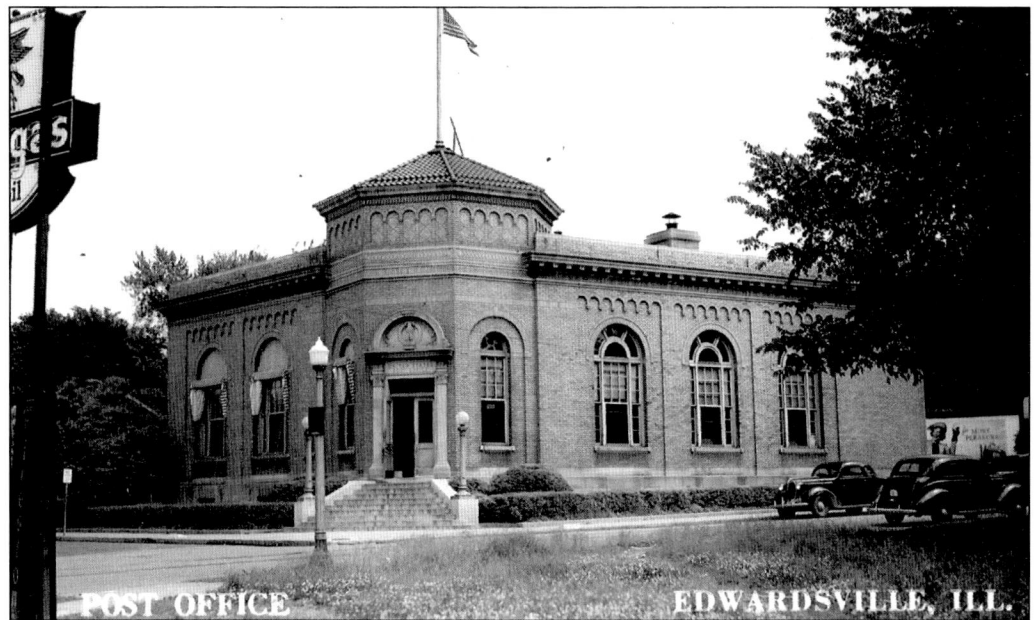

As the glimpse of the Mobil gas sign and the cars denote, the post office at Hillsboro and Commercial Streets continued to serve Edwardsville well into the 20th century. After 50 years of service, the building was relegated to housing county offices when a new post office was built nearby on Kansas Street. This building is now privately owned. (Courtesy of June Nealy.)

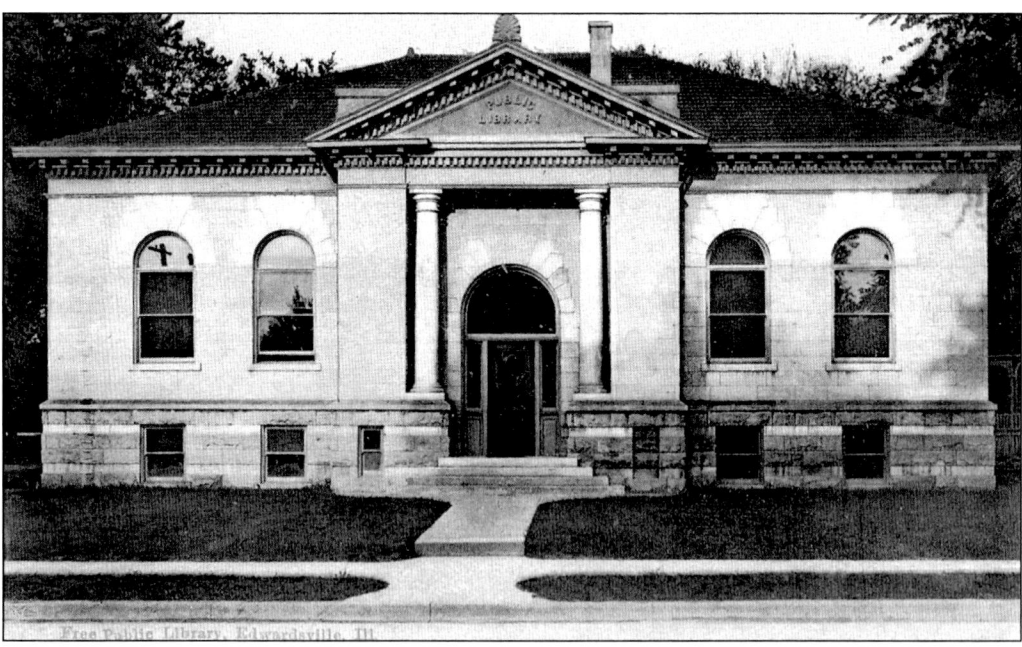

Charles Boeschenstein, former Edwardsville mayor and publisher of the *Intelligencer*, wrote to Andrew Carnegie in 1903, requesting funds for a public library. Carnegie responded with a $12,500 check to build the new library. The City of Edwardsville donated the land within Edwardsville City Park upon which to construct the new edifice and budgeted $1,250 per year for the library's expenses. (Courtesy of June Nealy.)

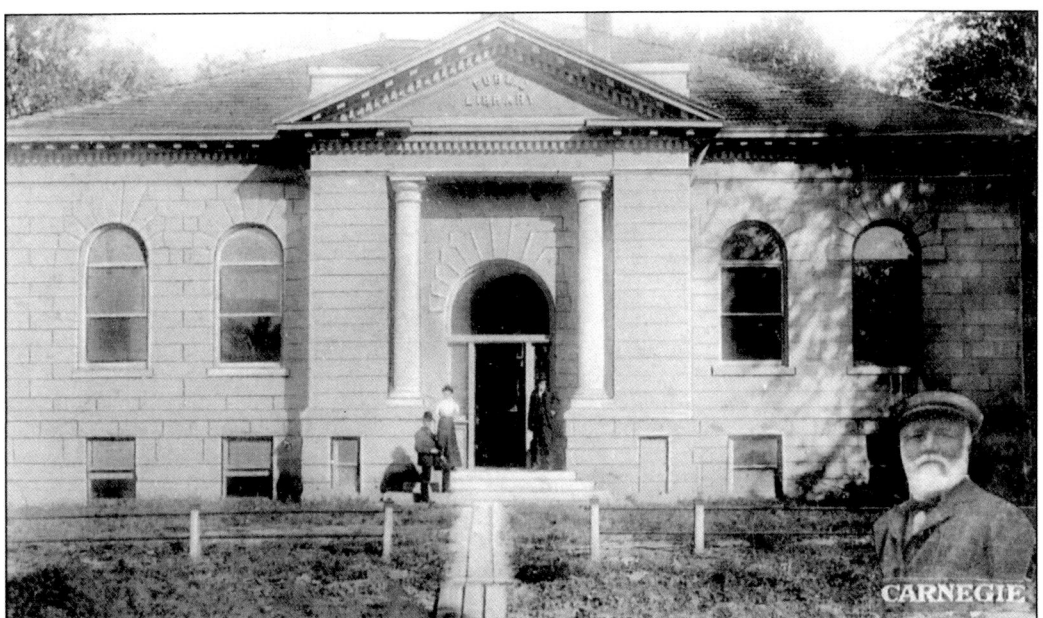

Andrew Carnegie, a Scottish immigrant who had worked his way from impoverished child to steel magnate, retired around the dawn of the 20th century from his steel company, selling it for close to $500 million. In an article written early in his life, Carnegie had stated that a man who dies rich "dies disgraced." To that end, he began his philanthropic phase, funding over 2,800 public libraries across the country. (Courtesy of June Nealy.)

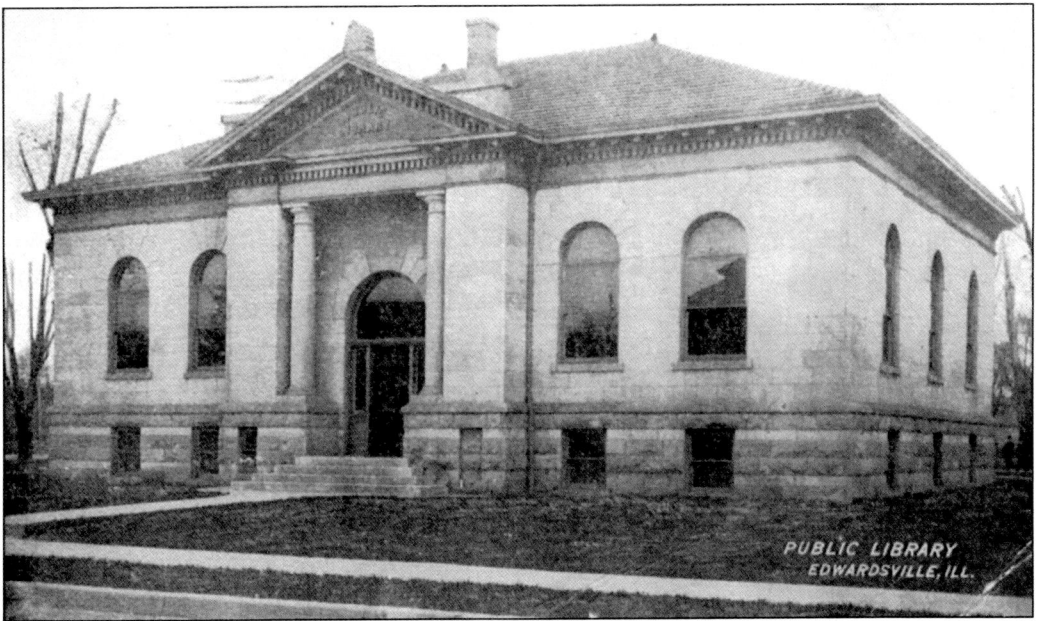

This handsome public library building was completed and dedicated in 1906, but the history of Edwardsville's libraries is much older. The city's first library was chartered in 1823 with over 100 volumes watched over by librarian John H. Randle. Although this library only lasted a short time, it stands as one of the state's oldest libraries. The collection was later looked after by a group of dedicated women as it was moved to various locations. (Courtesy of June Nealy.)

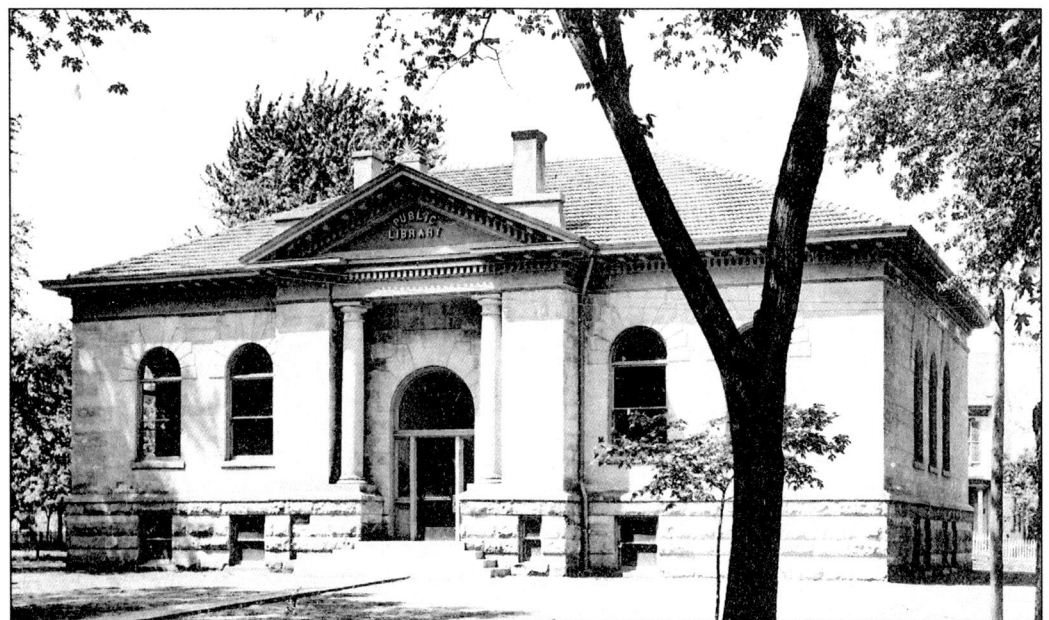

The library, although without a permanent home, was rechartered in 1879 and was fortunate to receive, in 1891, the lifelong dedication of Sarah Coventry, who served Edwardsville as librarian for almost a half century, until 1937. She bridged the gap between a small lending library moved from place to place and the building of the new library building and its establishment as a fixture of the city. (Courtesy of June Nealy.)

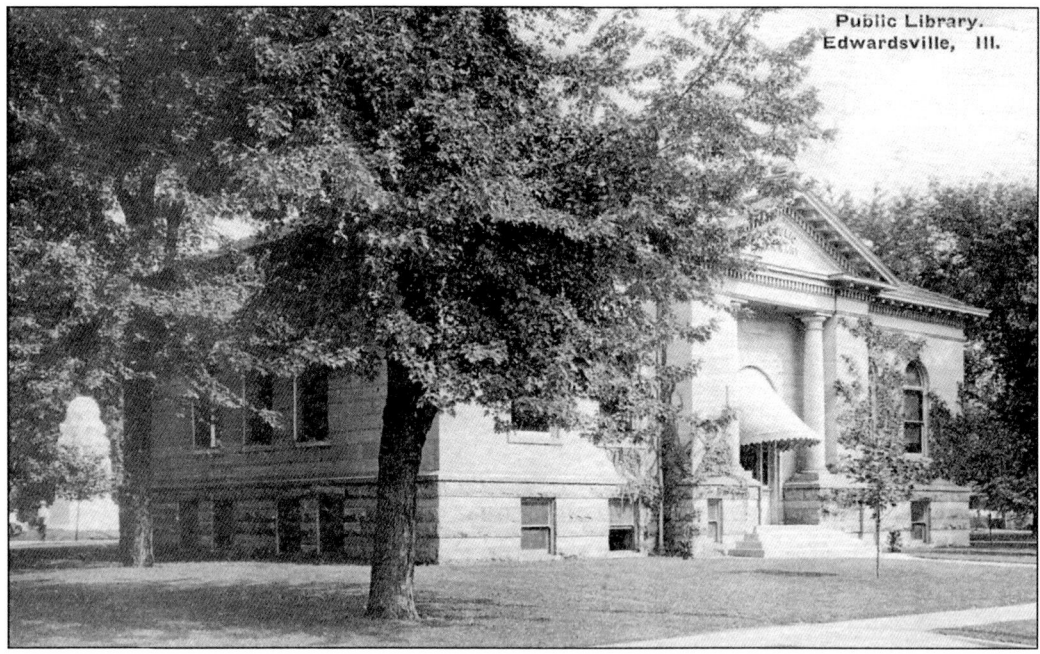

The new library began with a collection of about 500 books and some bookcases, which the women's library association had amassed. Charles Boeschenstein was appointed to lead the new Edwardsville Public Library Board. Fund-raisers and community events were held to assist with library expenses. (Courtesy of SJ Morrison.)

Four

Going to School

As early as 1809, there were "subscription schools," where only families with children who attended paid. The first recorded teachers included Joshua Atwood, John Barber, John Gibson, Miss Hastings, and Mrs. Stearnes. Several private schools also existed, some for short periods of time, including the Academy of Science, taught by Madame Jerome, and the Edwardsville Female Academy.

In 1855, Illinois passed legislation that required communities to establish property taxes to pay for free public schools. Consequently, several rural schoolhouses sprang up in the various townships in and around Edwardsville. These included Bohm, Center Grove, and Goshen in Edwardsville Township; Loos and Silvan in Pin Oak Township; and Progress in Fort Russell Township.

A later subscription school, the German Language School, established by German families, was active from 1855 to 1863. It was closed and sold, with the money being donated to the public library, after the Dale Public School opened in 1864.

In 1877, a free school for the African American children of Edwardsville was established at the corner of North Main and Liberty Streets in the former county clerk's building. This tract of land had been the site of the public square and the donation courthouse. Ironically, on this site, Gov. Edward Coles was sued by his political opponents in 1824 for freeing the slaves he had brought specifically from Virginia to free. In 1912, a handsome new brick building was constructed on the site as a grade school for the African American children. A two-year high school department was later added, but unfortunately any African American student who wished to complete his or her high school education was forced to go out of town to do so. Many went to the Lincoln School in Jefferson City, Missouri, where they could board until they graduated.

The St. Boniface Catholic congregation constructed its present school and hall in 1912; in 1889, there were 103 students. Trinity Lutheran built its first school building in 1915, after holding classes in the church basement for 14 years. By 1916, 48 students were enrolled in eight grades.

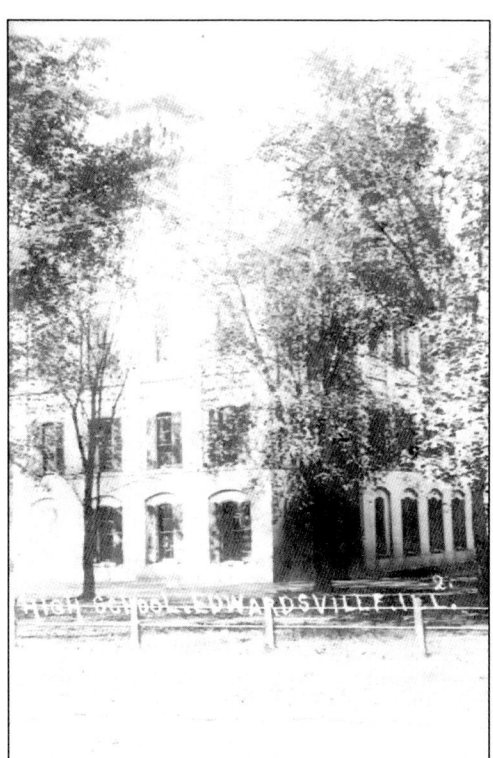

The Dale School was built in 1864 on Kansas Street and named for county court judge Michael G. Dale. The three-story white brick structure could hold 350 students and served all grades, including a high school department. Five teachers covered all the grades. Dale had come to Edwardsville in 1853 to serve as the last registrar of the U.S. Land Office, a post he closed out in 1857. (Courtesy of Neal Strebel.)

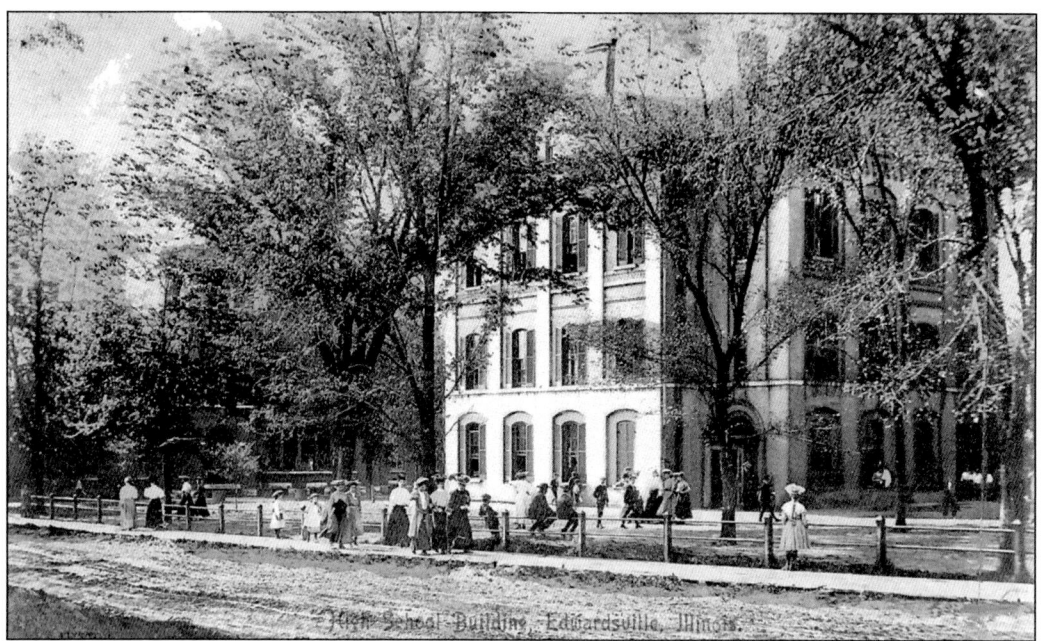

This view of the Dale School shows the older students in the school yard. The Dale School was designed by local architect Charles H. Spilman, who provided the designs for numerous buildings and houses in Edwardsville, including the home of attorney William H. Krome. Spilman was a member of the local Masonic lodge and in 1915 took over the local newspaper, the *Intelligencer*, from Charles Boeschenstein. (Courtesy of June Nealy.)

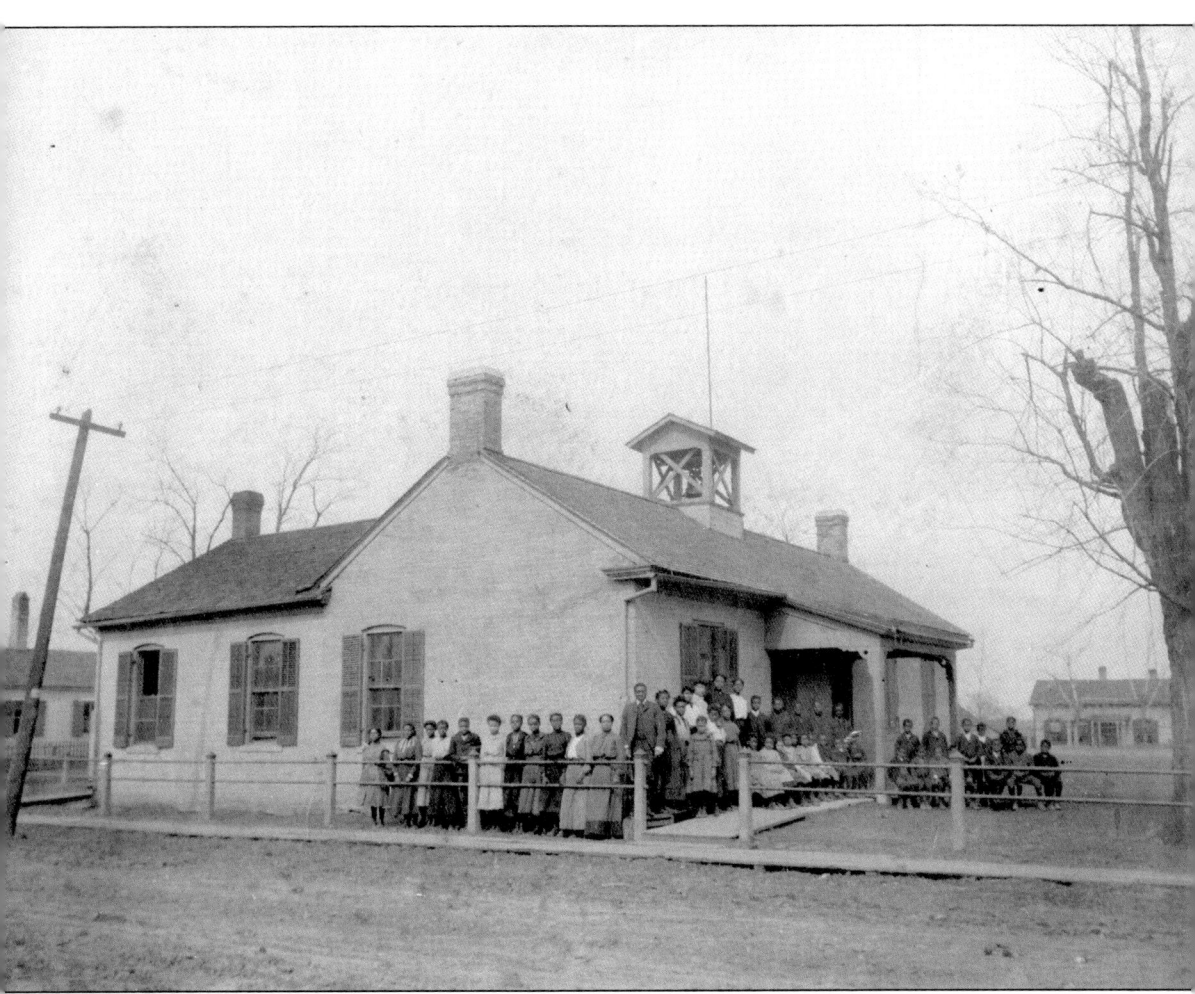

The free school for African American children, established in 1877, is shown here in 1910. Christopher Columbus Jones dedicated his life to giving African American children an education and served as principal from 1902 in this school until 1950 in the new Lincoln School, which replaced this building. Anna C. Harper was another early teacher who served in this building. (Courtesy of Madison County Historical Society.)

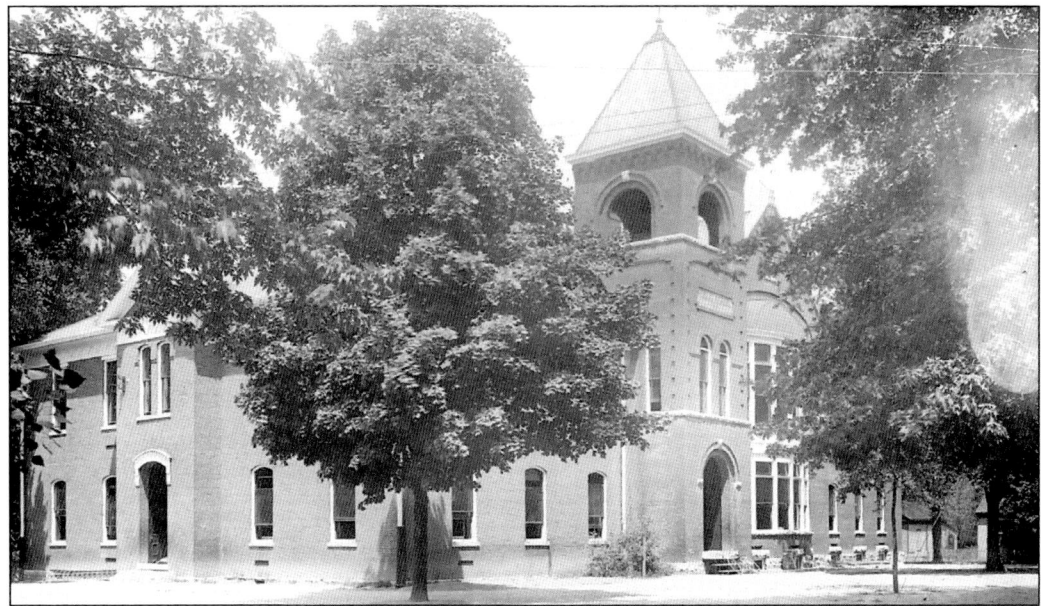

In 1886, the portion of the Columbus School to the left was built as the new public school for elementary students, allowing more room in the Dale School for the older students. This building was constructed adjacent to the Dale School. Charles H. Spilman again served as architect. (Courtesy of Michael A. Sporrer.)

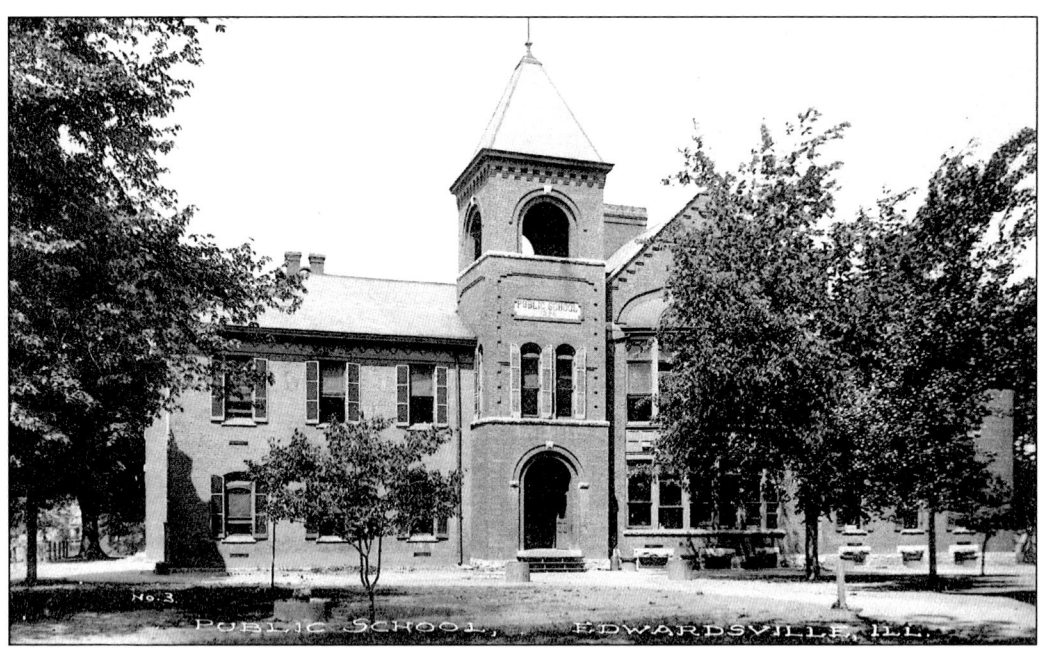

Again in 1896, reflecting the growing population, more classrooms were needed to accommodate students. The bell tower in the center of the building and the large section to the right were added onto the 1896 Columbus School building, providing eight more classrooms. Charles H. Spilman again provided the architectural design. (Courtesy of June Nealy.)

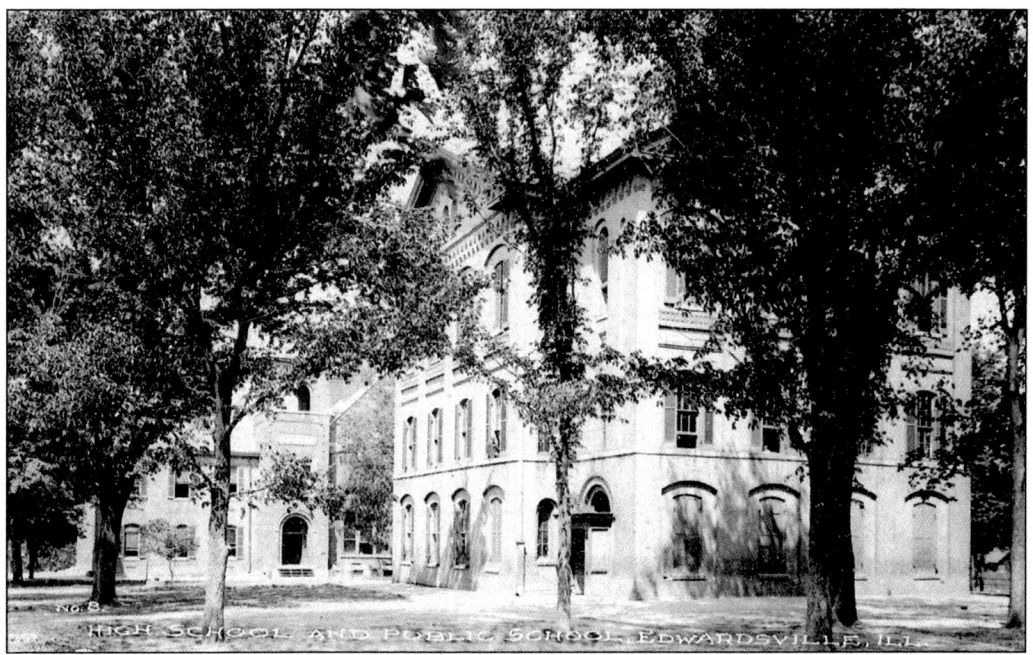

Dale School is shown in front in these photographs facing North Kansas Street, with the 1886–1896 Columbus School in the background. The Columbus School still exists and is in use, and is the Edwardsville Community Unit School District's oldest building. It is accessed on East College Street, the street to the left in the lower photograph. In 1900, the board of education listed desirable qualities for Edwardsville teachers as including professional equipment, appearance, voice, initiative, use of English; outside activities; resourcefulness; industry; enthusiasm; optimism; loyalty; definite aims; sincerity; self-control; tact; sense of justice; understanding of children; and skill in stimulating thought. (Above, courtesy of June Nealy; below, courtesy of Neal Strebel.)

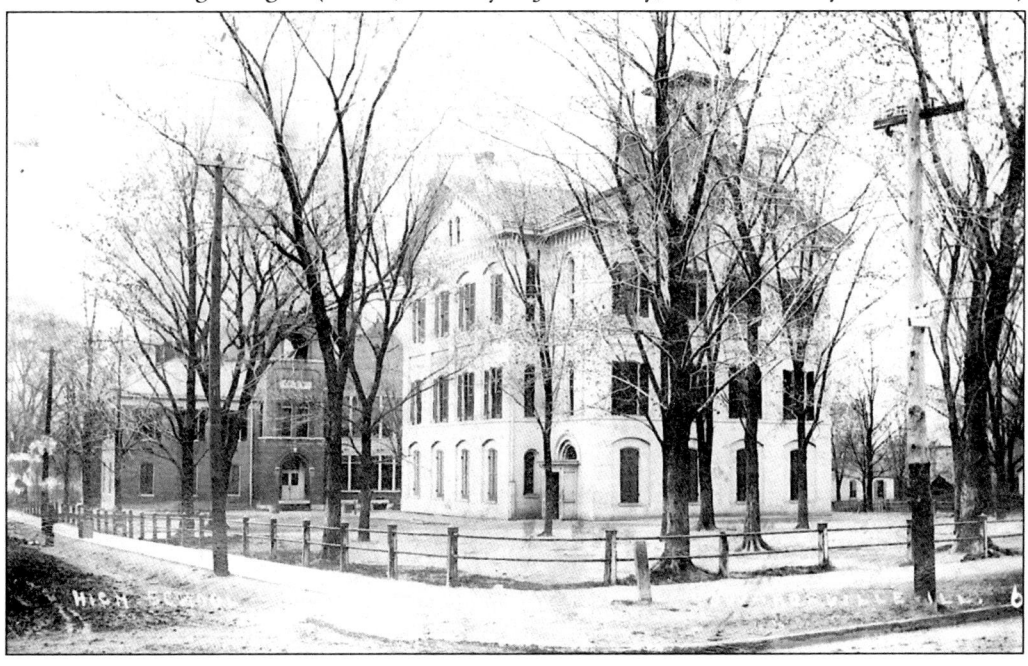

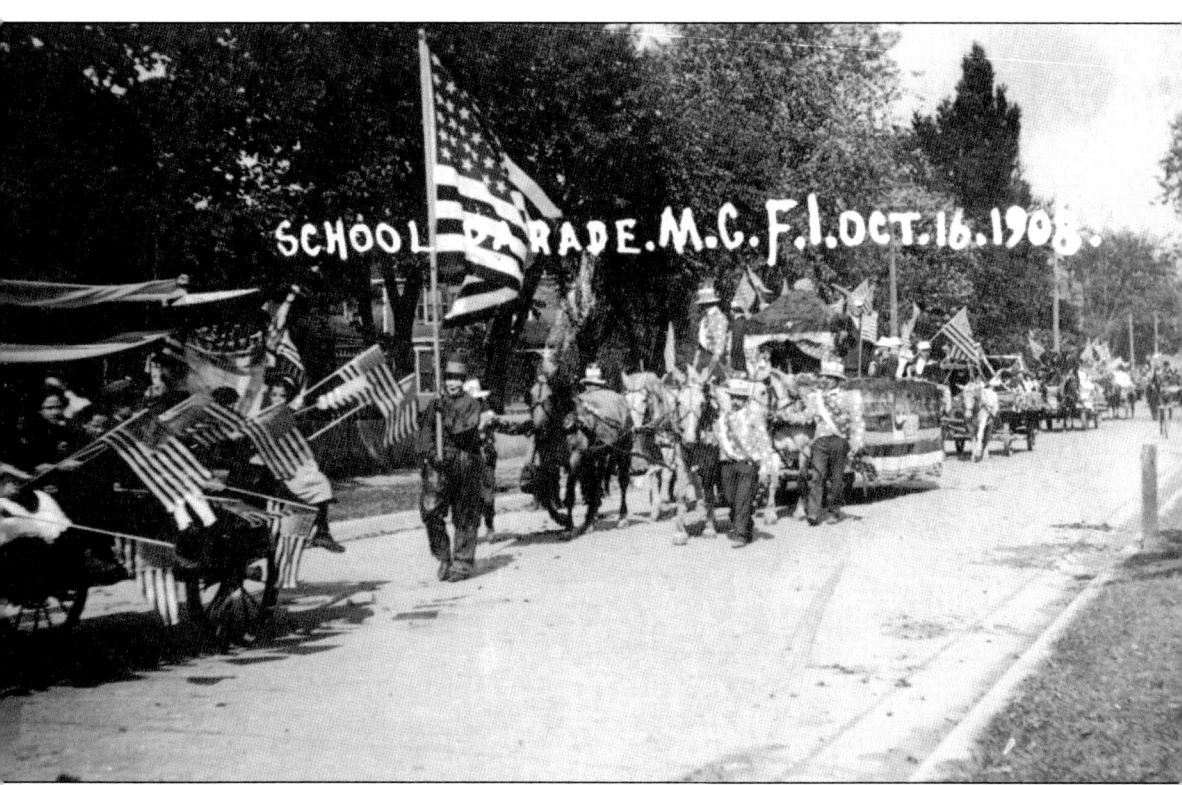

On October 16, 1908, Madison County schools closed for a holiday on the closing day of the annual Farmers' Institute and participated in a huge parade down Main Street. The parade had a total of 45 classrooms participating, which amounted to over 2,000 students. An article in the *Intelligencer* stated, "If there is anything that warms the heart and evokes enthusiasm, it is the schools and the view of the future citizens who are 'coming on.'" (Courtesy of Madison County Historical Society.)

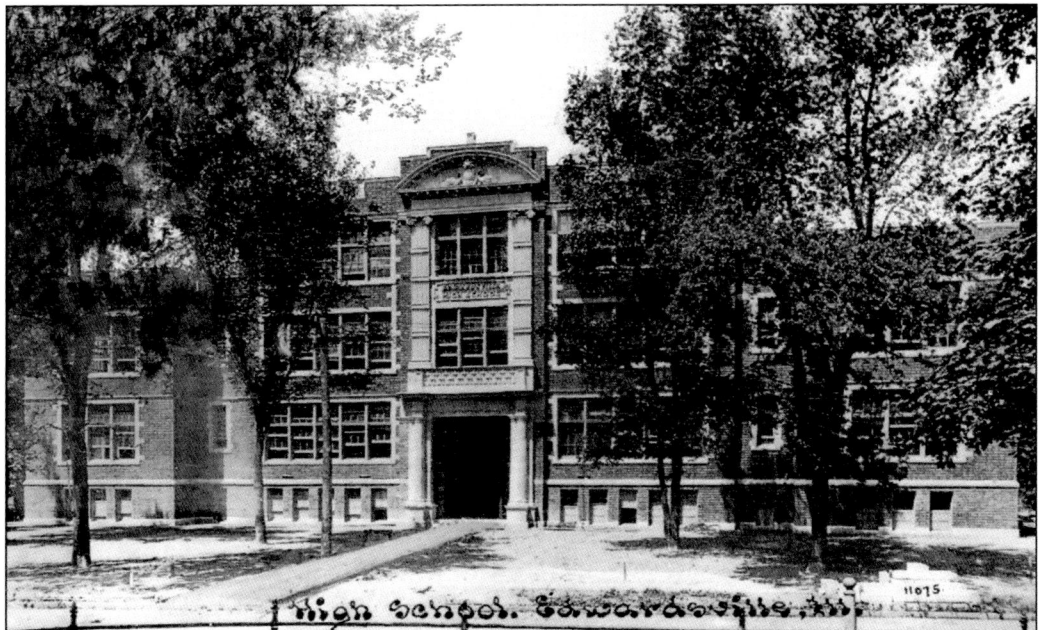

By the early 1900s, the community began to realize the need for a larger, separate high school. Edwardsville School Board president Judge W. P. Early and school board members expressed their support in statements in the *Intelligencer* in 1909. In 1910, the 1864 Dale School was razed and construction began on this three-story high school on the Dale School site. Of Tudor design, this school was named Edwardsville High School. (Courtesy of June Nealy.)

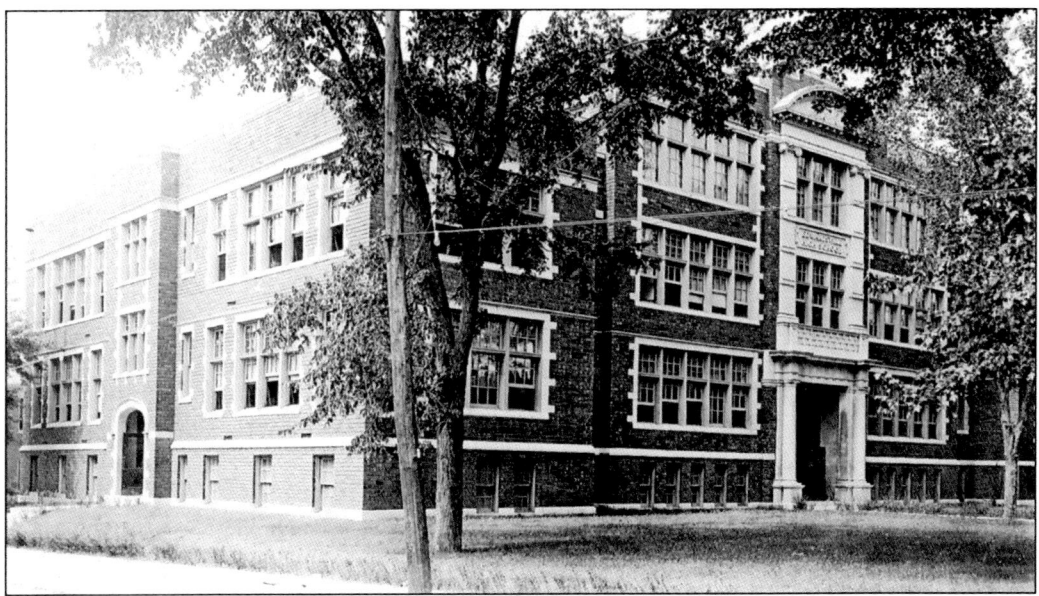

On May 22, 1909, a $50,000 bond issue was voted on. The new school carried a contract price of $47,194, and with the plumbing, heating, and fixtures cost added in, the total came to $62,000. The school dedication was held on August 30, 1911, and school opened for classes on September 1. The new building contained about 30 rooms, including modern laboratories, classrooms, offices, and a gymnasium. (Courtesy of June Nealy.)

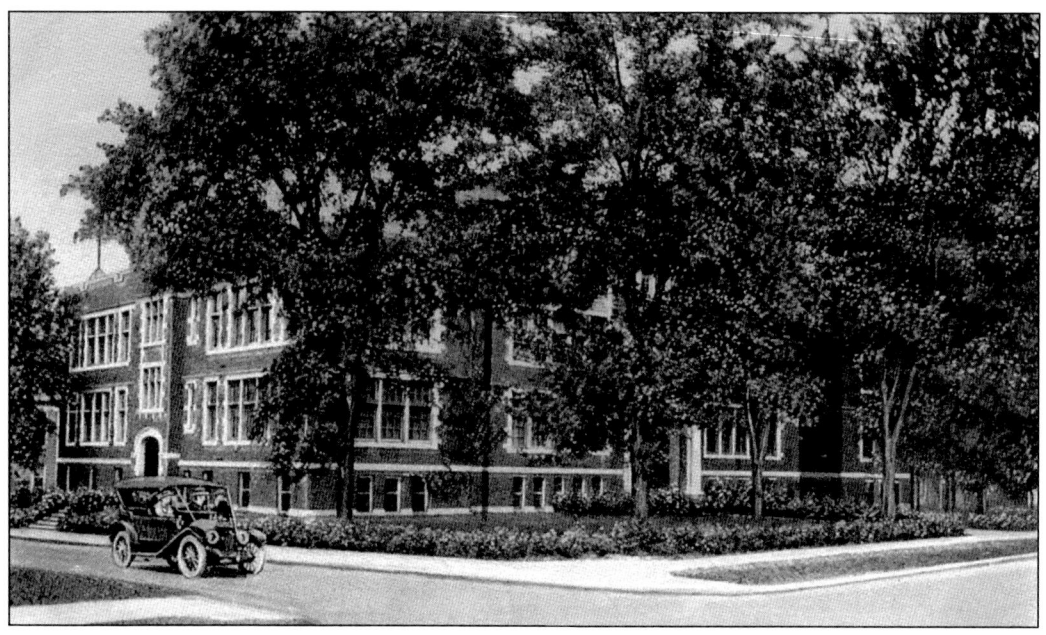

As the earliest automobiles came into use, the high school on Kansas Street that replaced the Dale School building was still in use until the new high school building was constructed in the late 1920s at another site. This building then went into service as the junior high school. Today it serves as part of the Columbus Elementary School. (Courtesy of June Nealy.)

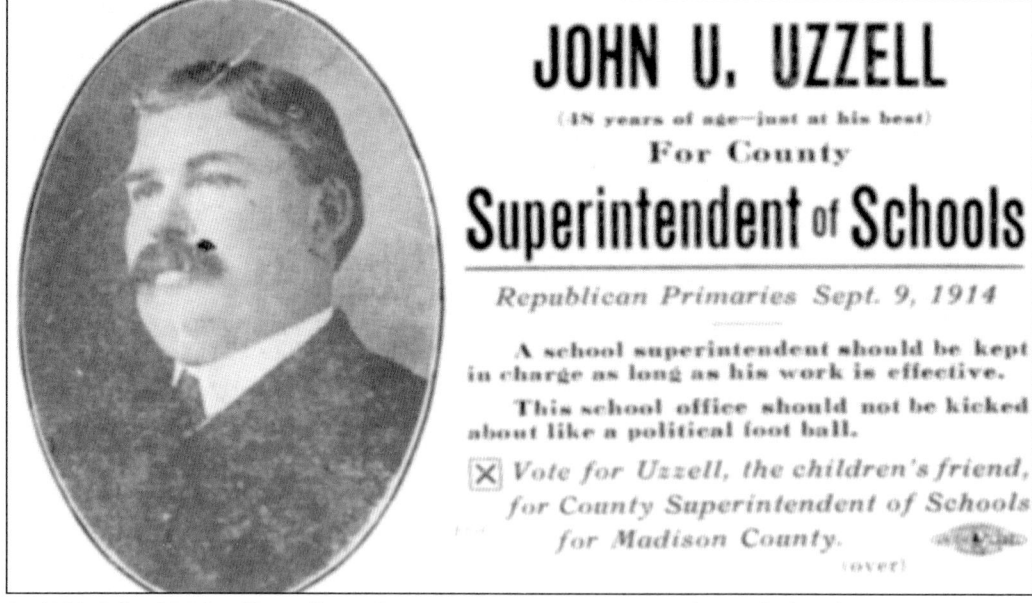

In 1914, John U. Uzzell ran for reelection as county superintendent of schools. He touted some of his accomplishments as county spelling and arithmetic matches, standardizing of rural schools, a 200 percent increase in eighth-grade graduation, a county course of study with uniform textbooks, and a boys' corn growing club. Before becoming superintendent, Uzzell was a teacher in the nearby Bethalto school system. (Courtesy of June Nealy.)

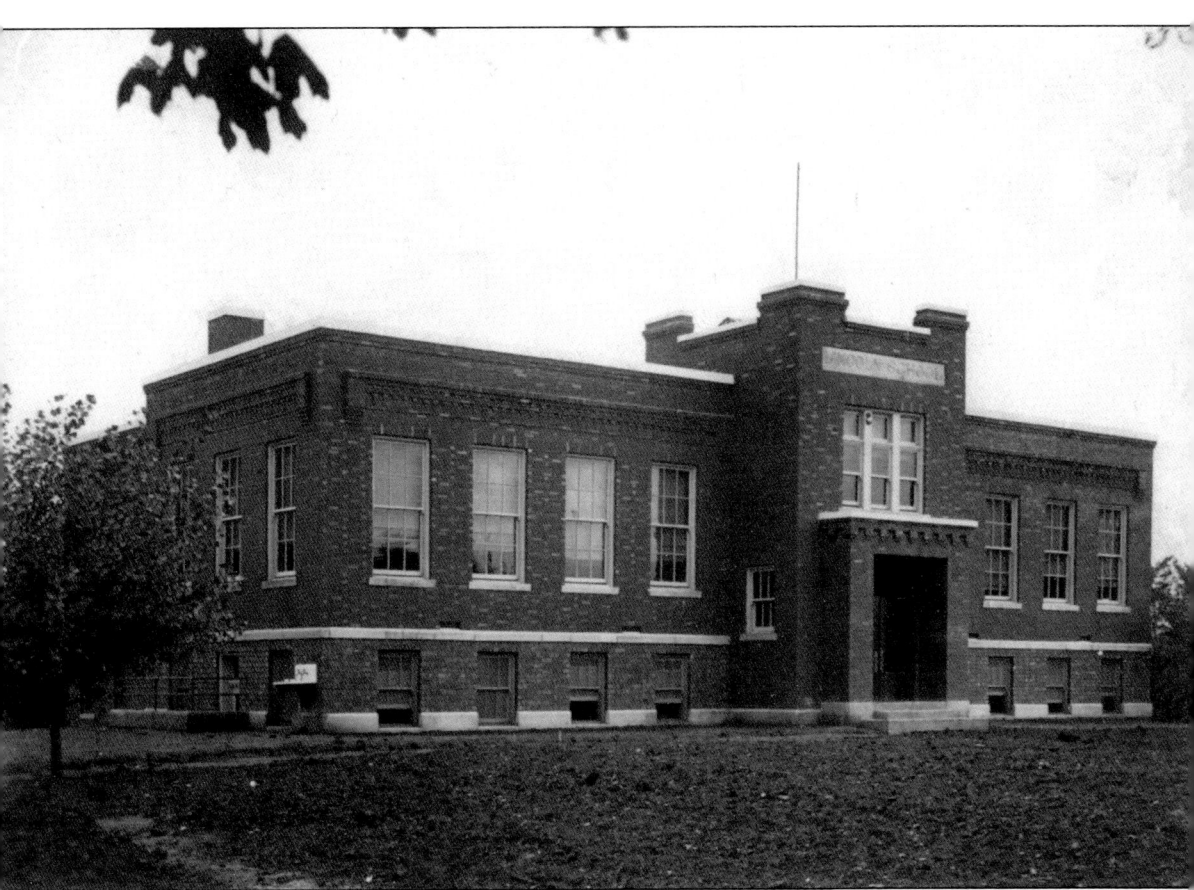

A petition was brought before the school board in 1911 to build a new school for the African American children to replace the old 1833 county clerk's office, which had been used since 1877. Lucas Pfeiffenberger and Sons architectural firm of Alton was hired to design the school, which was completed in 1912. It served as the black school of Edwardsville until it was closed in 1951 for renovations to reopen in 1952 as an integrated elementary school. (Courtesy of Madison County Historical Society.)

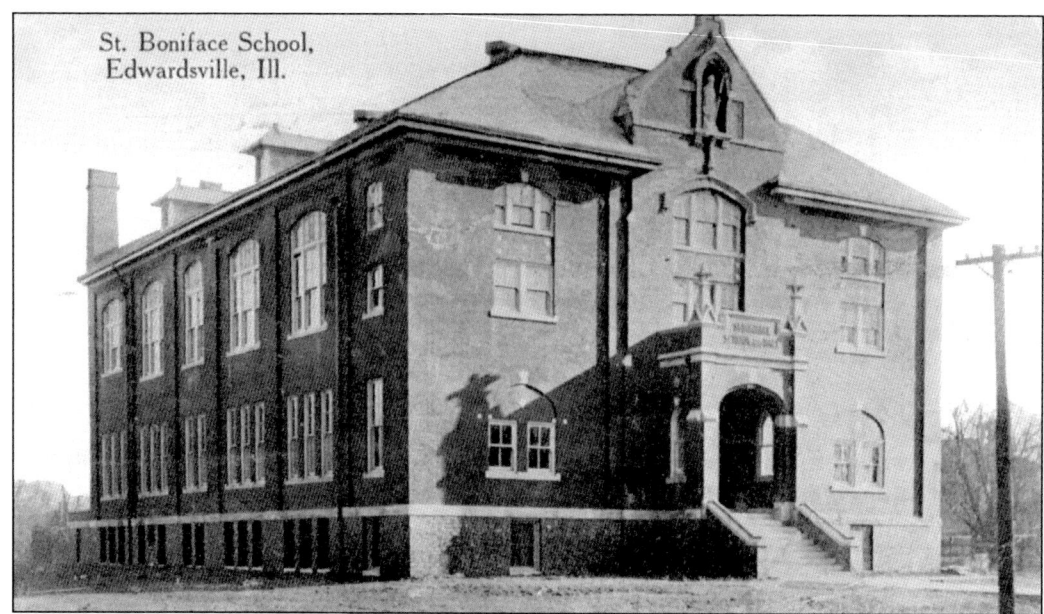

St. Boniface Catholic School and Hall was constructed in 1912, replacing its first school, which had been established in 1871. Its modern amenities included large classrooms, a kitchen, a dining room, playrooms, and a 600-seat auditorium on the third floor. Administrators and teachers were Sisters of the Precious Blood (1871–1896), Sisters of St. Dominic of Racine (1896–1904), and Poor Handmaids of Jesus Christ, beginning in 1905. (Courtesy of June Nealy.)

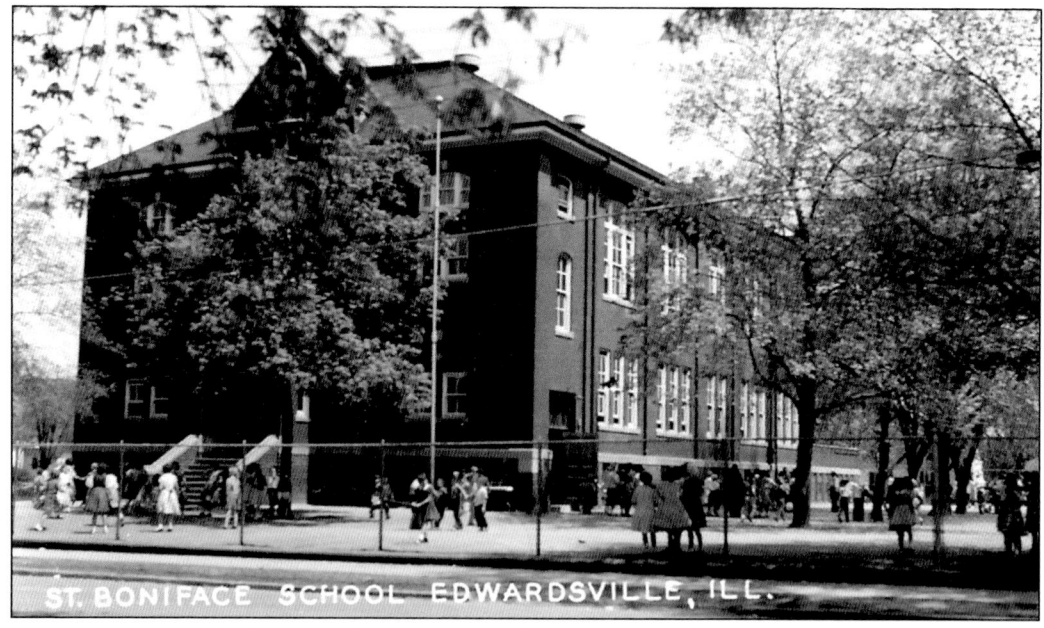

During Fr. Ernest J. Eckhard's 35-year tenure at St. Boniface, he initiated wholesome recreational activities for the students and had bowling lanes installed in 1928 in the basement of the St. Boniface school. Advertisements read, "Edwardsville's finest bowling parlor," and "wholesome entertainment for young and old." The 1912 building serves to this day as the congregation's day school. (Courtesy of June Nealy.)

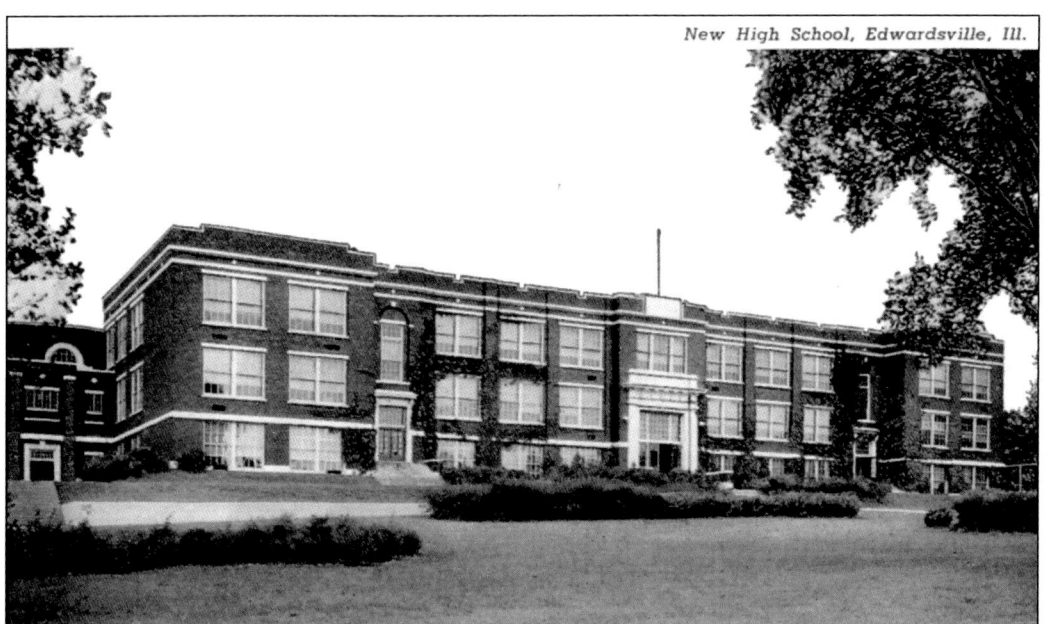

By 1921, the ever-growing school enrollment in Edwardsville again created crowded conditions at the high school building on Kansas Street. The school board looked for a larger tract of land on which to build the new high school and settled on acreage on West Street between St. Louis and Schwarz Streets. The architect of this three-story edifice was M. B. Kane, one of several generations of Edwardsville architects. (Courtesy of June Nealy.)

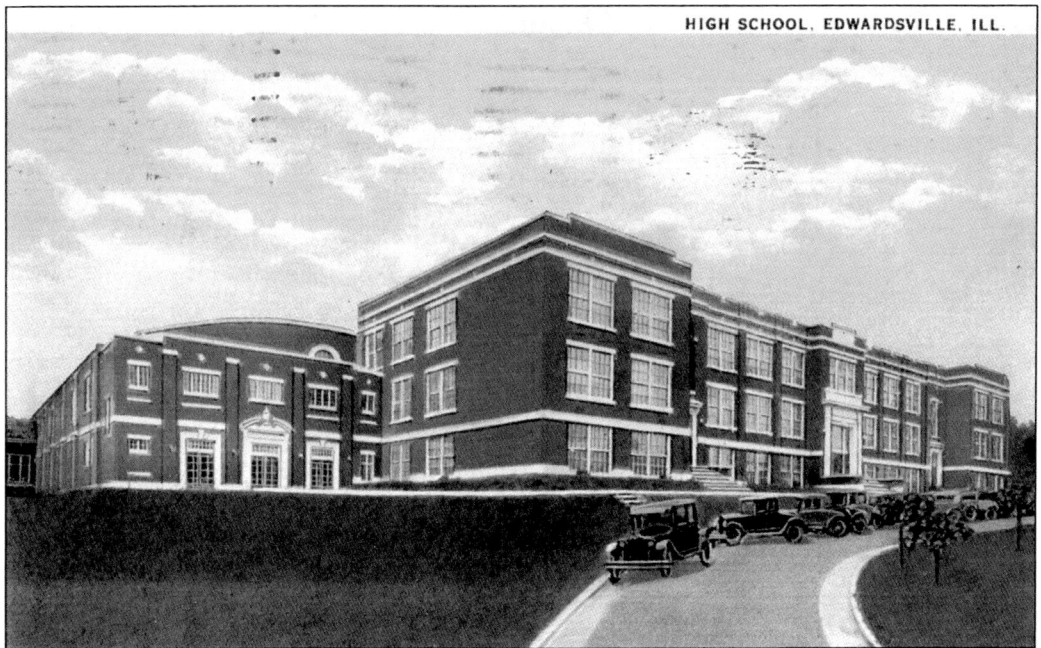

The main building of the new high school on West Street was completed in 1925; however, the gymnasium was not added on until 1928 because of low funds. As the new high school was put to use, the old 1910 high school building on Kansas Street became a junior high school. (Courtesy of June Nealy.)

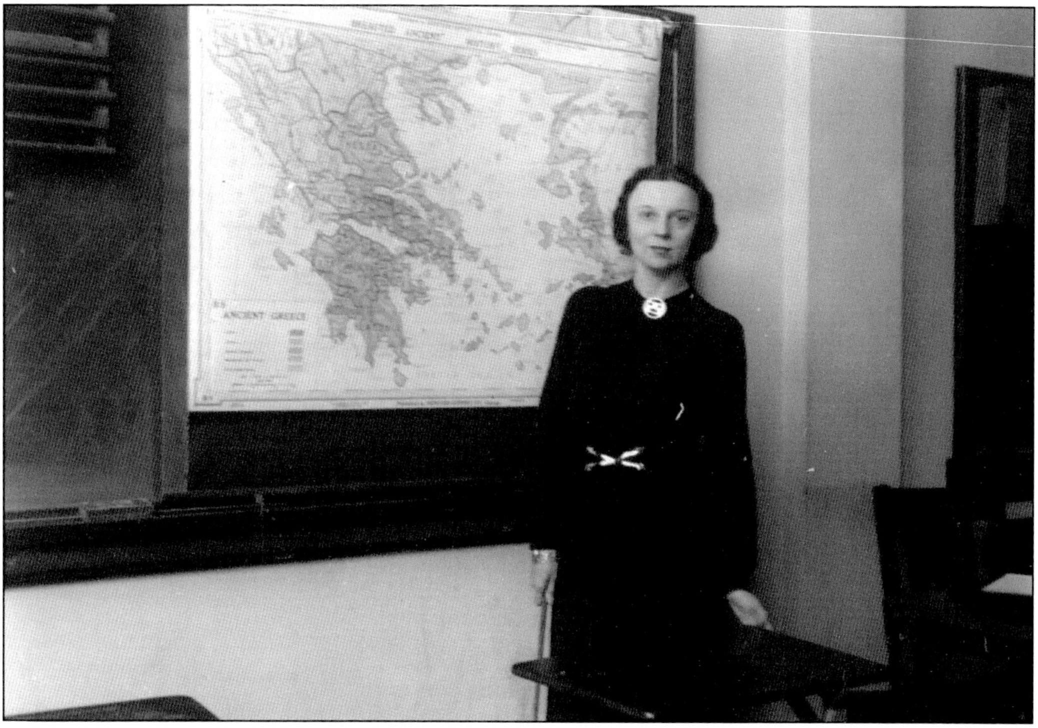

Ila Oliver, one of Dr. Adam Hale Oliver's two daughters, graduated from Washington University at St. Louis in 1922 with a bachelor of arts degree and proceeded to teach history at the Edwardsville High School. She resigned in 1938, perhaps to care for her aging father; he passed away the following year. By 1846, she had resumed her teaching position at the high school. In 1929, Olga Oliver temporarily replaced library director Sarah Coventry when she was struck with influenza. The girls' mother died in 1956. Neither Ila nor Olga ever married. They both lived out their lives in the family home on Vandalia Street. (Courtesy of Madison County Historical Society.)

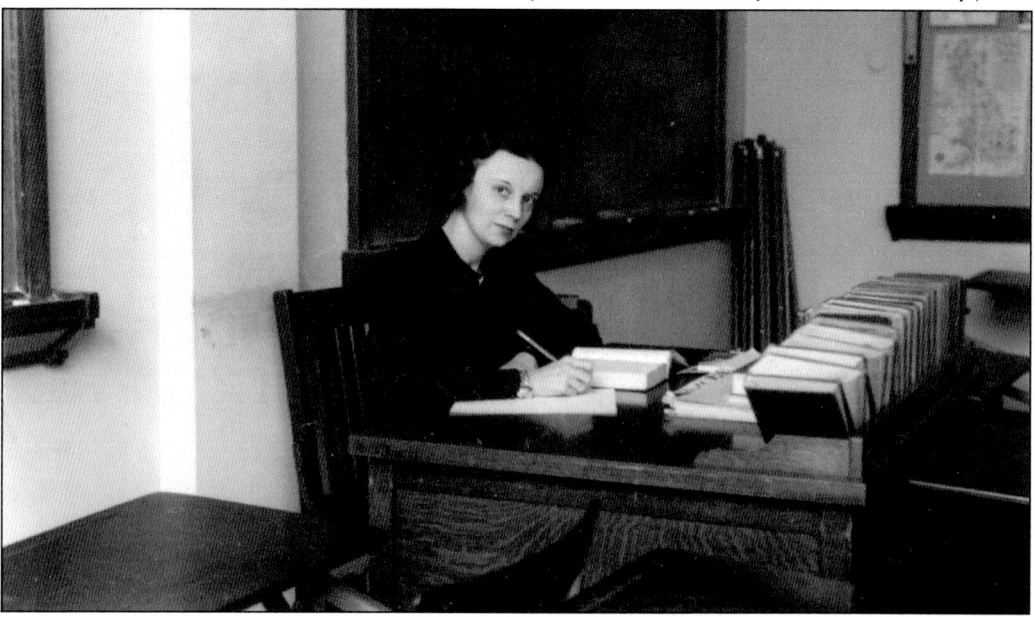

Five
RESIDENTIAL STREETS

The elegant homes that still grace St. Louis Street (now a national historic district) characterize the Gilded Age, during which many of them were built. However, St. Louis Street began as a humble dirt road traversed by early settlers and farmers, perhaps from other farms in the American bottoms or to a ferry with service to St. Louis. Log cabins were the first structures to dot the land along the road, the first being built by early pioneer John Lusk in 1809.

The Madison County Agricultural Society was formed in 1854 by John A. Prickett, William T. Brown, Thomas Judy, and Jacob J. Barnsback, and the first Madison County Fair was held in 1855 on what is now known as St. Louis Street. The street was then called Fairgrounds Road. As the farmland was developed and subdivided, homes of varying architectural styles were built and the street was renamed St. Louis Street. To study the fine homes there is to learn the family stories of the prominent citizens of Edwardsville.

Main, Kansas, Vandalia, Buchanan, and Hillsboro Streets were other main streets along which fine homes were built. At 409 South Buchanan Street stands the imposing 1820 Stephenson residence, the oldest brick home in Edwardsville. Col. Benjamin Stephenson was one of the founding fathers of both Edwardsville and the state of Illinois. He served as a merchant, sheriff, bank president, Indian agent, road commissioner, militia colonel, member of the Edwardsville Board of Trustees, and member of the U.S. House of Representatives.

Residences of important citizens on Main Street included those of Matthew Gillespie, where a reception for Abraham Lincoln was held; Dr. John Weir; businessman Henry Trares (later the home of Dr. Edward William Fiegenbaum and now the Weber Funeral Home); William H. Krome, first full-term Edwardsville mayor, 1873–1875; and Charles H. Bartels, barber and photographer.

Many outstanding historical residences still stand in Edwardsville. Some are on the National Register of Historic Places, some are Edwardsville local landmarks, and others have been put to new uses. However, many of the houses are still used according to their original intention, that of home to an Edwardsville family.

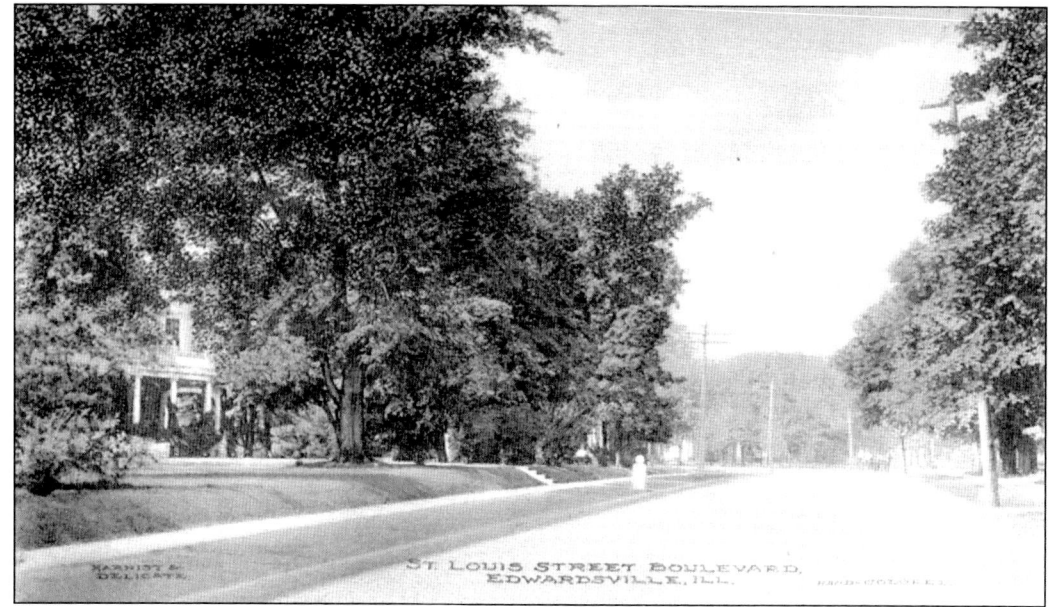

On the left is the Hadley house at 708 St. Louis Street. This home on 10 acres was a wedding gift to Mary and W. F. L. Hadley from her parents, Edward and Julia West, across the street from Mary's childhood home. Originally of Italianate style, renovations over the years added Queen Anne, chateau, and Romanesque elements. W. F. L. was an Illinois state senator (1886–1890) and a delegate to the 1888 national convention. (Courtesy of June Nealy.)

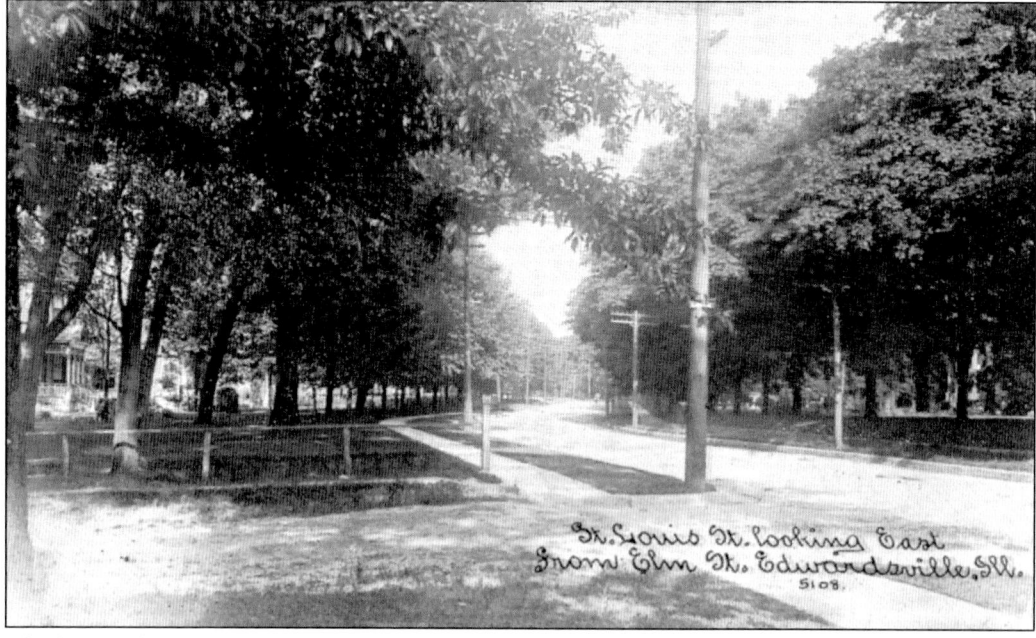

The home of attorney Edward C. Springer at 923 St. Louis Street is at the left in this photograph, on the north side of the street. L. E. Landis of Mount Vernon was contracted to build the eight-room Queen Anne–style home in 1893. Next behind it was another Queen Anne–style residence, the home of S. O. Bonner, a farmer, auctioneer, coroner, and businessman. (Courtesy of June Nealy.)

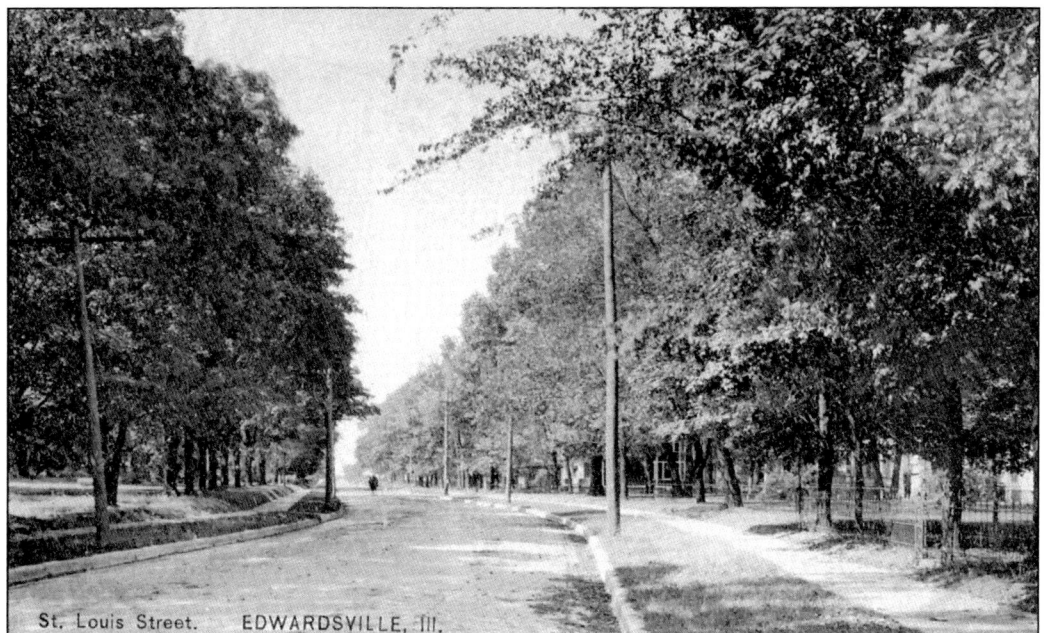

This view is believed to be looking west between Maple and Elm Streets. The early homes of successful men were built on huge lots with parklike settings. As families gave portions of their estates to family members, the land holdings began to break up. Judge Joseph Gillespie divided his land in 1883 and held a large sale of lots on the north side of the street. Homes built after that were consequently closer together. (Courtesy of June Nealy.)

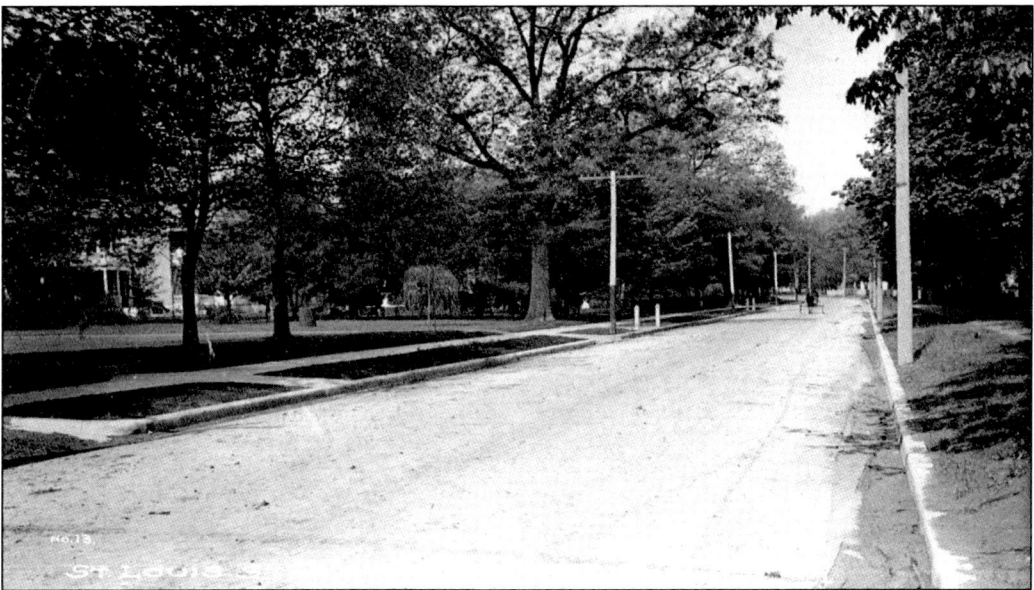

As fine homes were constructed beginning around 1860 up through the 1980s, an eclectic mix of architectural styles developed along the gently curving street. Although Queen Anne was the most popular style around the dawn of the 20th century, today one can spot Italianate, classical revival, chateauesque, craftsman, Mediterranean, Colonial Revival, and contemporary styles along the seven-block section of the St. Louis Street Historic District. (Courtesy of June Nealy.)

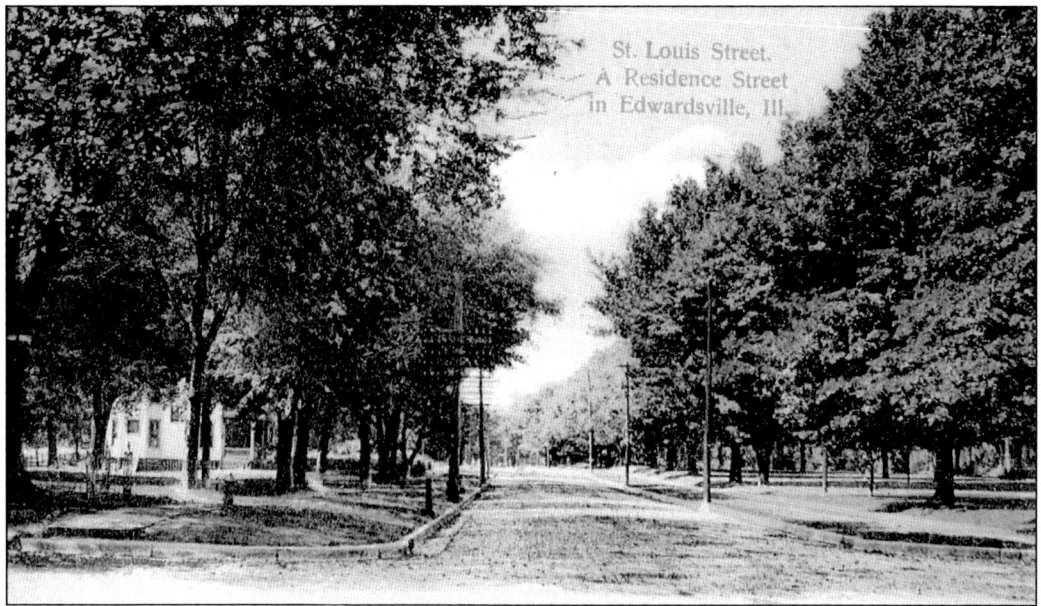

In 1911, "Helen" wrote to her friend "Amanda" on the back of this postcard, "This is a fine street for that auto of yours. When you get it, come over on this street for a merry spin." Edwardsville's most fashionable street was lined with the homes of successful businessmen, political figures, bankers, developers, and editor-publisher W. R. Brink, who authored the *Madison County Atlas* (1873) and *The History of Madison County* (1882). (Courtesy of June Nealy.)

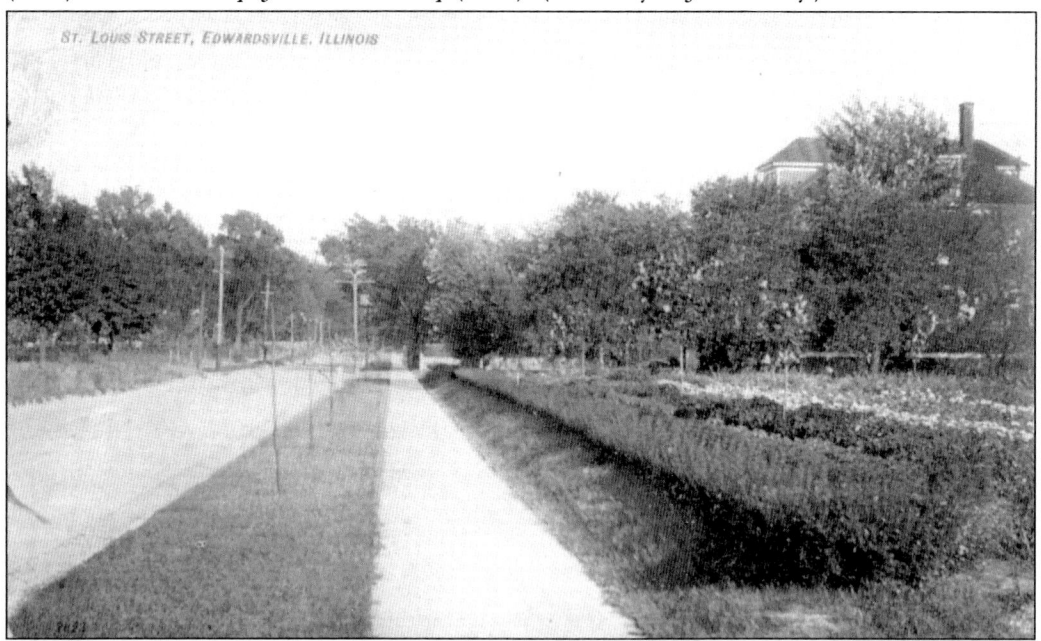

This view is probably somewhere between the 1100 and 1300 blocks on the west end of St. Louis Street. This portion of the street developed later than the rest as it was farther from downtown. As the automobile made its way into American life, homes were built along this section. Early residences like this one enjoyed huge lots with plenty of room for ornamental trees, flower beds, and vegetable gardens. (Courtesy of June Nealy.)

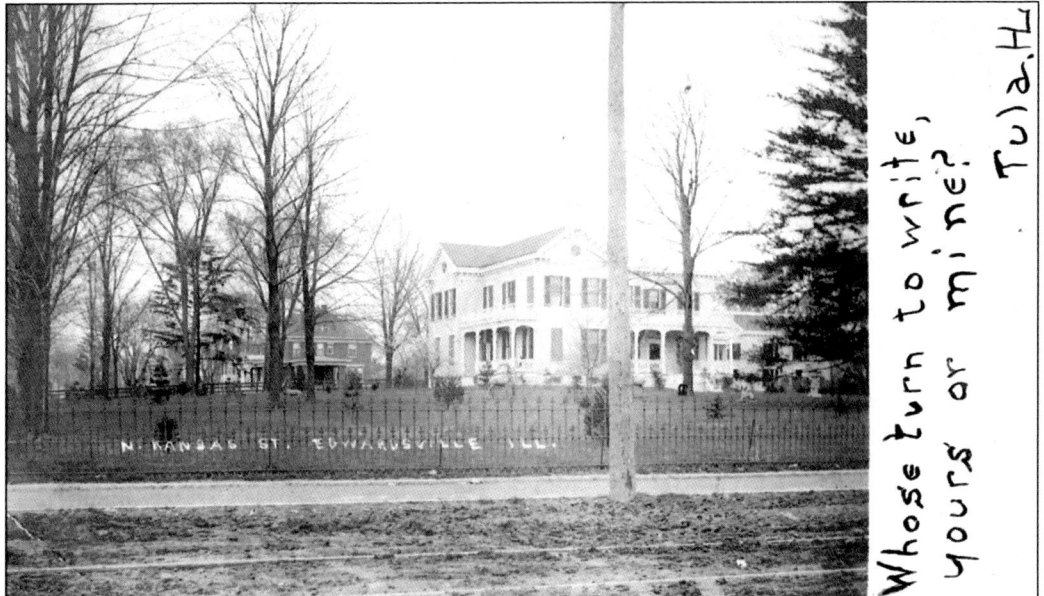

Kansas Street was also home to many fine early residences, such as this huge home at 210 North Kansas Street built by Col. Thomas Judy. It was constructed around 1854 in a combination of Greek Revival and Federal styles. Colonel Judy planned for his family to move into town from their farm. However, Mrs. Judy believed that the city would be a bad influence on their daughters and refused to leave the farm. (Courtesy of Neal Strebel.)

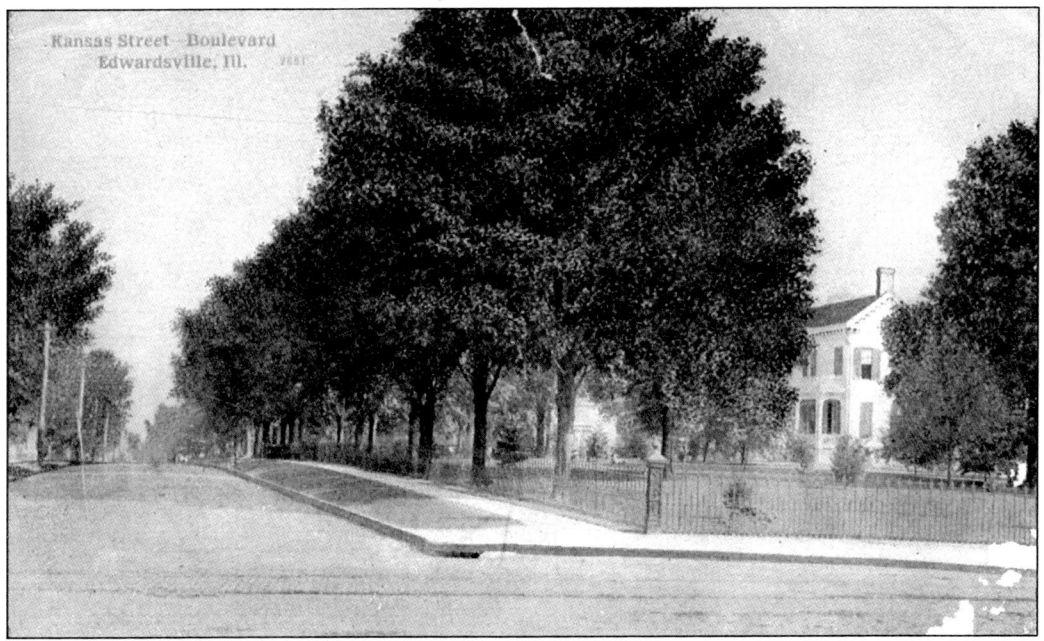

Since Mrs. Judy and her daughters would not move to their new home, Colonel Judy sold the house to Maj. William Prickett, who was the son of one of Edwardsville's earliest merchants and had served in the Civil War. Prickett married a daughter of banker Edward M. West and eventually became a prominent banker in his own right, serving as president of the Bank of Edwardsville. (Courtesy of June Nealy.)

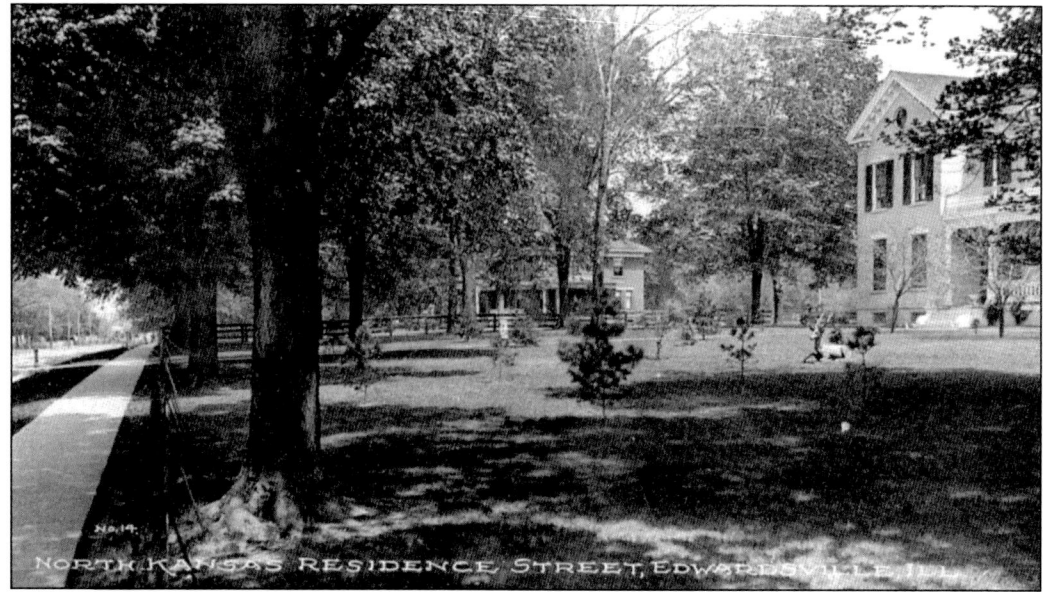

Maj. William Prickett was also active in politics and served two terms in the Illinois General Assembly and as a delegate to the Democratic National Convention of 1892, casting a vote for Grover Cleveland. He was honored in 1912 at the Madison County centennial as being the oldest living Edwardsville native at the time. (Courtesy of Neal Strebel.)

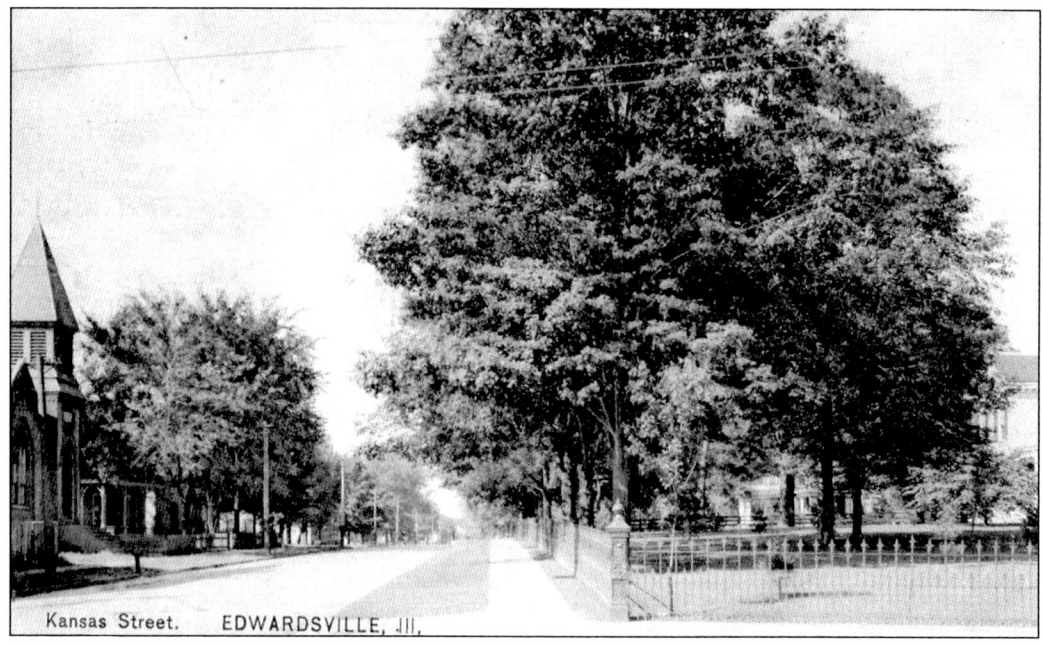

On the left is the First Presbyterian Church at 237 North Kansas Street, which was constructed in 1885 across the street from the Prickett residence. In 1930, the Mateer Funeral Home began operations in the Judy-Prickett home. Another prominent Edwardsville citizen, Mayor Henry P. Hotz, who served from 1903 to 1913, lived on North Kansas Street at No. 516.

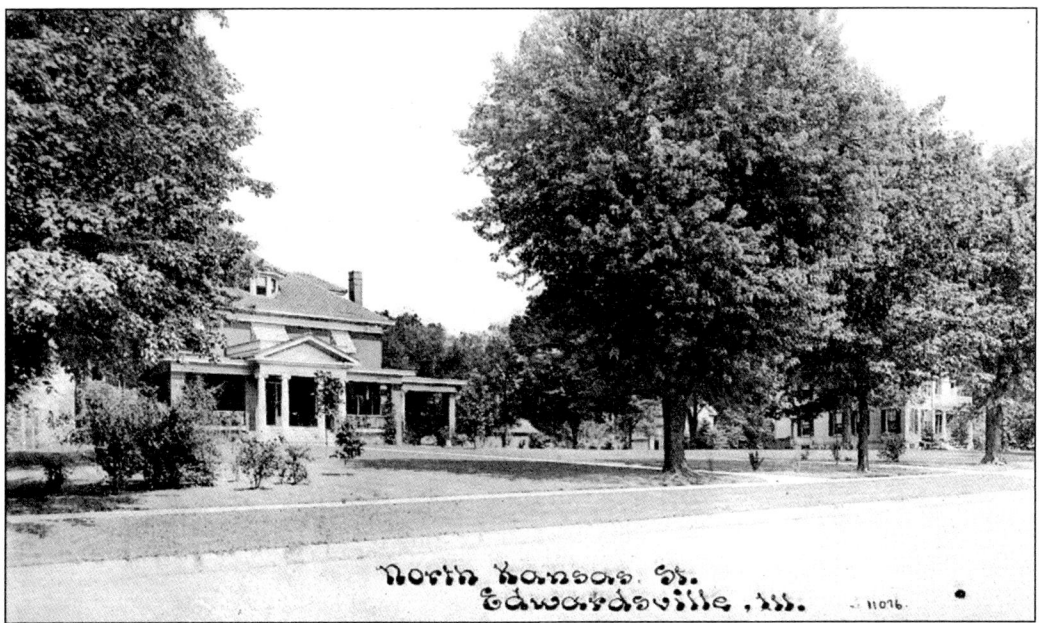

Also on North Kansas Street was the home of Charles Boeschenstein. As a young adult, Boeschenstein had been involved in the organization of the Southern Illinois Press Association. Later he served as editor of the *Intelligencer* and president of the Illinois Daily Newspaper Association. Boeschenstein was instrumental in locating the N. O. Nelson's manufacturing complex in Edwardsville in 1890 and was one of the main organizers of the Madison County centennial in 1912. It was Boeschenstein's letter to Andrew Carnegie that produced a $12,500 check to construct Edwardsville's new library. He then, appointed by the mayor, served as head of the new Edwardsville Public Library Board for 34 years. He also served as one-term mayor, county Red Cross chair, and vice president of the Bank of Edwardsville, and he spearheaded the organization of the Edwardsville Water Company. (Above, courtesy of June Nealy; below, courtesy of Neal Strebel.)

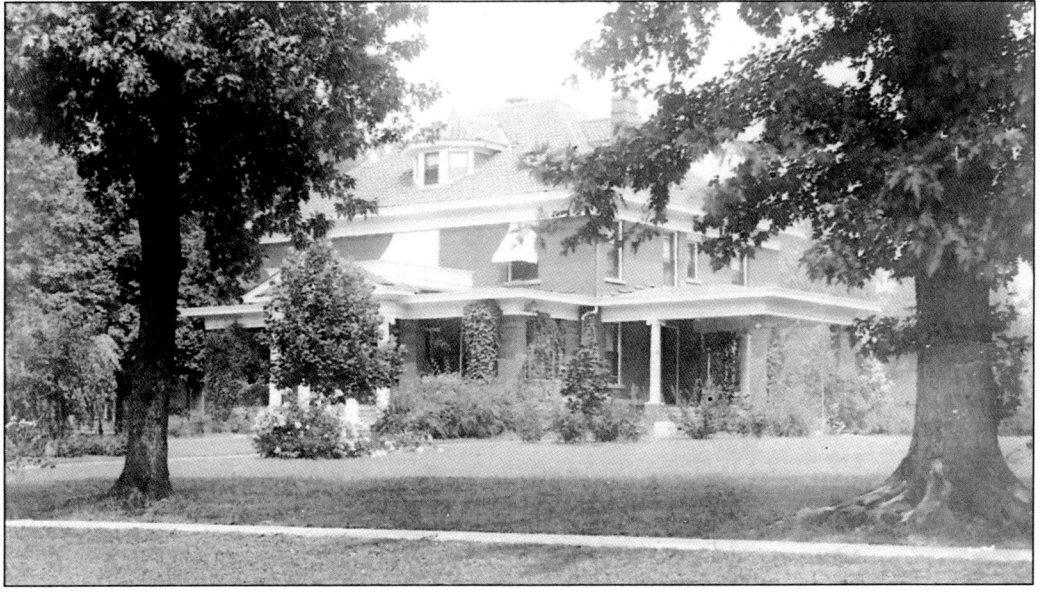

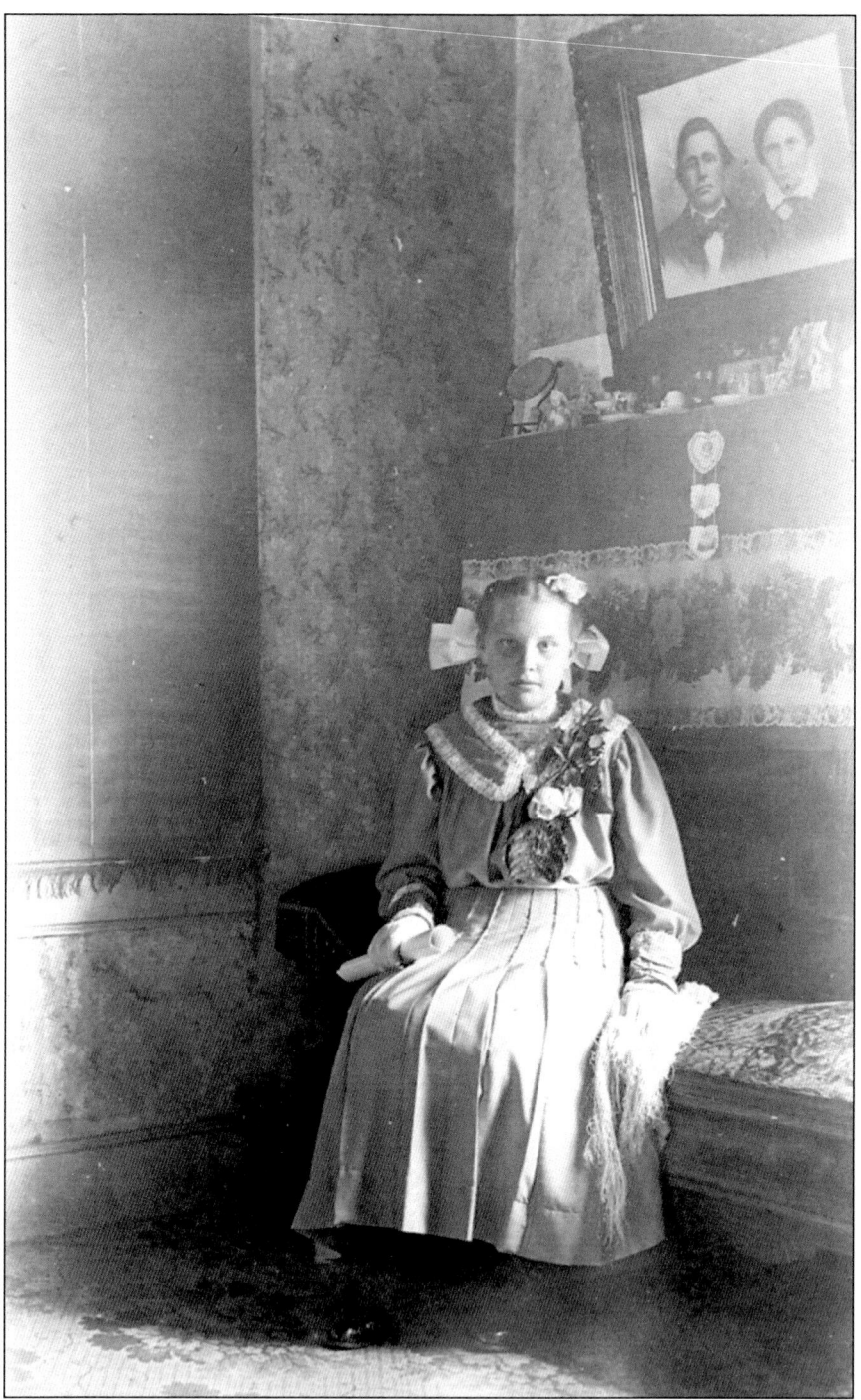

Here is a view of a typical Victorian home interior, with patterned wallpaper on the walls and a formal portrait, probably of this girl's parents, on the wall. Victorian interiors were meant to be beautiful refuges from the outside world, adorned with intricate patterns, beautiful stained glass, fretwork, and elaborate decorations. The Industrial Revolution made manufactured goods more affordable and also gave more consumers money to spend. (Courtesy of Neal Strebel.)

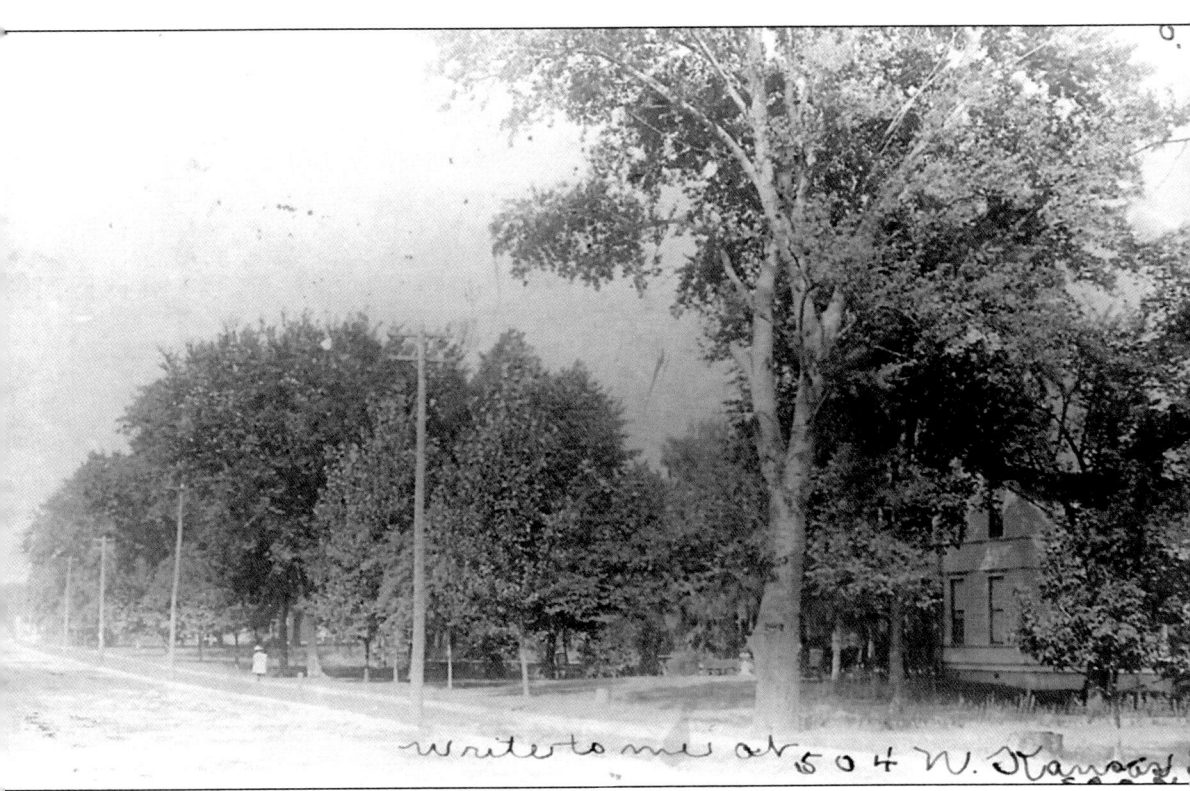

Other notable residences on Vandalia Street included those of Dr. Adam Hale Oliver at 121 East Vandalia, William Erastus Wheeler at 419 East Vandalia, and the Hotz home. Three members of the Hotz family served as Madison County Clerk—Joseph Hotz, son Norbert Hotz, and daughter Eulalia Hotz. She was the first female to serve as a Madison County elected official and remained in the county clerk position for 31 years, retiring in 1973. (Courtesy of Neal Strebel.)

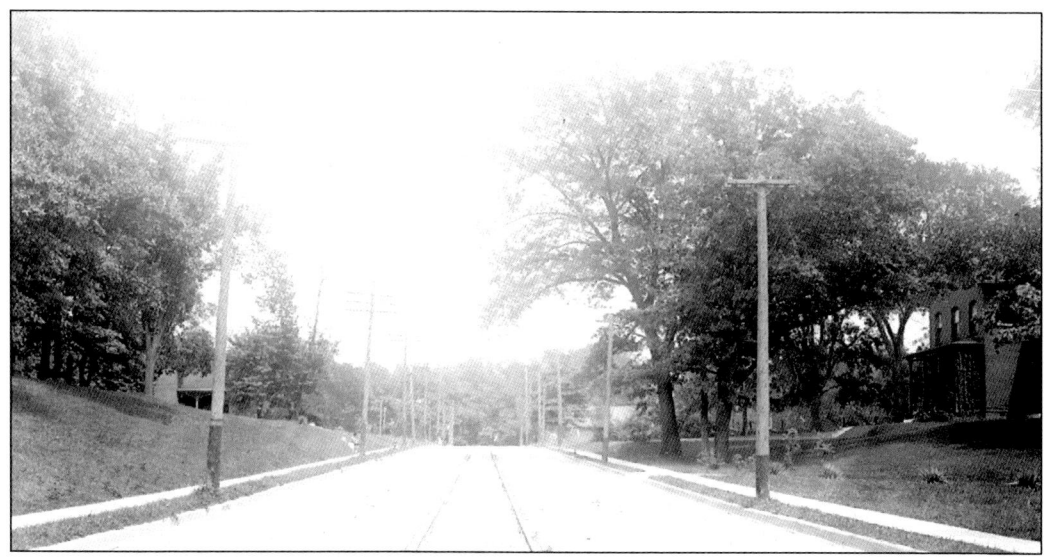

This unidentified street is probably Hillsboro Road. Notice the electric car tracks down the center. The Happy house, at 722 Hillsboro Road, was built by attorney Cyrus Happy, who served as lawyer for the Wabash Railroad and also partner with Judge David Gillespie and later with C. N. Travous. The Happy house has been designated a local landmark. (Courtesy of June Nealy.)

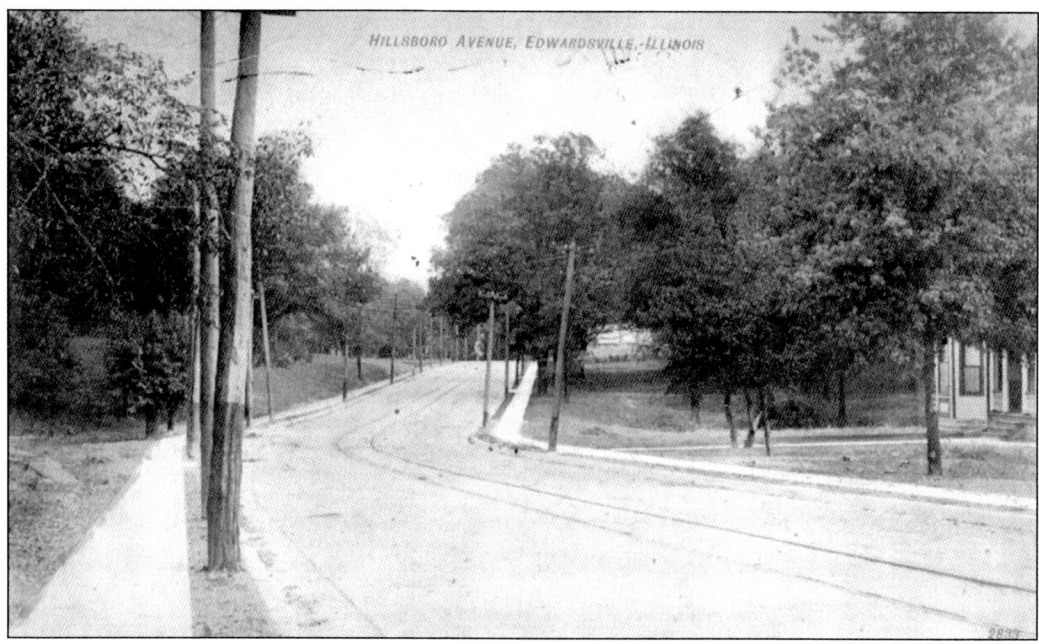

This view looking east on Hillsboro Road shows a house, visible through the trees at right, at 606 Hillsboro. Farther up the hill on the left still stands a large Italianate house. Just behind the photographer of this picture would have been the cross street of Columbia Avenue and the large residence of Dr. J. A. Hirsch, which was built in 1877. This beautiful home has been well restored and won a 1995 preservation award. (Courtesy of June Nealy.)

Six

Banks, Business, and Industry

The earliest stores in Edwardsville were those of Abraham Prickett, Benjamin Stephenson, and brothers Robert and George Pogue. Pogue's store on North Main Street shared the building with the Indian agency after 1819. Portions of the brick walls of that early building still survive, within the building known during recent years as Rusty's Restaurant, at 1201 North Main Street. In 1818, a state charter was issued to a Bank of Edwardsville, which later failed; although it bore the same name, it was not connected with the Bank of Edwardsville established in 1868. Edward West, later a banker, opened and operated a general store from 1835 until 1854. According to James T. Hair's *Gazetteer of Madison County,* in 1866 Edwardsville could claim "three flouring mills, two breweries, one distillery, one steam furniture manufactory, several dry goods, grocery and general stores that do a thriving business, two newspaper offices that issue weekly papers, together with several carriage, wagon, plow and other mechanical shops."

Two early hotels were the General Washington, opened by W. C. Wiggins in 1819 northeast of the public square, and one on the west side of Main Street known later on as the Wabash Hotel. By 1895, there were 10 rooming houses and hotels in Edwardsville. The railroads were regularly bringing passengers and cargo to town by that time.

Coal became an important industry in response to the railroad's arrival. From 1879 until 1905, the Madison Coal Company's Madison No. 3 Mine was the largest and most successful mine in town. It was located near the village of Leclaire west of Troy Road. The coal company was sold and reorganized after 1905 and finally abandoned in 1929.

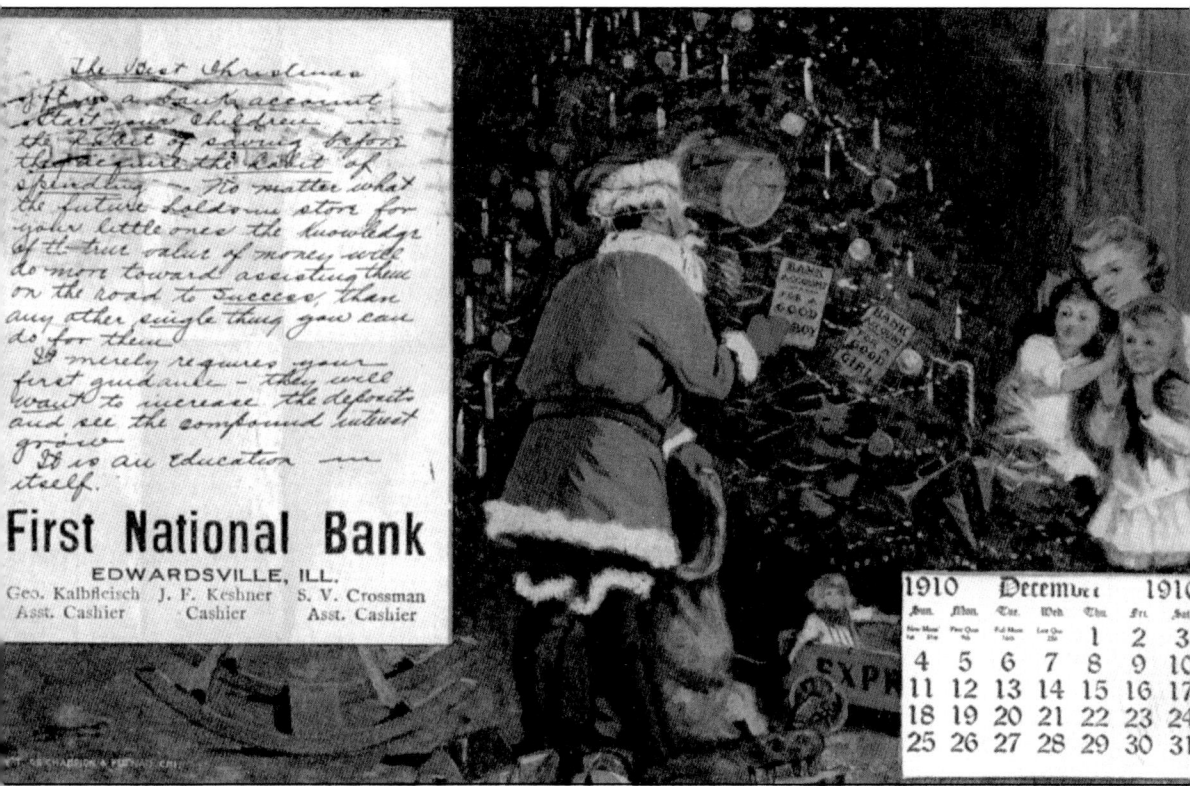

The First National Bank was located on the corner of Main and Purcell Streets. In the early 1900s, First National was absorbed by the Bank of Edwardsville and shortly thereafter, the Bank of Edwardsville built its new five-story facility on the former site of First National. (Courtesy of Neal Strebel.)

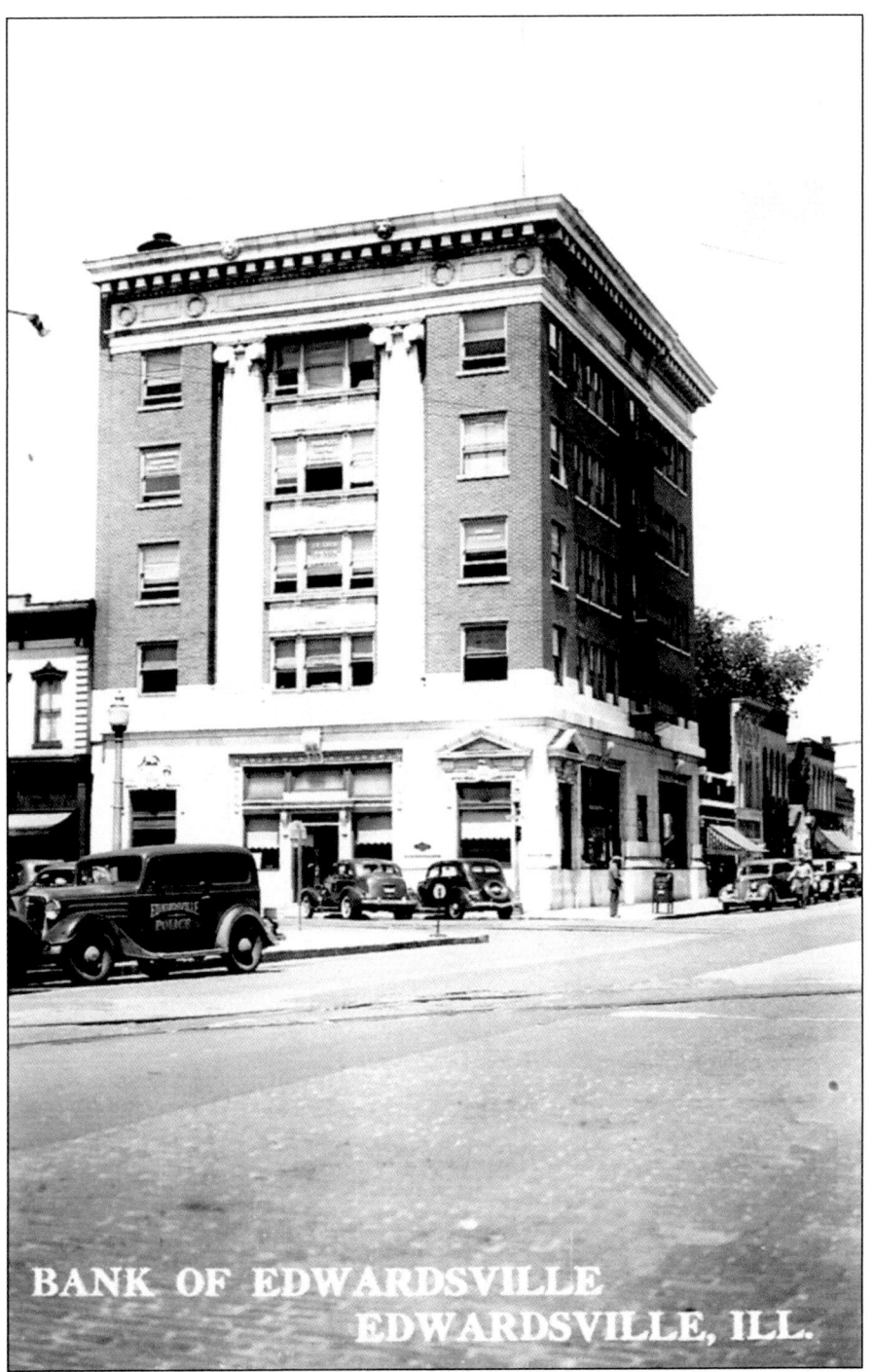

This five-story Bank of Edwardsville building was constructed in 1917 on the northwest corner of the intersection of Main and Purcell Streets. Edward M. West and his son-in-law Maj. William R. Prickett had founded West and Prickett, later renamed the Bank of Edwardsville, on January 1, 1868. It consolidated with the Madison County State Bank in 1899. (Courtesy of June Nealy.)

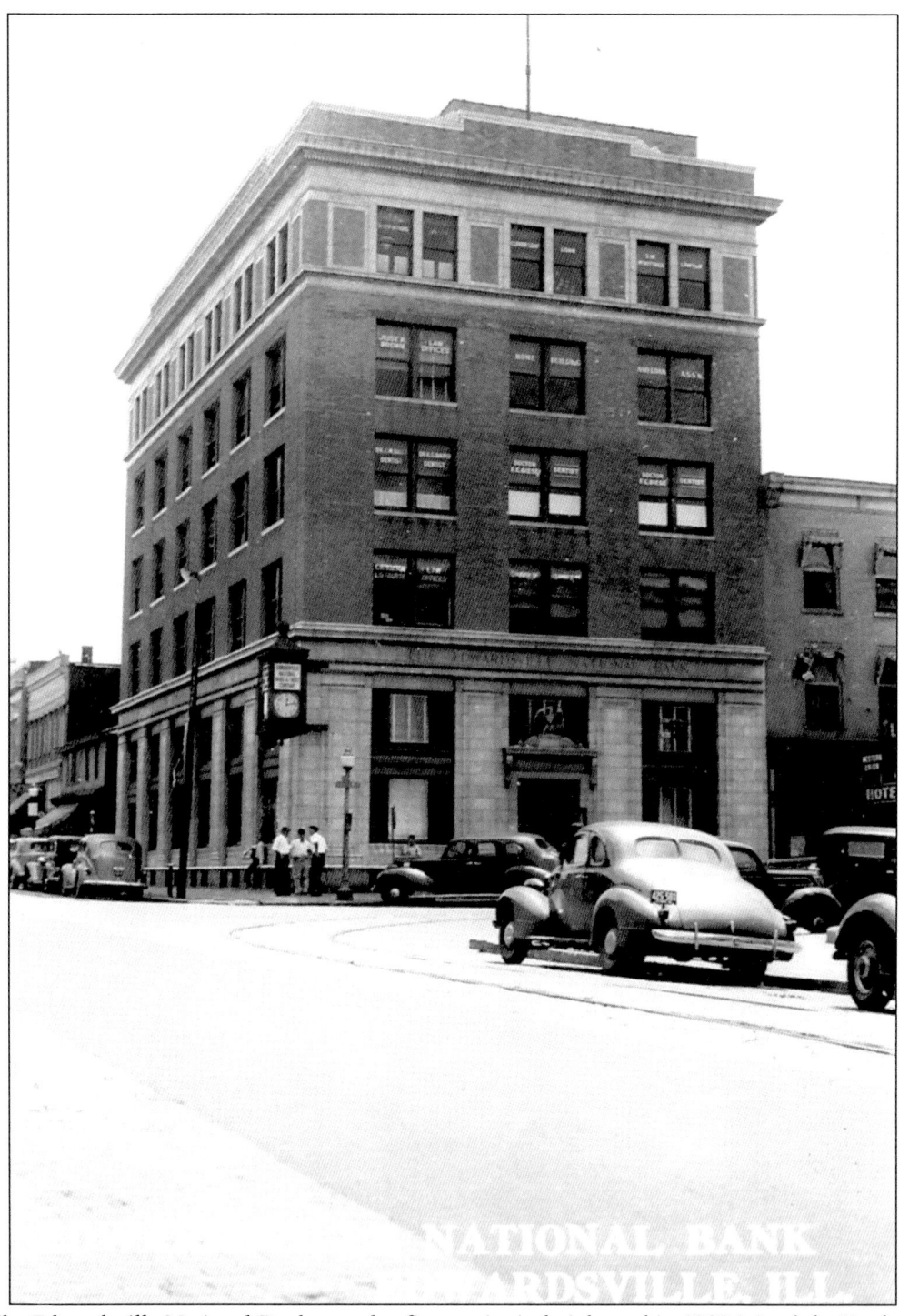

The Edwardsville National Bank was also five stories in height and in 1923 joined the Bank of Edwardsville as another modern building flanking the courthouse. The Edwardsville National Bank was on the corner of North Main and St. Louis Streets. The large clock on the corner of this bank made it very recognizable. (Courtesy of SJ Morrison.)

Community banks often mailed out commercial postcards, such as this one advertising the Christmas Club, thank you, or calendar cards. This card states, "Our Friend the Squirrel Knows How—In fact if he were human he would make a fine member of our Christmas Club." (Courtesy of June Nealy.)

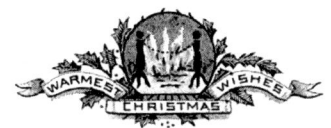

The Citizens State and Trust Bank was consolidated with the Edwardsville National Bank on August 15, 1929, under the title of the Edwardsville National Bank and Trust Company. (Courtesy of June Nealy.)

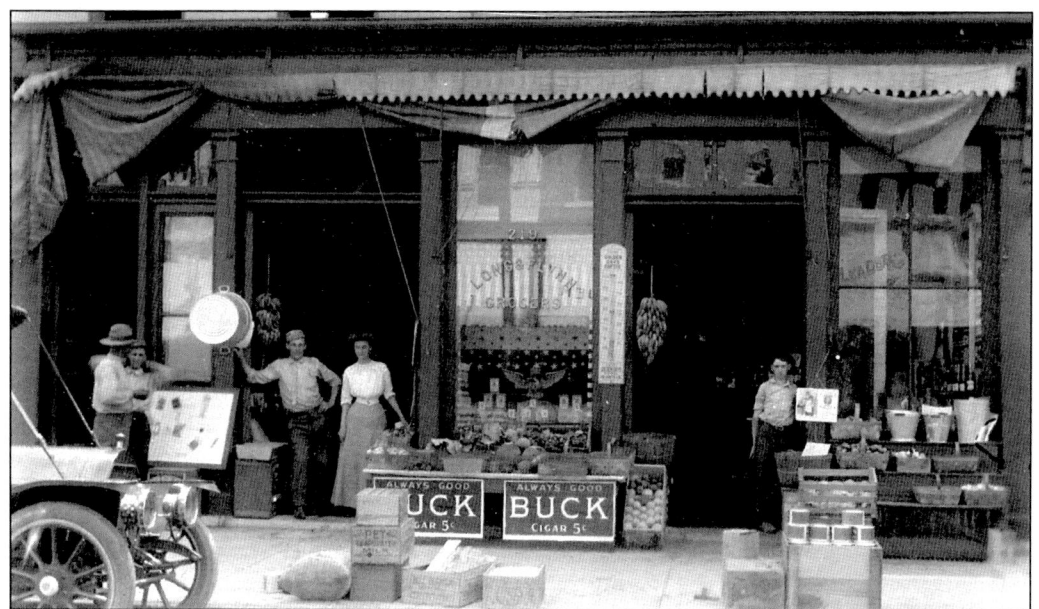

In the 1890s, Long and Flynn Grocers advertised "choice eating potatoes at 75 cents per bushel" and "White House brand canned California fruits and vegetables." When the circus came to town in May 1893 and set up in Wolf's Pasture near the coal mine, the *Intelligencer* reported that Long and Flynn "took advantage of a novel way of advertising by placing banners on the elephants." (Courtesy of Neal Strebel.)

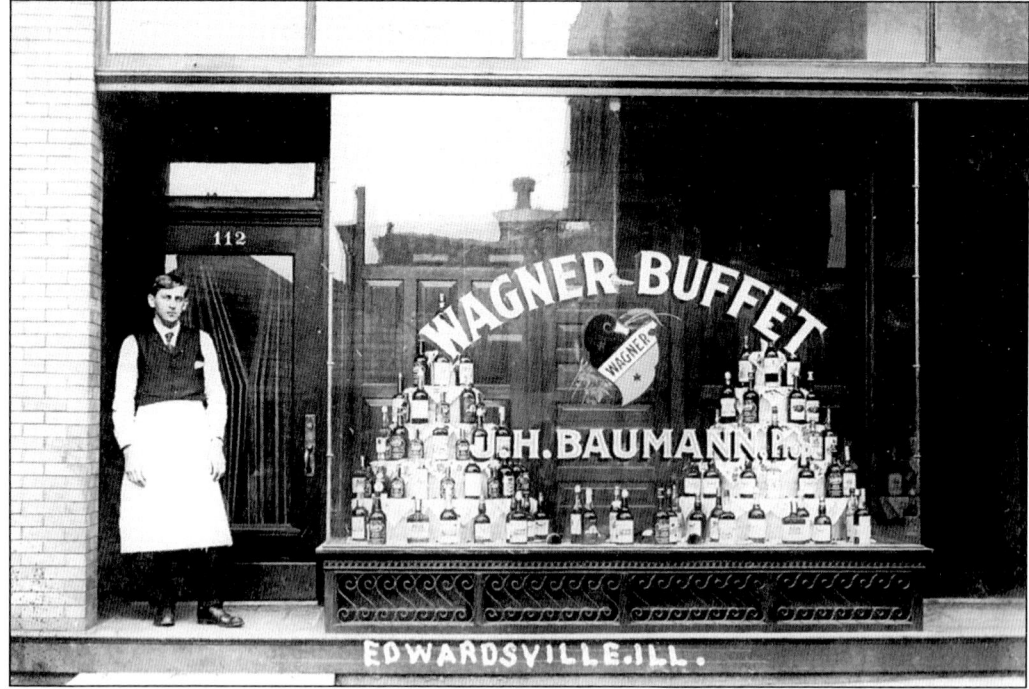

In the mayor's report in the February 10, 1909, *Intelligencer*, Joseph H. Baumann, proprietor, was approved for a grocery bond to open his business, the Wagner Buffet, at 112 North Main Street. (Courtesy of Neal Strebel.)

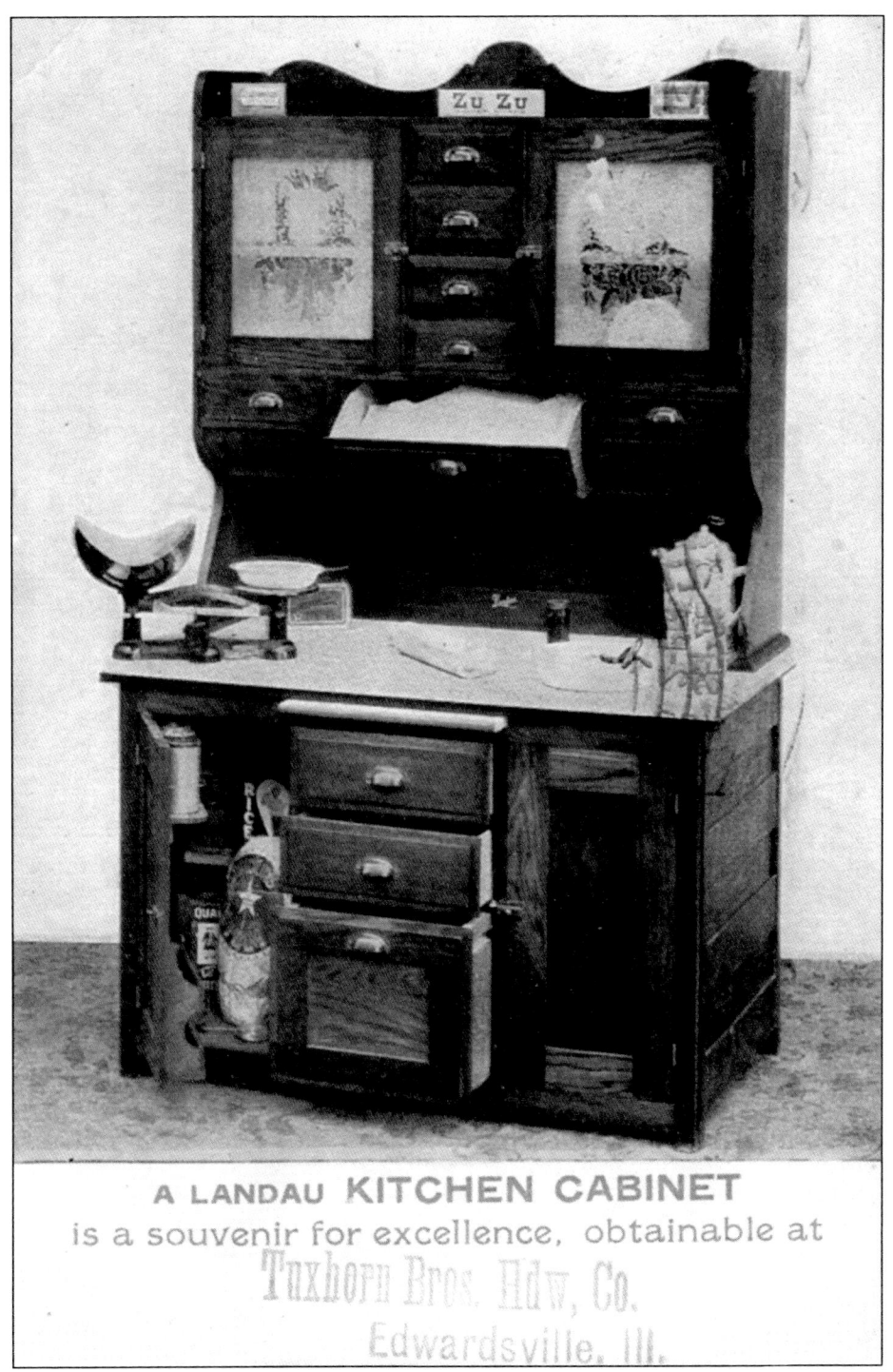

The Tuxhorn Brothers Hardware Store at 228–230 North Main Street sold a variety of household goods. This card was mailed out in September 1908 to offer a "special prize" of "Tuxhorn's 'Utryme' sewing machine for best pound of butter" at the Farmer's Institute October 14–16 of that year. The card also carried the slogan, "Make our store your headquarters."

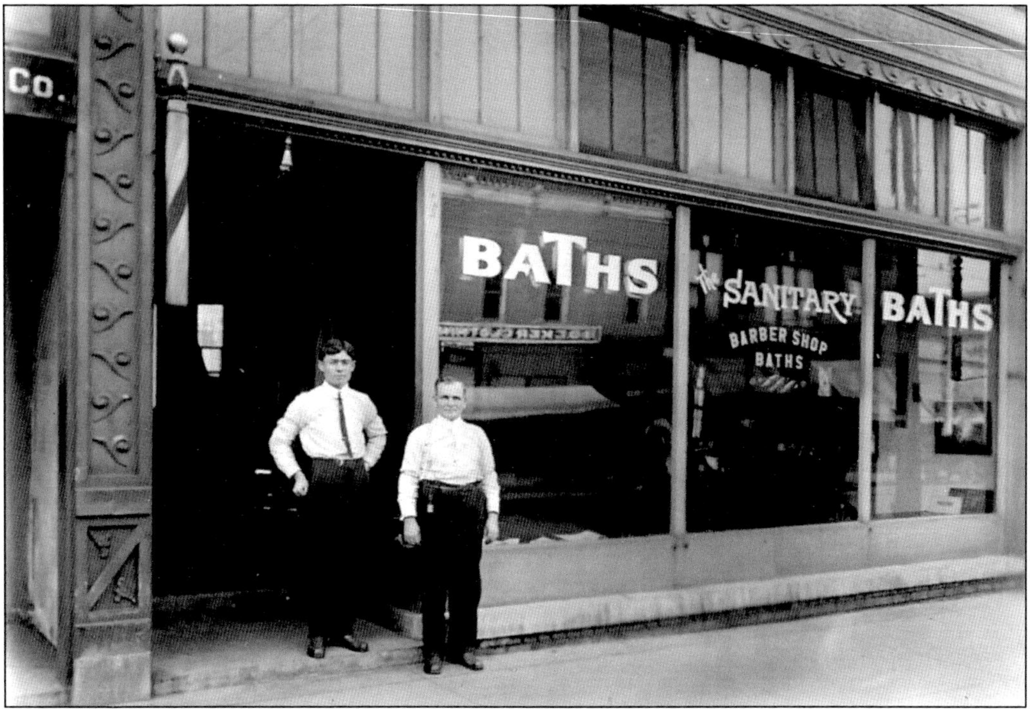

The F. W. Hartung Barber Shop was listed in the 1914 Edwardsville city directory at 115 North Main Street. Barbershops at that time also offered shaves and "sanitary baths." Another member of the Hartung family, Louis, owned a shop on Vandalia Street. On March 31, 1901, a German woman named Regina Schmid Hess fell ill while passing Louis's shop and sat down on the steps. Someone took her inside, where she died a few minutes later. (Above, courtesy of June Nealy; below, courtesy of Neal Strebel.)

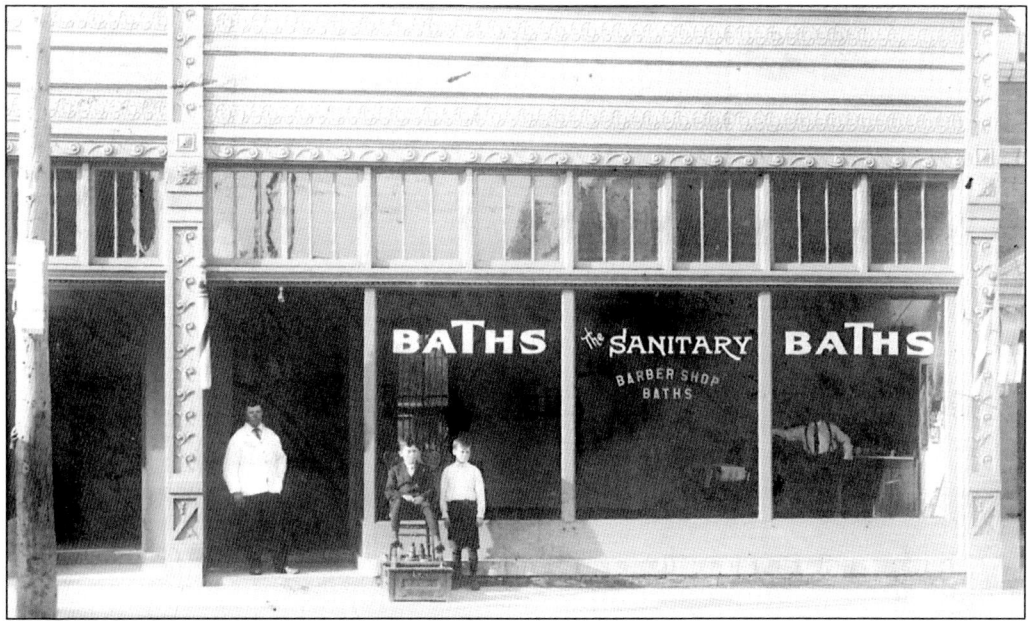

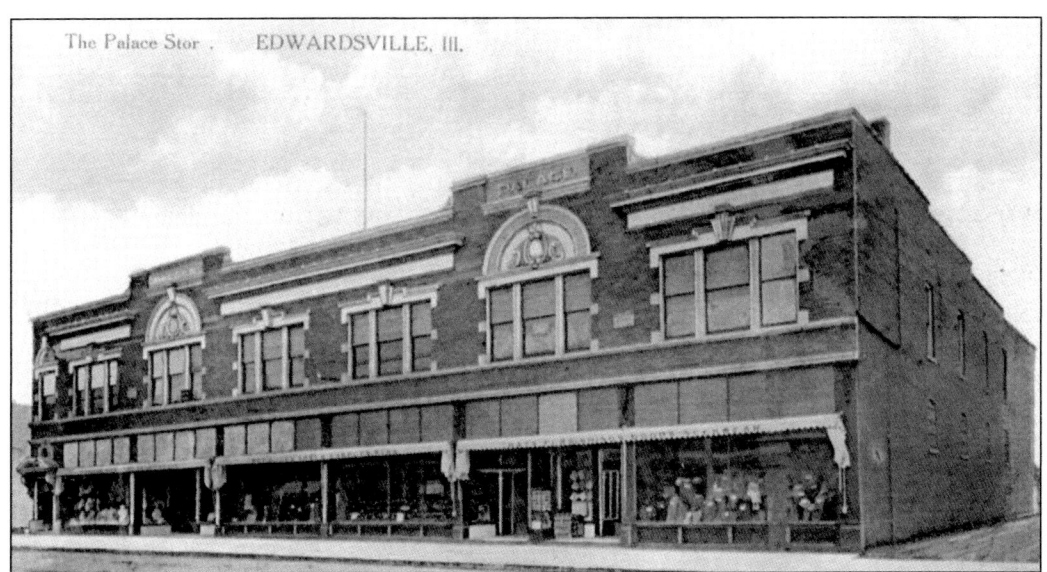

In 1912, the *History of Madison County* claimed the Palace Store on the west side of the 100 block of North Main Street to be the "largest mercantile establishment at Edwardsville." John Trares, a German immigrant, arrived in Edwardsville in the 1860s and began a career in retail. He entered into several business partnerships and acquired more than one building downtown. He retired from retail in the late 1800s to concentrate on his real estate interests. (Courtesy of June Nealy.)

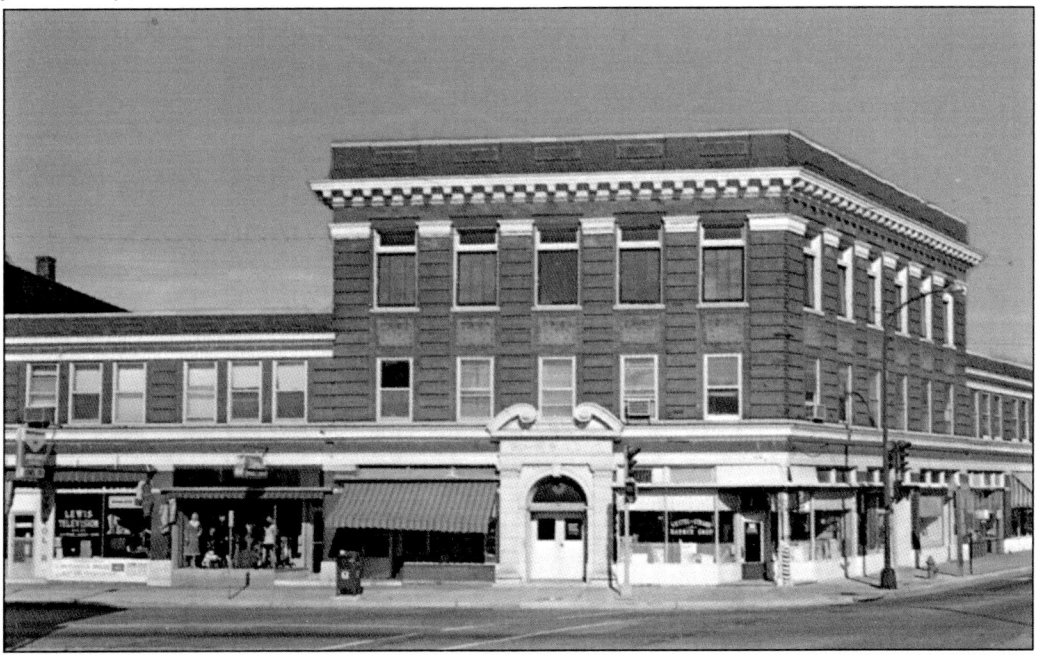

The Bohm Building is an Edwardsville landmark at the corner of Main and Vandalia Streets. It was built in 1910 by William Bohm, a farmer and local businessman, and the building served as Edwardsville's first office building. The third floor was added on later to provide a ballroom for Bohm's son, Clarence, in which to give ballroom dance lessons. Clarence had attended ballroom dance school in California and was eager to share his prowess. (Courtesy of June Nealy.)

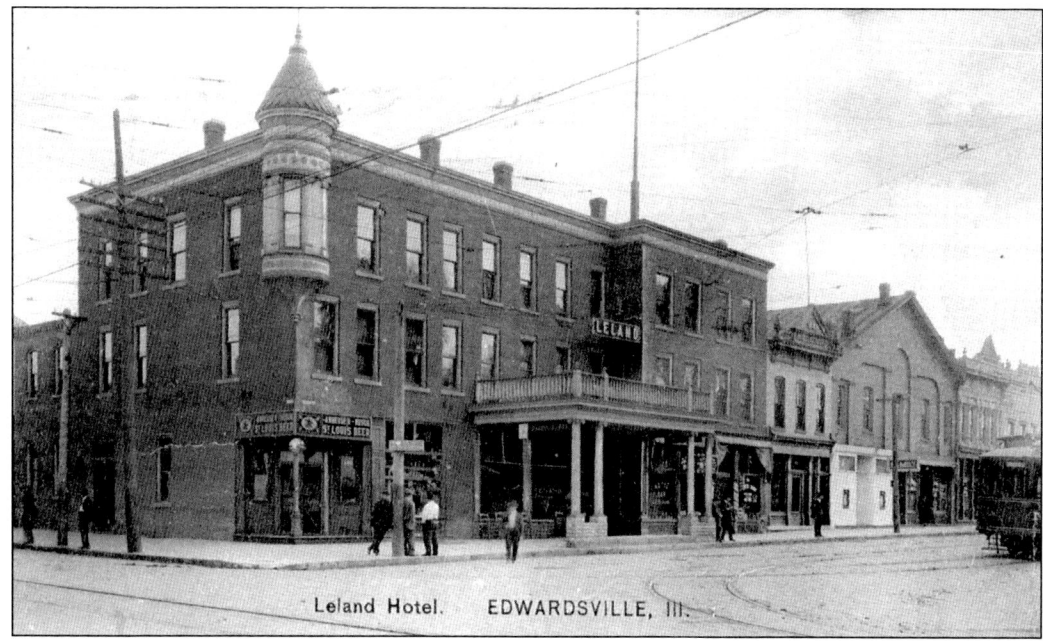

Leland Hotel. EDWARDSVILLE, Ill.

The Leland Hotel with its distinctive corner turret graced the intersection of Main and St. Louis Streets for many years. When the Leland was finally torn down to make way for the Edwardsville National Bank Building, the Leland Barber Shop, to the right of the columned overhang, was left there for another 50 years, at which time it was torn down and replaced with a small park. A fire in the hotel in 1905 nearly ended an actress's career. Victoria Bateman, a stage actress, was visiting members of the *Dr. Jekyll and Mr. Hyde* company, which was playing down the street at the Tuxhorn Opera House. Someone saw smoke coming from around the door to Bateman's room and called the proprietor. Bateman was said to be unconscious and required medical attention. (Courtesy of June Nealy.)

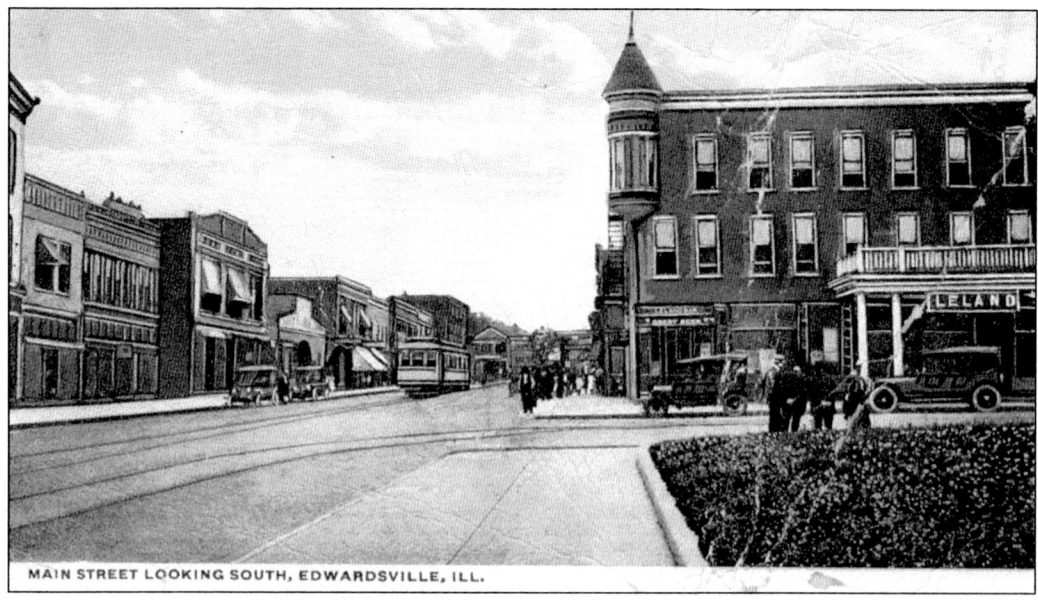

MAIN STREET LOOKING SOUTH, EDWARDSVILLE, ILL.

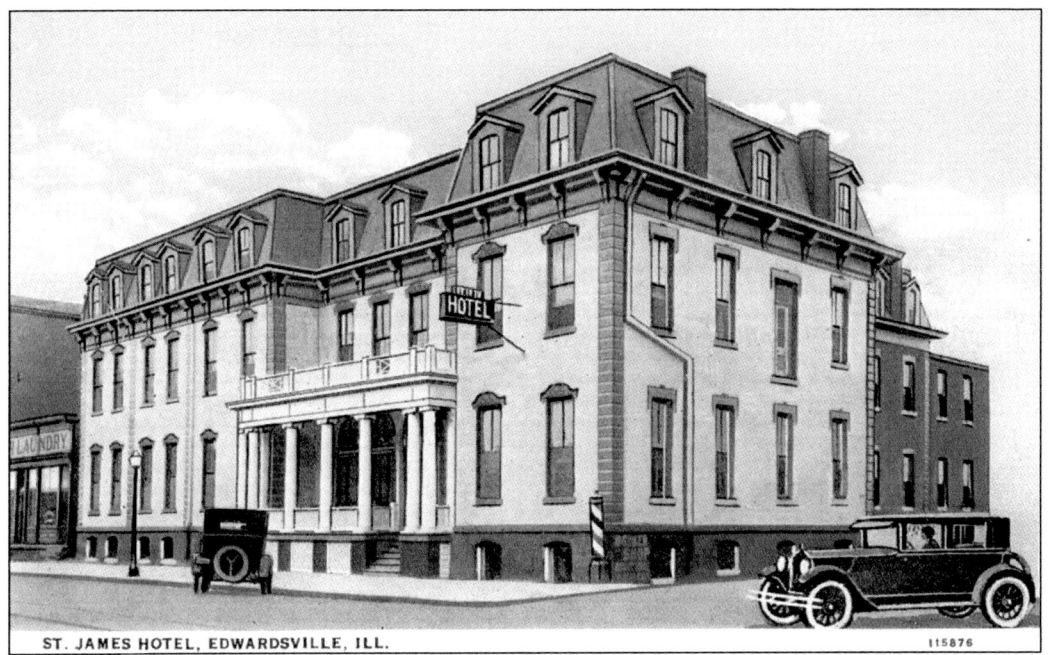

The St. James Hotel was connected by a second-floor walkway to the second-floor, 800-seat Tuxhorn Opera House in the 200 block of North Main Street. J. E. Tunnell was serving as proprietor of the St. James in 1907. Sadly, the hotel was razed and the site is now a parking lot. (Courtesy of June Nealy.)

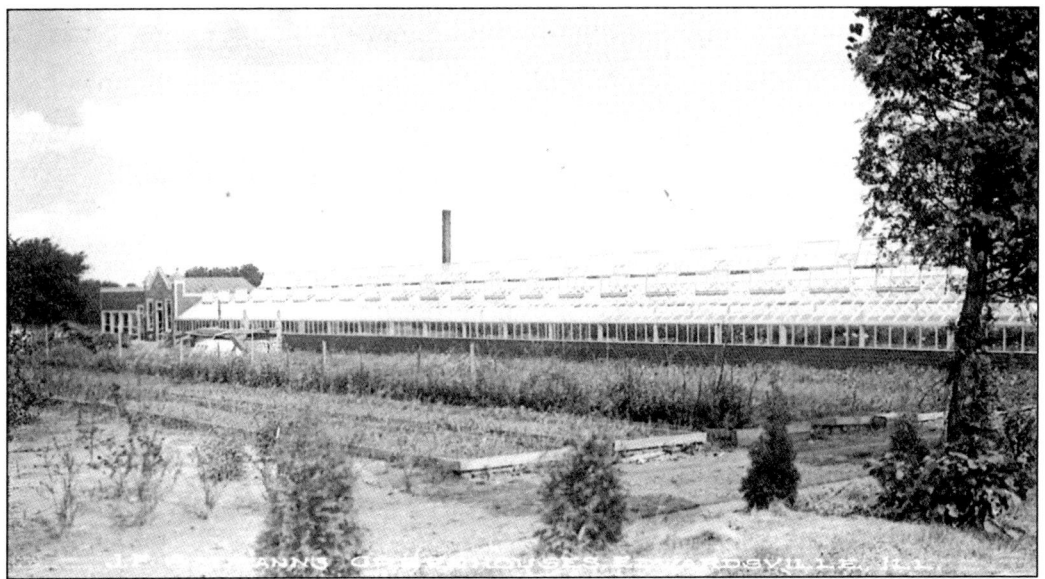

J. F. Ammann began a greenhouse and floral business on seven acres at 1308 St. Louis Street in 1890. He produced flowers year-round in his greenhouses and wholesaled them to stores in surrounding communities as well as Edwardsville. Ammann was active in local politics and a member of Eden Church. He served as a delegate to the Progressive Party at the convention that nominated Theodore Roosevelt for president. (Courtesy of Michael A. Sporrer.)

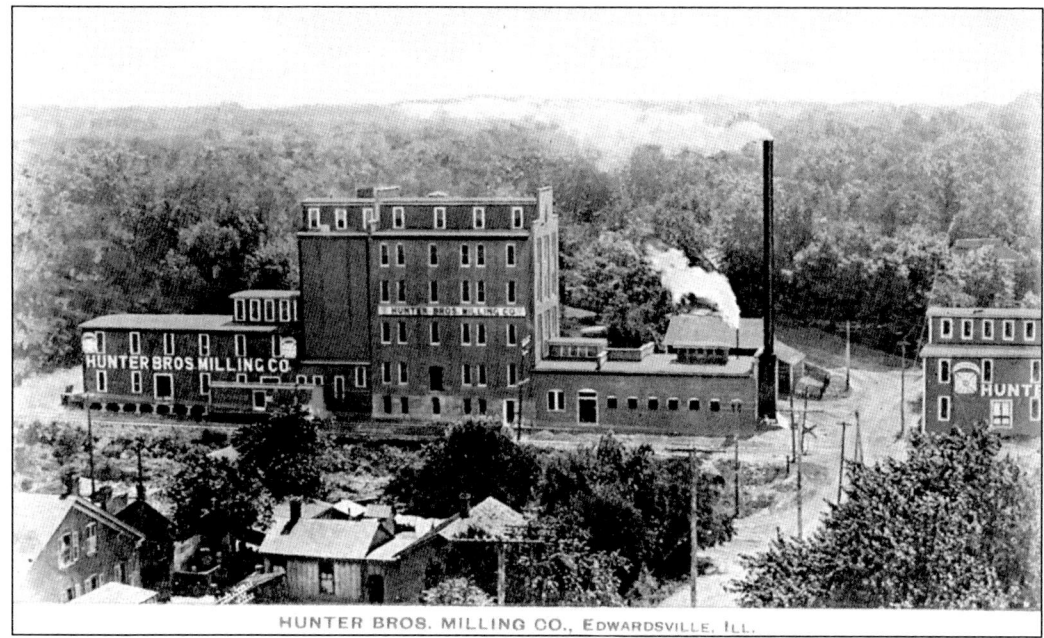

HUNTER BROS. MILLING CO., EDWARDSVILLE, ILL.

Hunter Brothers Milling Company was the last big flour mill in Edwardsville; it was established in 1905 by a group of St. Louis investors and local bankers. Located at West High and Second Streets, a millpond fronted the mill where a parking lot exists now. On the back of one of these postcards is the advertising message, "Ask your grocer for the flour of Edwardsville—ALMA." Edwardsville had become such an important milling center for the region that farmers from Logan County were said to have traveled by night to reach the Edwardsville mills, because the flies were so bad during the day. (Courtesy of June Nealy.)

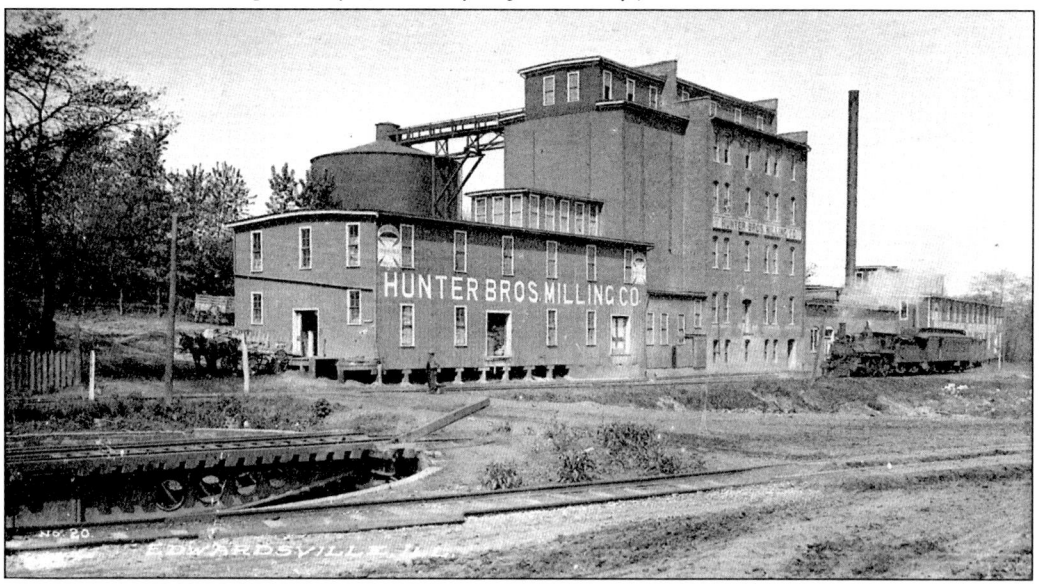

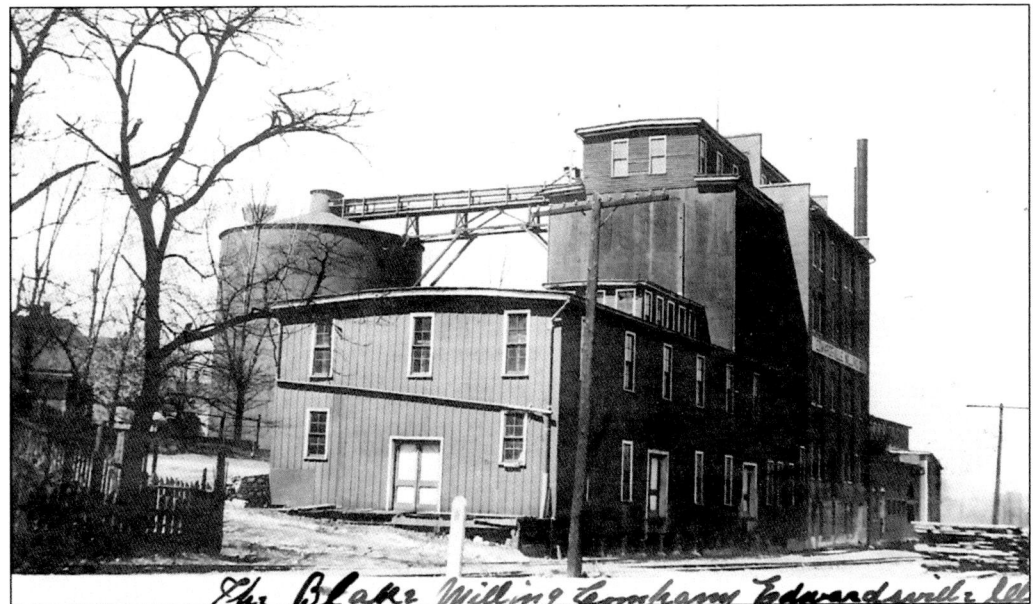

This 1919 view of Edwardsville's last big mill was taken five years after the name was changed from the Edwardsville Milling Company to Blake Milling Company. Looking closely at the front of the building (right in photograph), one can see the name "Edwardsville Milling Company" is still visible. Most of the mill complex burned down in 1926; one building, in use today as a retail shop, is all that remains. (Courtesy of Neal Strebel.)

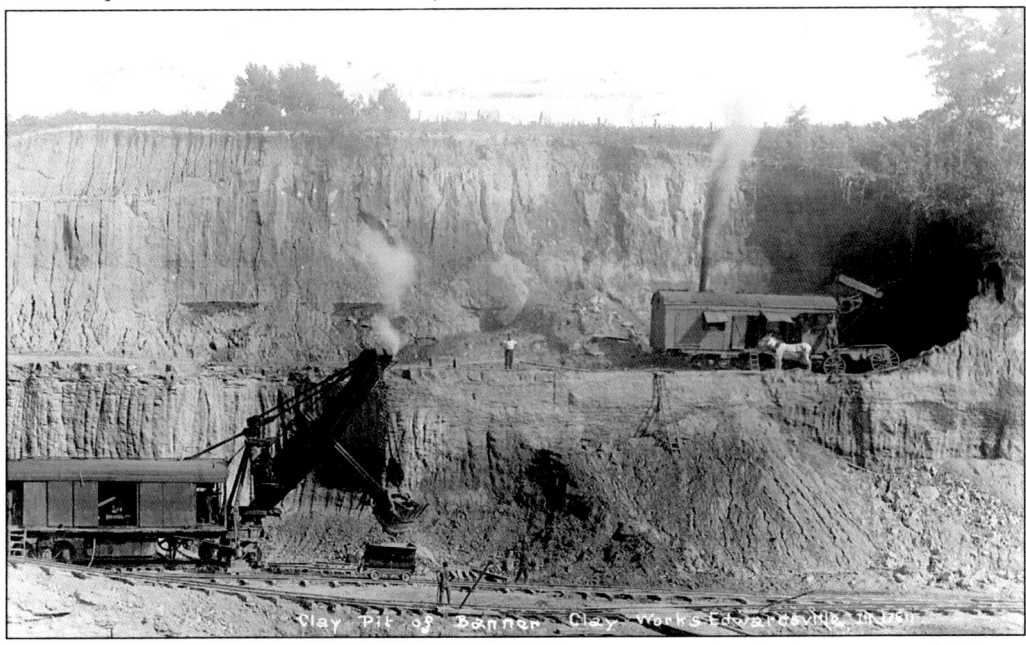

The Banner Clay Works on St. Louis Road produced paving bricks for streets, which are harder than building bricks. Banner Street on the west side of Edwardsville is named for the company. A severe thunderstorm hit Edwardsville in July 1912, causing an estimated $50,000 in total damages, with the heaviest losses suffered by Banner Clay Works, which was a St. Louis corporation. (Courtesy of Neal Strebel.)

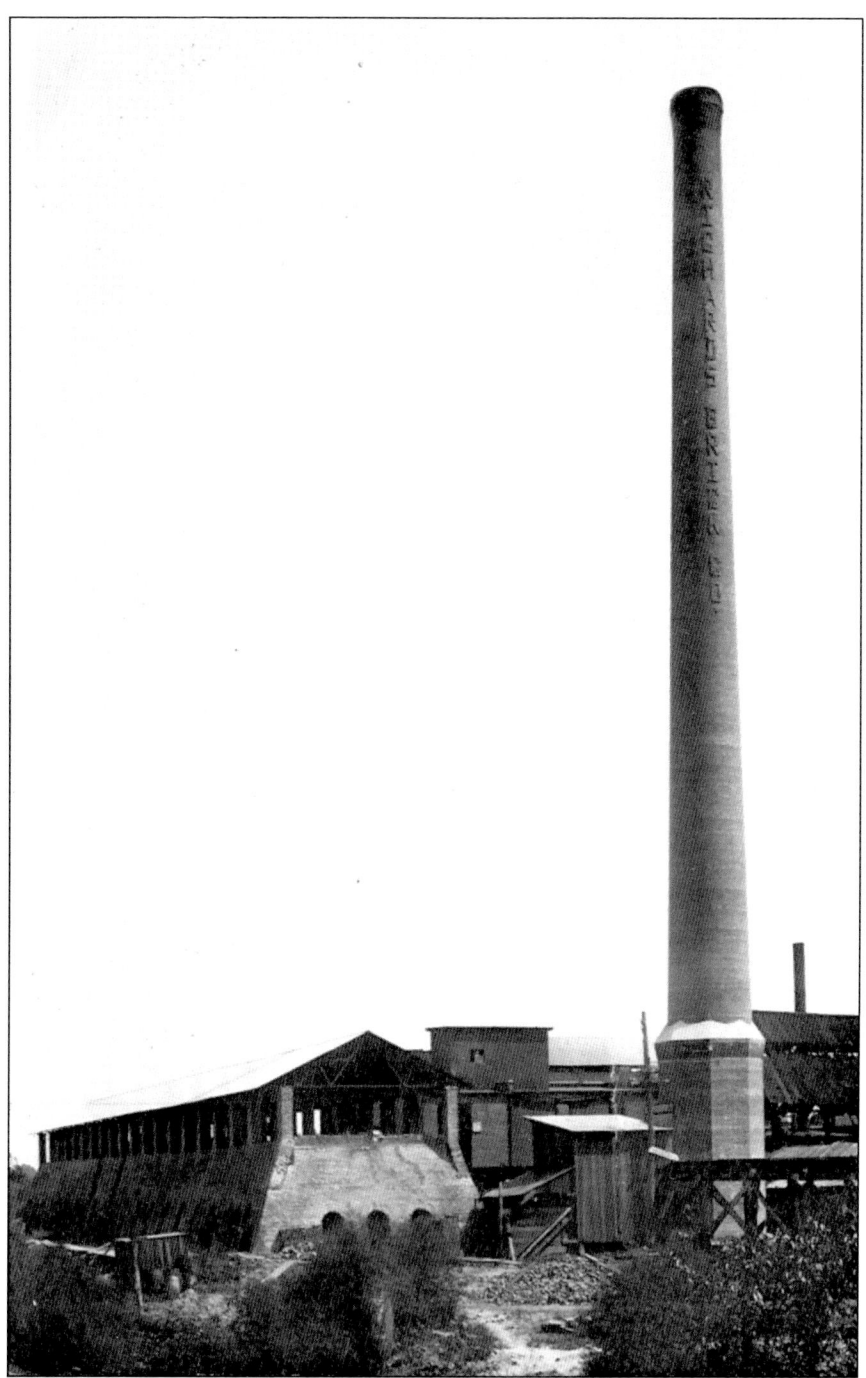

Richards Brick Company was founded in 1890 by Ben H. Richards and Thomas W. Springer at the east end of Schwarz Street, not far from where Leclaire was established. Richards lent his name to the company and Springer to the street where the company located. The bricks for the building of Leclaire were produced by this company. By 1912, Richards Brick Company was producing 10 million bricks per year. The company is still in business. (Courtesy of Neal Strebel.)

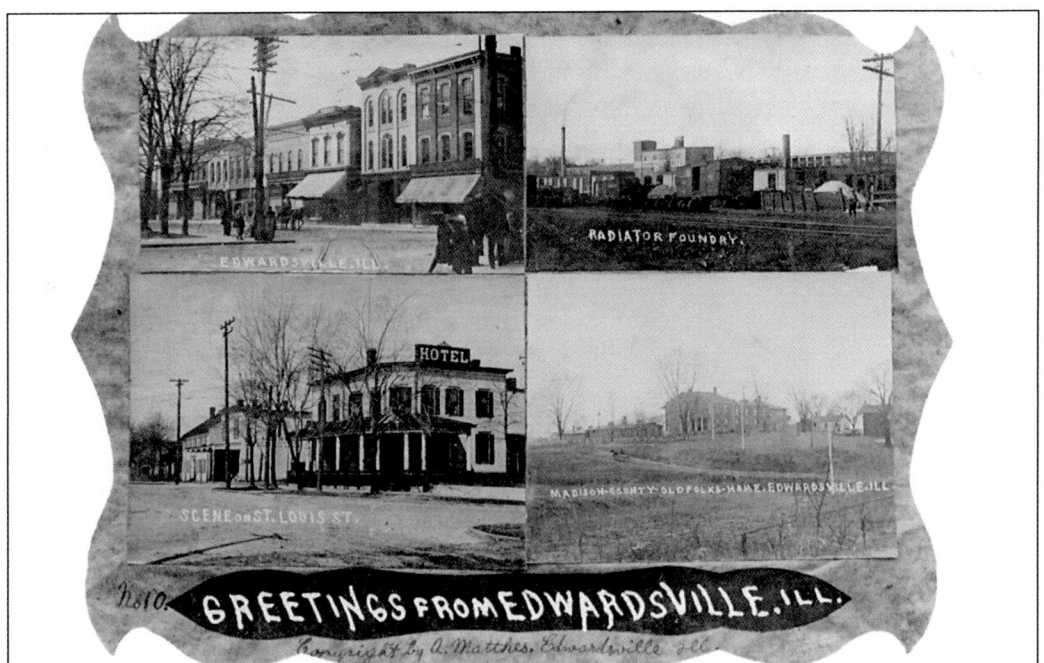

On this multiview postcard, the radiator foundry is shown at the upper right. Established as the U.S. Radiator Corporation, the company manufactured cast-iron steam radiators in its plant on East Vandalia Street. (Courtesy of Neal Strebel.)

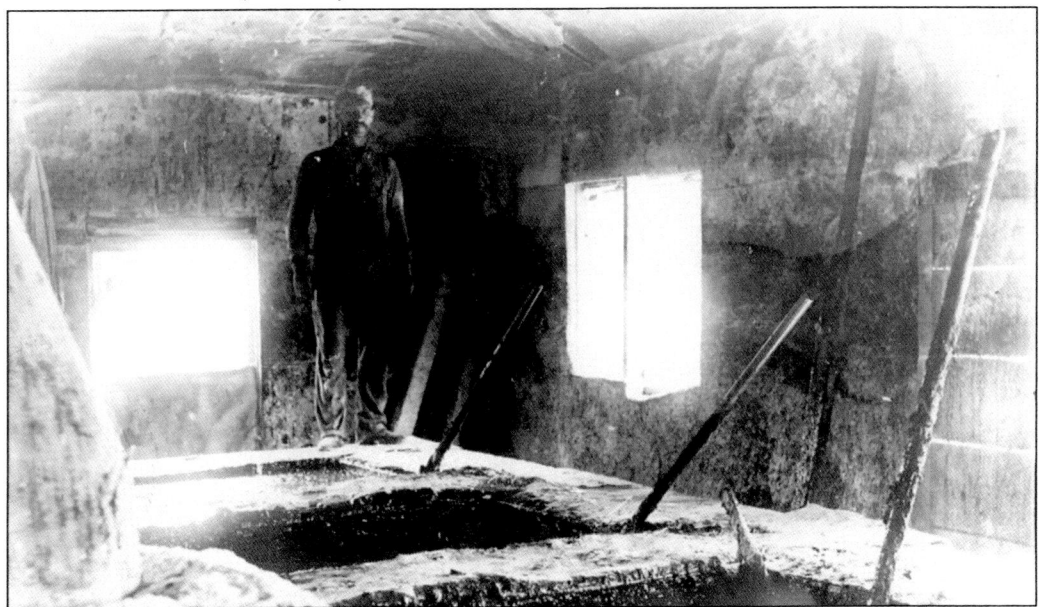

This worker is on the job at the National Mastic Roofing Company, which was located at the southern edge of Edwardsville near the Clover Leaf Railroad and the Madison Coal Company. The notation on the back of the postcard reads, "ware [sic] Dad worked in Edwardsville making roofing." Mastic asphalt is a product that combines limestone and refined bitumens to make a waterproof coating. The process was patented by a Frenchman in 1860. (Courtesy of Neal Strebel.)

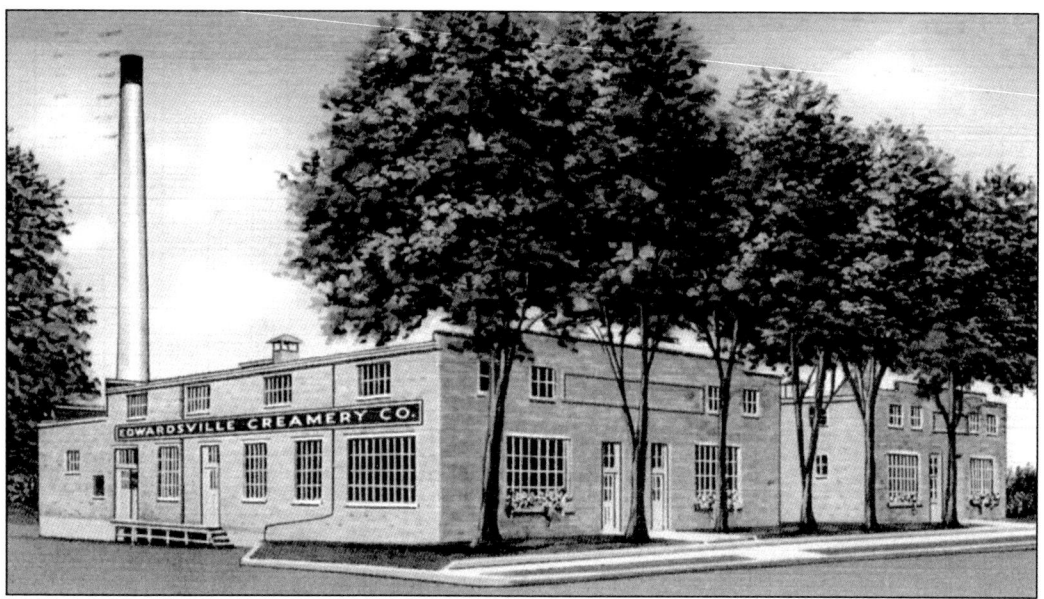

Martin Jensen founded the Edwardsville Creamery Company (ECCO) in 1927 at Park and Johnson Streets and remained at that address for half a century. The operation began by producing butter and milk powder and later expanded to include bottled milk and other dairy products. Milk was sold wholesale to groceries and also was available through home delivery to consumers. (Courtesy of June Nealy.)

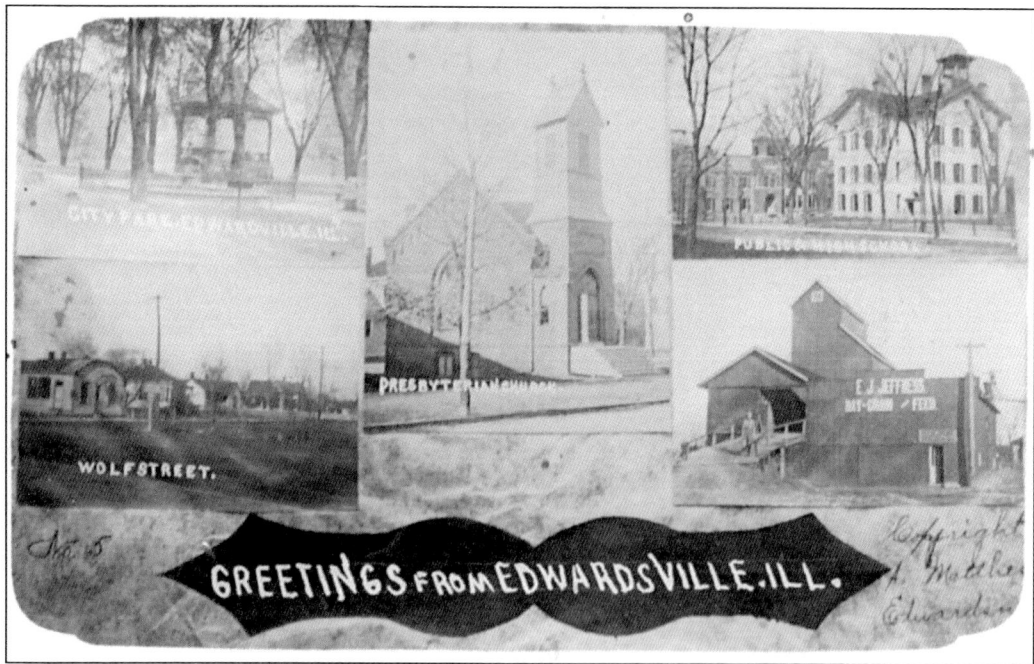

The E. J. Jeffress Hay, Grain, and Feed Company is shown at the lower right on this multiview postcard. Other feed businesses and grain elevators included the A. and B. Feed and Seed Store, Inc., on West Vandalia Street and Dippold Brothers Feed and Grain at Randle and St. Louis Streets. (Courtesy of Neal Strebel.)

Seven

N. O. NELSON AND LECLAIRE VILLAGE

After the Civil War, city populations swelled as workers sought factory jobs. Unsafe working conditions, which existed well into the 1900s, led to workplace tragedies like the Monongah, West Virginia, coal mine explosion and the Triangle Shirtwaist fire in New York City. Poor wages and overcrowding in city tenements resulted in unsanitary conditions and disease. Dissatisfaction and strikes ensued, but were soon quelled due to the fear and poverty that ruled the workers and to the sheer numbers of immigrants eager to take on any job.

Amid the great discrepancy between the rich and the poor that characterized the Gilded Age, Norwegian immigrant N. O. Nelson humbly began his business career in St. Louis and in 1877 established the N. O. Nelson Manufacturing Company. His awareness of the conflict between capitalism and the working class grew as he served as a strike arbitrator and read *On Profit Sharing between Capital and Labor* by Sedley Taylor. The idea of a model company town inspired him to begin a search for suitable land.

Edwardsville won out with nearby coal, water, and railroad lines and a community that recognized the value of attracting the factory there. After negotiations, it was agreed that the Edwardsville businesses and residents would voluntarily contribute $20,000 to secure the land, with Nelson paying the remaining $3,385. Nelson named the new village Leclaire after French profit-sharing pioneer Edme Jean Leclaire (1801–1872) and broke ground in 1890. Six guiding principles were to influence all planning for the new company town—work, education, recreation, beauty, homes, and freedom.

Two years after Leclaire was established, investigative reporter Nellie Bly, who had exposed the squalid living conditions of the so-called model company town of Pullman, visited Leclaire. She reported in the July 29, 1894, issue of *The New York World* that, "There is one place in America where the labor question seems to have been solved. That is in Leclaire, Ill., one hour's ride from St. Louis, Mo."

The cooperative village of Leclaire remained a peaceful independent community until 1934 when, in need of infrastructure improvements, it was annexed to Edwardsville.

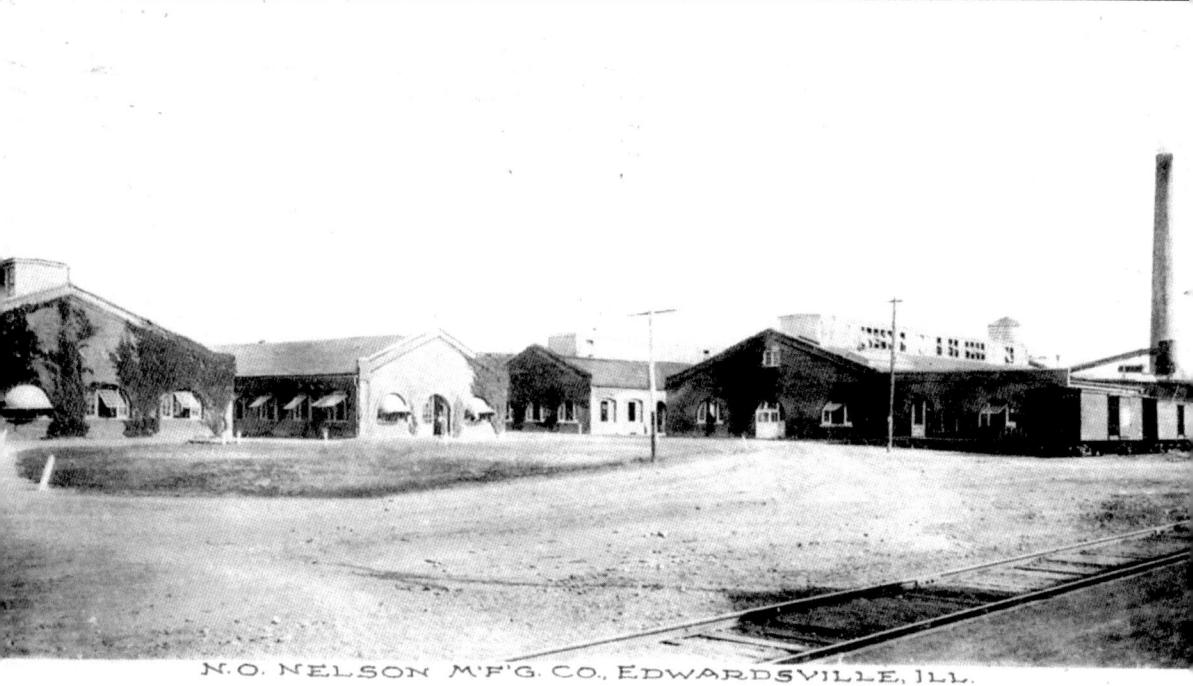

The Leclaire shop buildings were designed to make workers as safe and comfortable as possible, with large windows and plenty of light and air. The buildings had electric fans, steam heat, fire sprinklers, and electric lights. Ivy, flowers beds, and green lawns were planted around the shop buildings. Architect Alexander Cameron of St. Louis designed the factory. (Courtesy of June Nealy.)

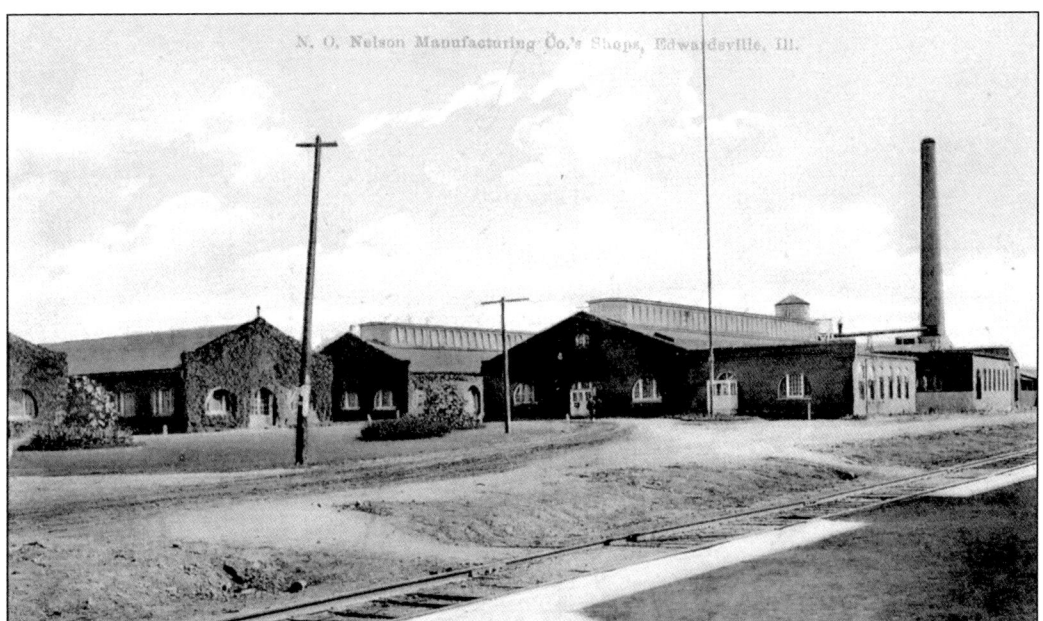

Besides the residences that were sold to employees, the company owned all of Leclaire, which included, besides the factory, a 50-foot-tall water tower, a bowling alley and clubhouse, tennis courts, Leclaire Park, and a school. The entire tract of land upon which Leclaire was located consisted of 150 acres just southeast of Edwardsville. Workers were paid fair wages and were encouraged to purchase company stock and shares of the cooperative store. (Courtesy of June Nealy.)

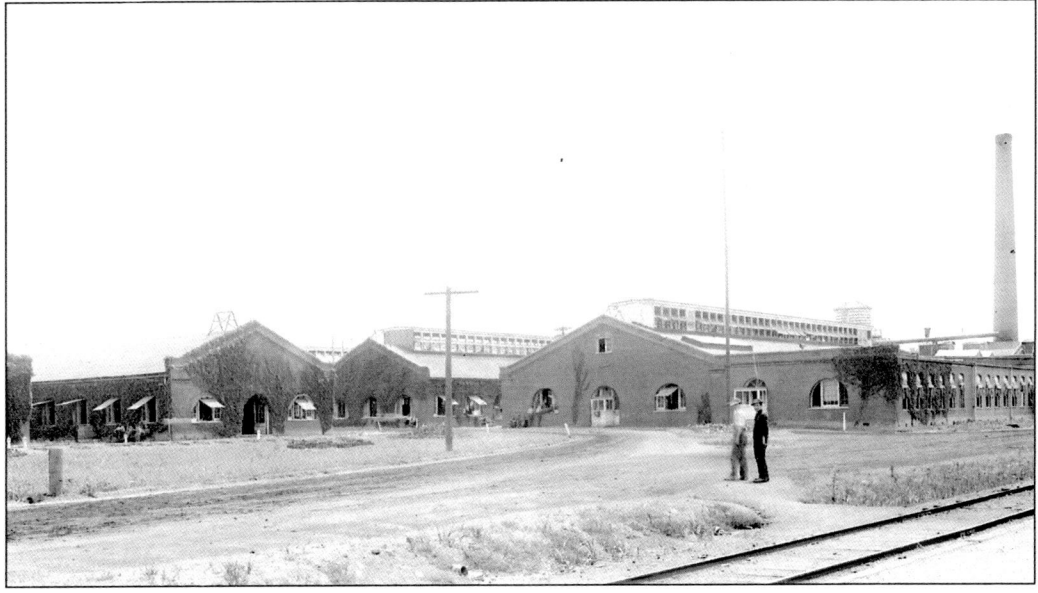

The N. O. Nelson Manufacturing Company shops included a bathtub mill (160 by 60 feet); a copper shop (160 by 40 feet); a cabinet mill (160 by 80 feet); a varnishing and finishing shop (60 by 60 feet); the boiler, dynamo, and pumping house (72 by 60 feet); a dry house (30 by 40 feet); a warehouse; a machine shop; and a marble shop. All the buildings were built of red brick and were capped with steel truss roofs. (Courtesy of Neal Strebel.)

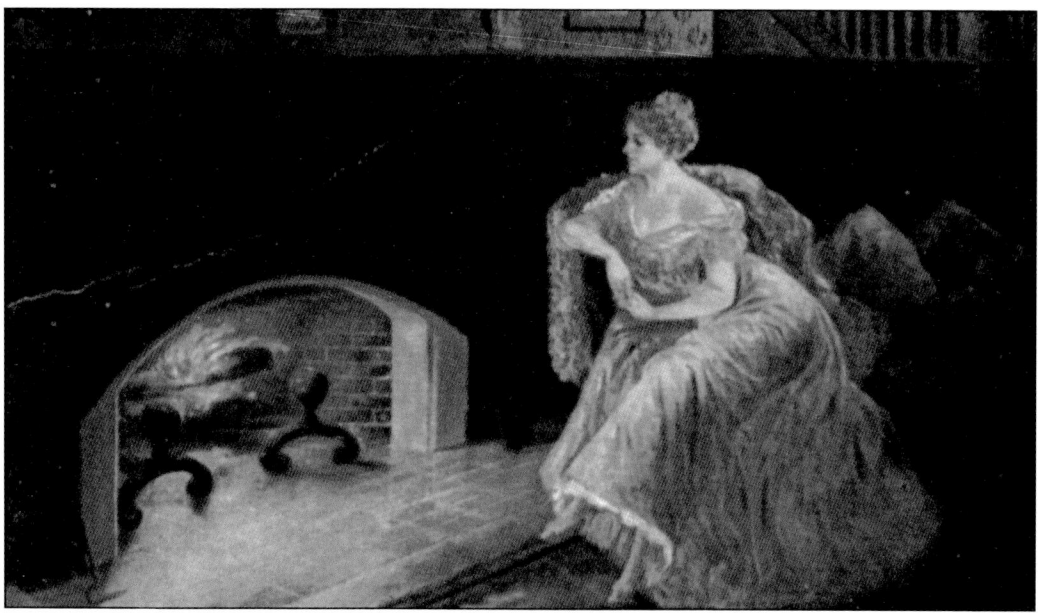

This early-1900s commercial postcard shows N. O. Nelson products. Marble works manufactured and installed by N. O. Nelson graced the entrance to the Wright Building in St. Louis, the main stairway in the Illinois State Trust Company in East St. Louis, the main waiting room in the New Orleans Terminal Station, and the State Stairway in the state capitol in Jackson, Mississippi. (Courtesy of June Nealy.)

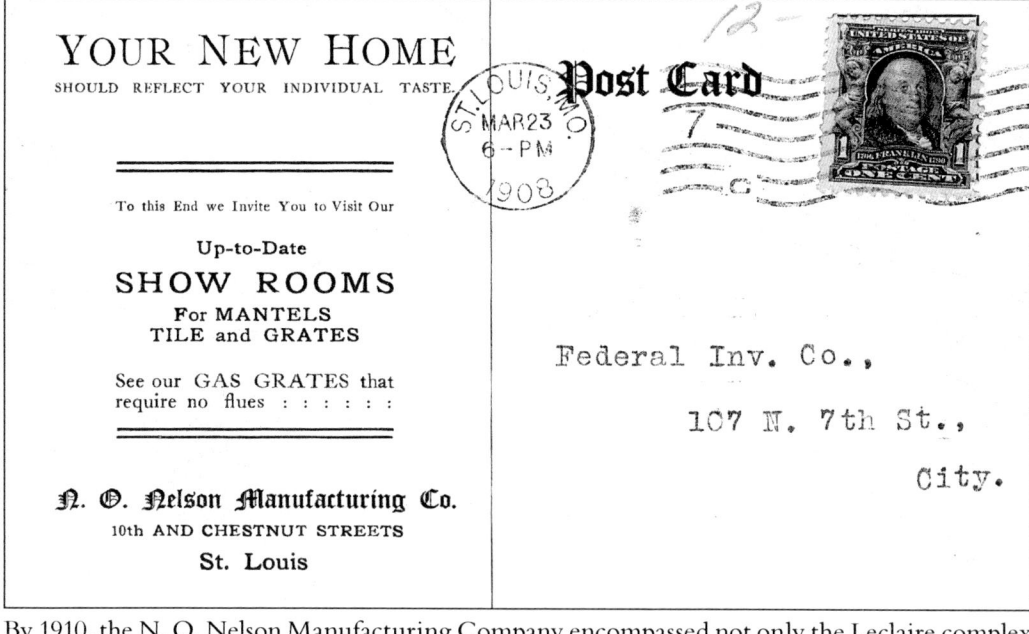

By 1910, the N. O. Nelson Manufacturing Company encompassed not only the Leclaire complex and the St. Louis headquarters and distribution center but additional manufacturing facilities in Bessemer, Alabama, and Noblesville, Indiana, and branch houses in Memphis, Houston, Los Angeles, Salt Lake City, Pueblo, Joplin, Butte, Spokane, and Birmingham across the United States. (Courtesy of June Nealy.)

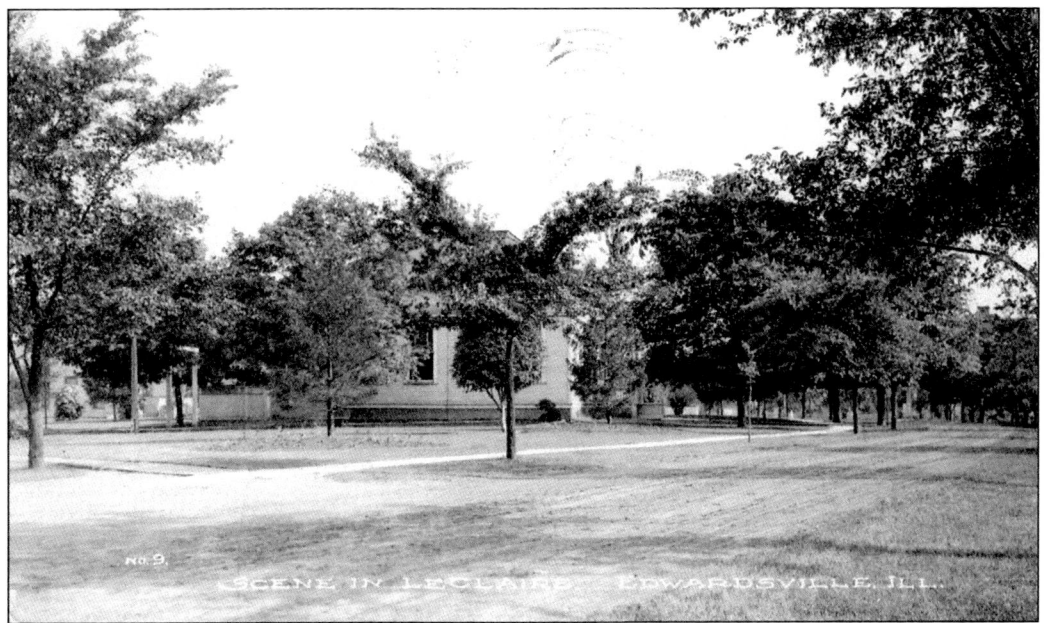

The Leclaire School House, partially visible behind the trees, was built in 1895 to serve not only the inhabitants of Leclaire Village but citizens of Edwardsville as well. The building was constructed with a library and four classrooms, with sliding walls that allowed the facility to also function as a community center for lectures, meetings, and family gatherings. Lecturers included Jane Addams, Nellie Bly, and Rev. Edward Everett Hale. (Courtesy of June Nealy.)

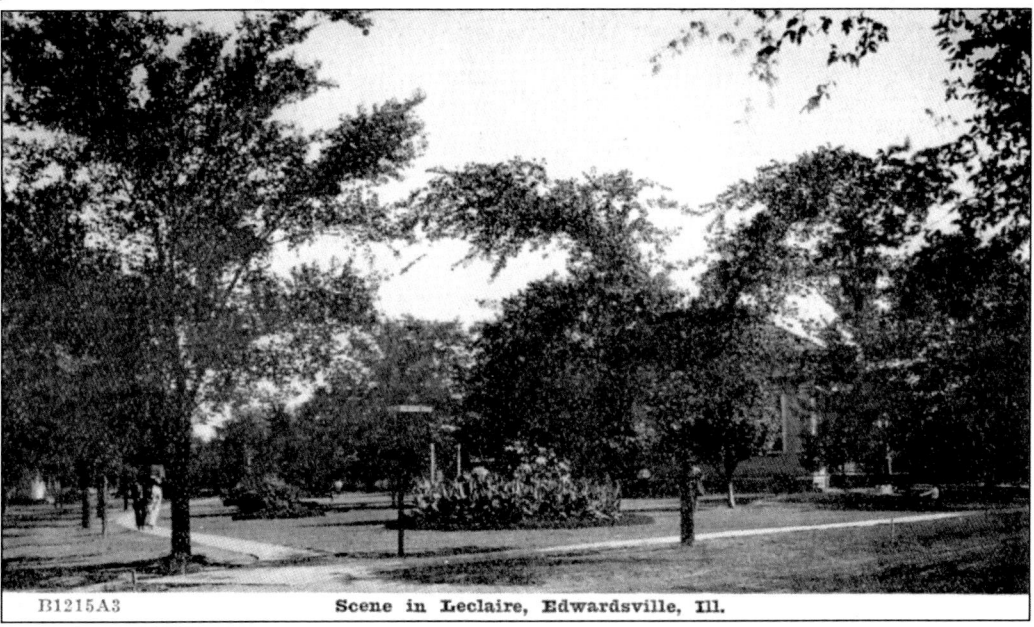

The Leclaire School House was built in a mixture of styles, including classical, Italianate, and Queen Anne. N. O. Nelson remarked, "Every brick and every board and every nail that is put into this building is for the benefit of humanity." To that end, Nelson encouraged the community to use the 1,200-volume library. Older students learned trade skills in the shops for half the day and academic subjects in school the other half. (Courtesy of June Nealy.)

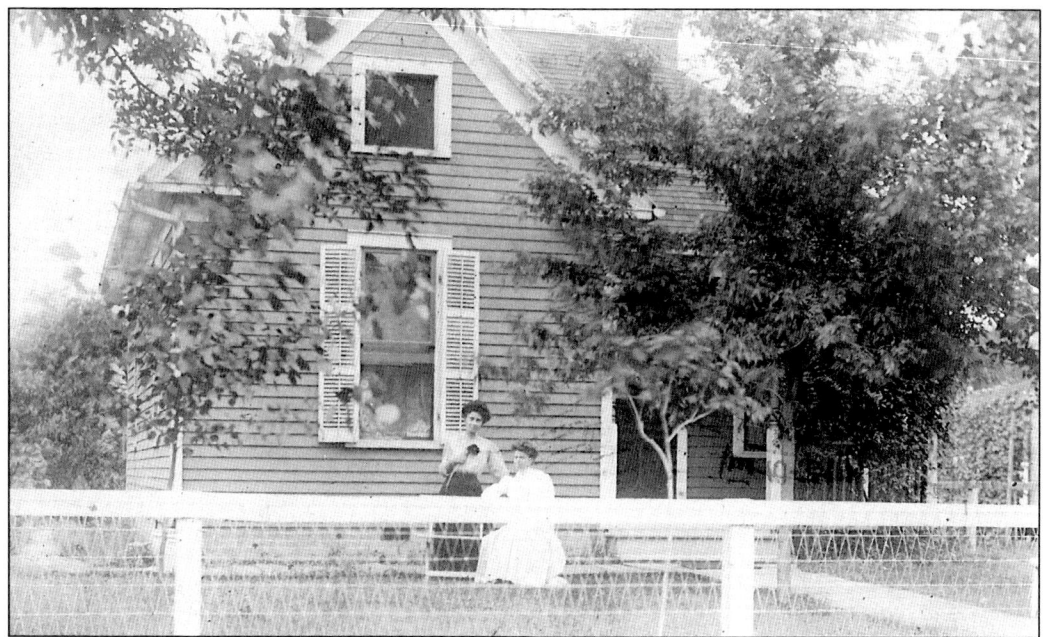

Leclaire's 150 acres were planned with the six guiding principles in mind. To ensure aesthetically pleasing surroundings, N. O. Nelson hired Julius Pitzman, who had supervised the layout of Forest Park in St. Louis, to plan Leclaire. The early streets were laid out in a winding fashion with large lots and generous setbacks. Residents enjoyed free water, street lighting, and street cleaning and in 1894 paid 25¢ per month for electricity. (Courtesy of Neal Strebel.)

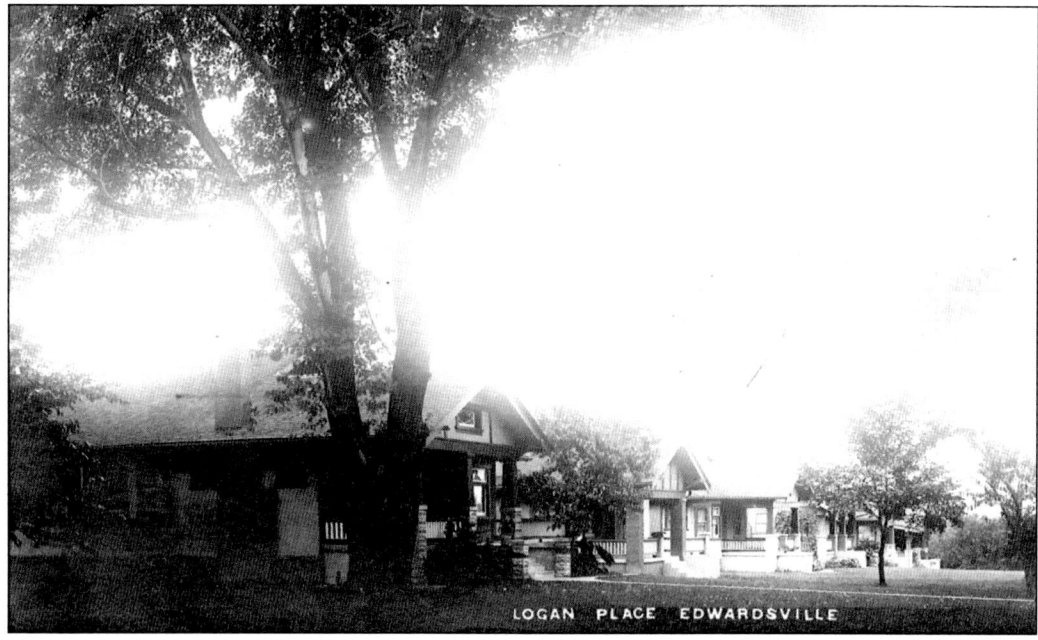

Eventually additional neighborhoods built up around the original 150-acre planned community of Leclaire. This line of early-1900s arts and crafts–style bungalows was built on Logan Place, a short residential street just east of the N. O. Nelson manufacturing complex. (Courtesy of Neal Strebel.)

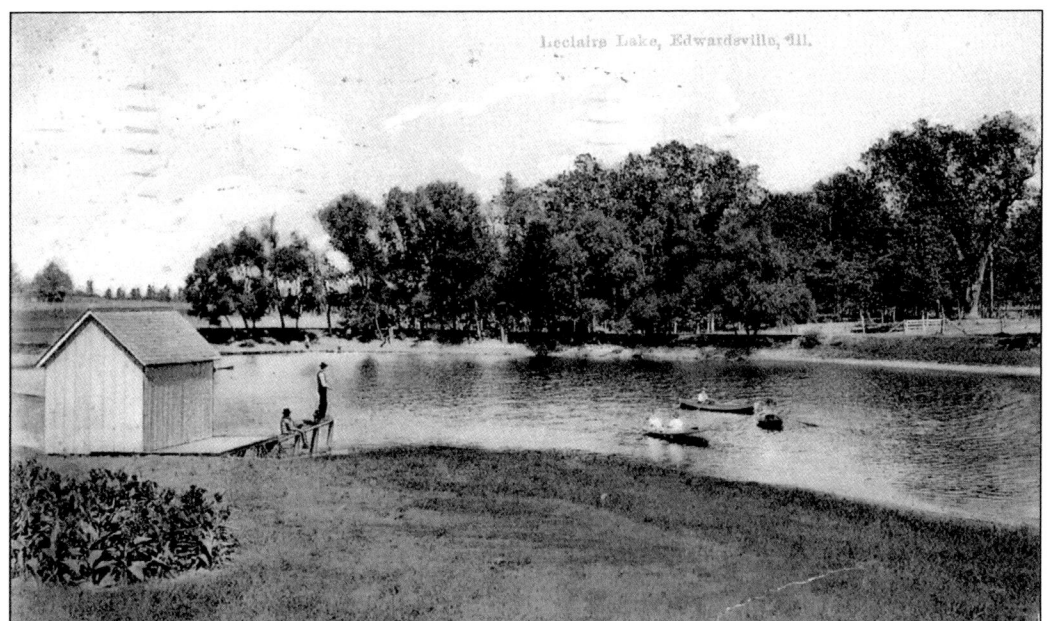

N. O. Nelson's belief in recreation as one of the six guiding principles of a community led him to create numerous recreational facilities for the village of Leclaire. The seven-acre Leclaire Lake offered opportunities for boating, swimming, fishing, and ice-skating. The lovely Leclaire Park that surrounded the lake boasted a building for family gatherings, a bandstand, and boat facilities. (Courtesy of June Nealy.)

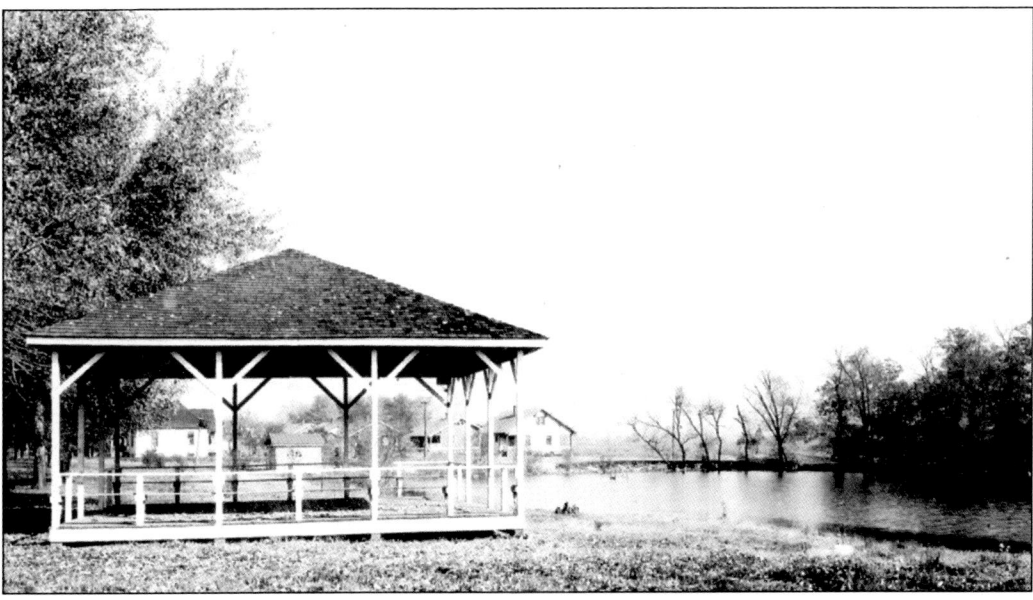

Leclaire Park enabled families to gather and children to play within the community. In 1892, W. B. Thomas organized a six-member musical group with Edward Weber, George Ryan, Fred Pfeiffer, Roland Van Hyning, and William McNeilly; Thomas served as bandleader. All six musicians were employees of the company. In later years, the band grew to 23 musicians. The band often provided music at company barbecues. (Courtesy of June Nealy.)

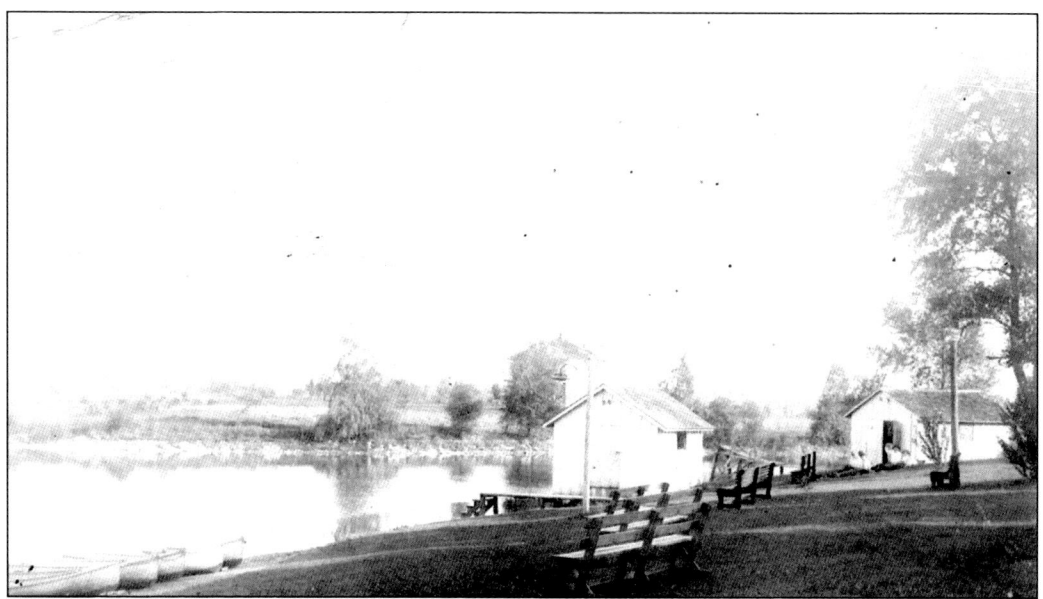

Other recreational activities provided to Leclaire residents included a bowling alley, billiard tables, and a baseball and football field. Leclaire boasted its own baseball team. In 1906, the Leclaire Blues ball team included players William Russel, Frank Rotter, Robert Hamor, Norbert Hotz, George Judd, Skeet Hentz, Dall Rizzolli, Pete Rotter, Fats Crossman, Fred Healy, and Frank Fink. (Courtesy of Neal Strebel.)

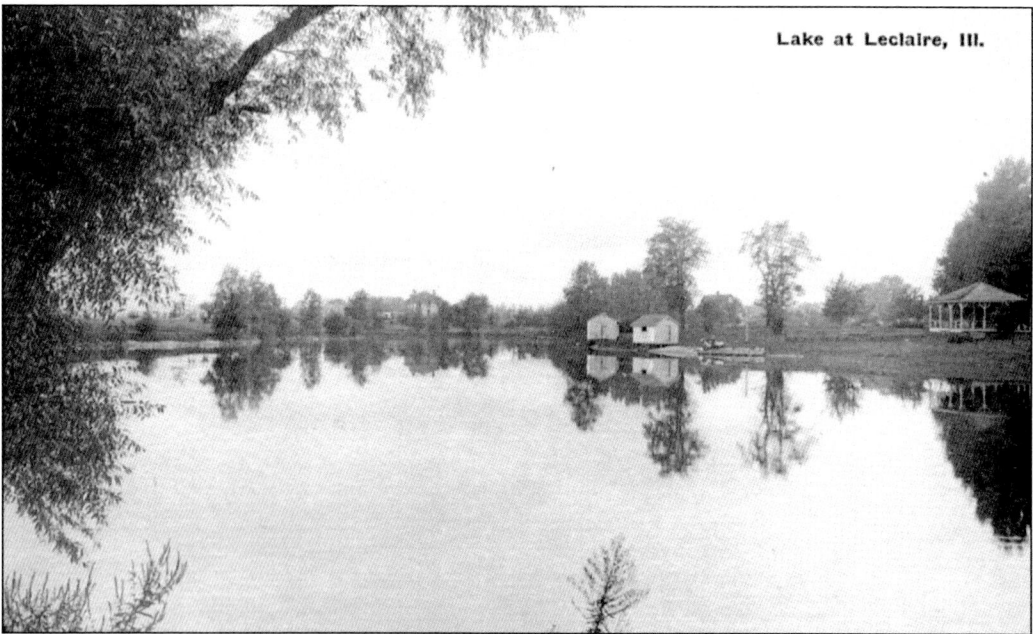

In 1911, employee Tom Trigg took on added responsibilities when he agreed to care for Leclaire Lake, the bowling alley, and the baseball field for an additional $15 per month. Wanting to keep the young people in Leclaire and out of trouble, he eventually built an ice-cream cart, built rafts for the boys, increased the safety of the boats and the lake, and bought and rented out swimsuits. (Courtesy of June Nealy.)

Eight

GETTING THERE

Edwardsville area transportation began with Native American trails and the traces used by early settlers. The first step toward a maintained system of roads began in 1813 with a county meeting at the house of Thomas Kirkpatrick, an early Edwardsville settler. At this gathering, overseers were appointed to be responsible for the various roads. In 1849 and 1850, two main plank roads were built to allow commerce in and out of Edwardsville. One of these ran west to Venice, and the other was a north-and-south road between Edwardsville and Collinsville, which Route 157 now roughly follows.

The railroad reached Edwardsville after the Civil War due to the efforts of Judge David Gillespie, Judge Joseph Gillespie, and Capt. J. F. Lusk. Under their leadership, Edwardsville raised $75,000 to build a railroad to connect with Alton. However, rival railroad companies, foreclosures, and leases complicated the process. The Wabash Railroad and the Illinois Terminal Railroad finally came to an agreement in 1899 that enabled a rail connection between Alton's eastern city limits and Edwardsville Crossing. It finally became operational in 1899. Another line was constructed in 1904 to Leclaire to make a direct connection with the Litchfield and Madison and the St. Louis and Western Railroads. The Illinois Terminal Railroad acquired the rights in 1910 to operate on tracks owned by the St. Louis and Illinois Belt Railroad to secure additional regional connections. According to the *History of Madison County*, in 1912 Edwardsville boasted stations for the Chicago and Alton; Toledo, St. Louis and Western; Big Four; and Wabash Railroads.

By 1912, four electric railroads were servicing Edwardsville, including the Alton, Granite and St. Louis; the East St. Louis and Suburban; the Edwardsville Belt Line; and the St. Louis, Springfield and Peoria.

In downtown Edwardsville, Main Street ceased to be a dirt road and became a brick-paved street with a concrete foundation in 1904. Other streets in town followed suit. Within the next score of years, automobiles and delivery trucks began to appear on city streets. In 1928, Edwardsville's first traffic lights were installed at the intersection of Main and Vandalia Streets.

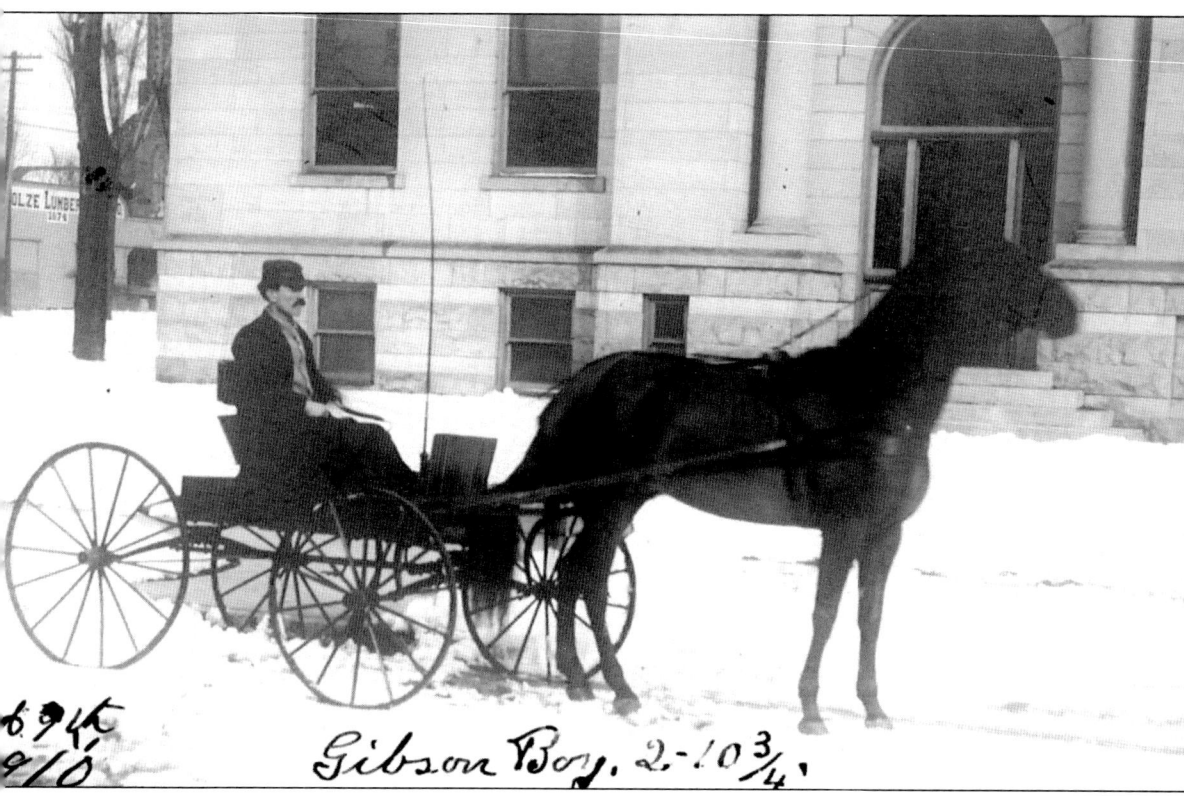

In 1910, the horse and buggy was still a prime mode of transportation. This photograph was taken in front of the library at Edwardsville City Park. A note on the back of the postcard states that the horse belonged to Phoebe Montgomery, who resided at 829 St. Louis Street. The sign on the building at the left identifies the Stolze Lumber Company at 225 East Vandalia Street, established in 1874. (Courtesy of Neal Strebel.)

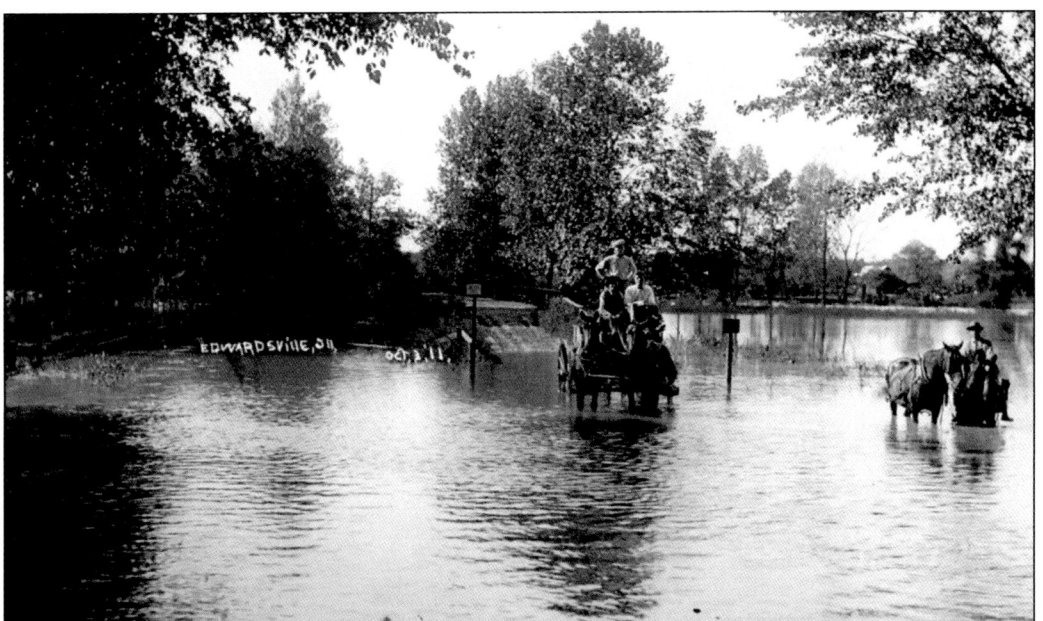

Floods ravaged parts of the United States in the fall of 1911, including this unidentified spot in Edwardsville. The message on the back of this postcard reads, "How do you like this change of weather? Note picture on this side. It is Pa driving the team. It was taken during the last flood." The card was postmarked November 14, 1911. (Courtesy of Neal Strebel.)

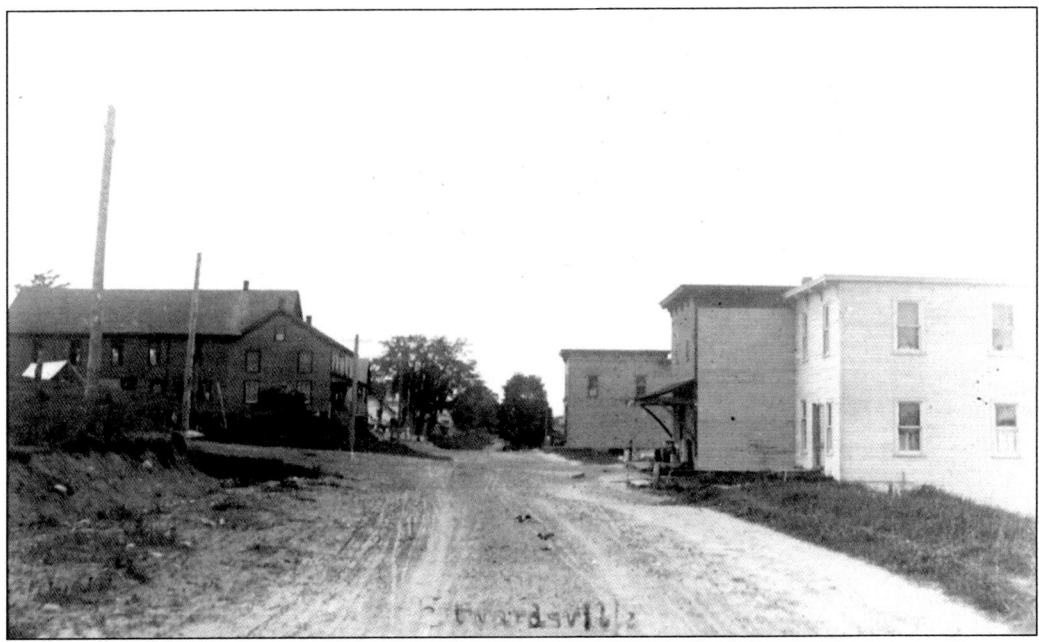

Unpaved streets were the norm until well into the 1900s. An article in the *Intelligencer* stated that, "We know not what to say in regard to the present condition of the thoroughfares leading to this mud-bound town. To say that they are simply muddy, would be complimenting them to the highest degree." Another said, "Our street crossings are almost impassable. Lady pedestrians might as well attempt to ford the Mississippi." (Courtesy of Michael A. Sporrer.)

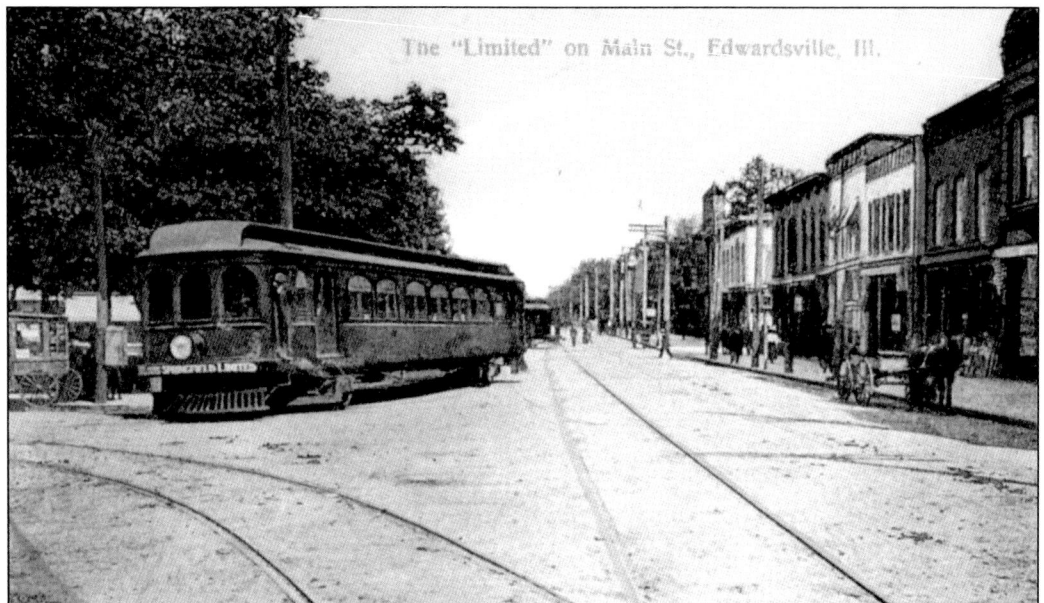

The Illinois Traction System served central Illinois to St. Louis, Missouri, and was popularly known by several names—"the Terminal," "the Traction," and "the Interurban." Businessman William B. McKinley consolidated a series of interurban railroads into the Illinois Traction System in the early 1900s; the railroad was reorganized and the corporate name was changed in 1937 to the Illinois Terminal Railroad. (Courtesy of June Nealy.)

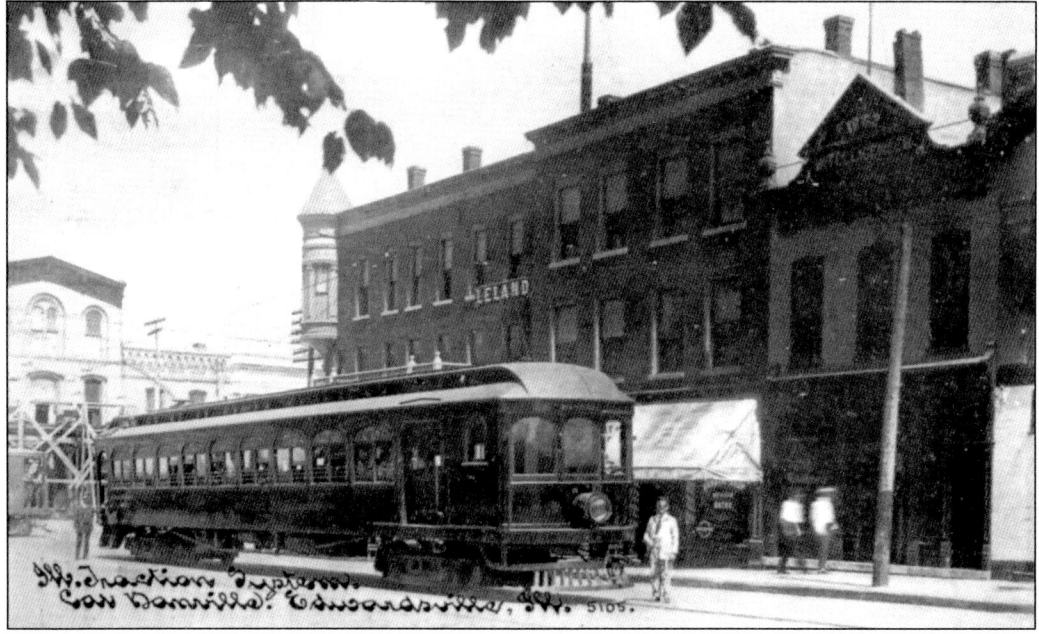

In the early 1900s, these cars probably belonged to the Edwardsville–Alton–East St. Louis interurban line and were bought out by the Illinois Traction System about 1928. The McKinley Bridge across the Mississippi River was originally built by William B. McKinley's company to carry the trolley cars of the Illinois Traction System back and forth from Illinois to St. Louis, Missouri. (Courtesy of June Nealy.)

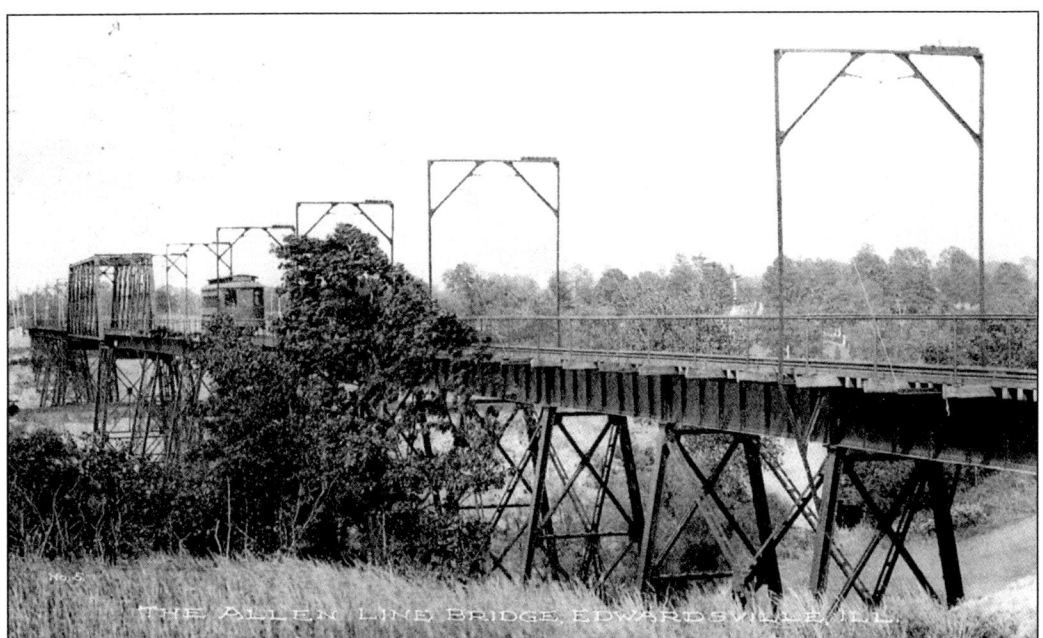

The Allen Line Bridge was constructed 1.5 miles south of Edwardsville around 1900 by the Illinois Traction System, later known as the Illinois Terminal Railroad. Known as a "pratt through truss" design, the bridge was removed after the line was discontinued. Note the electric car passing over the bridge just behind the trees. (Courtesy of June Nealy.)

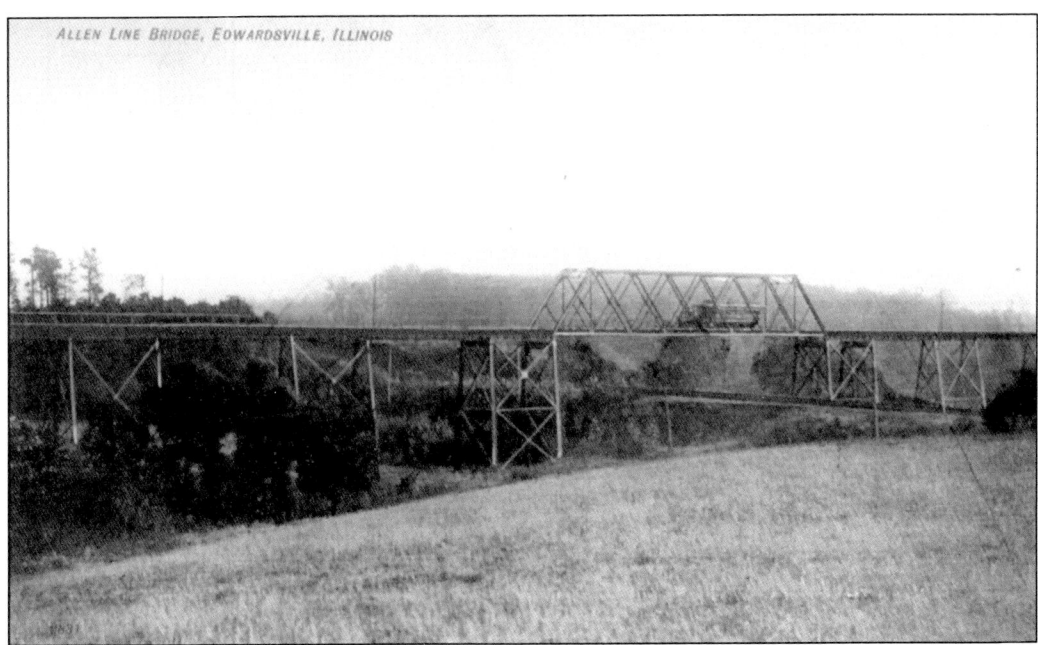

In another view of the Allen Line Bridge, the hilly landscape on the south side of Edwardsville can be seen. The Allen line was a branch line owned by the Illinois Terminal Railroad, which ran from Mitchell to Edwardsville. A message on the back of one of these postcards reported, "Arrived home all okay. The train was only four hours late, that's all." (Courtesy of June Nealy.)

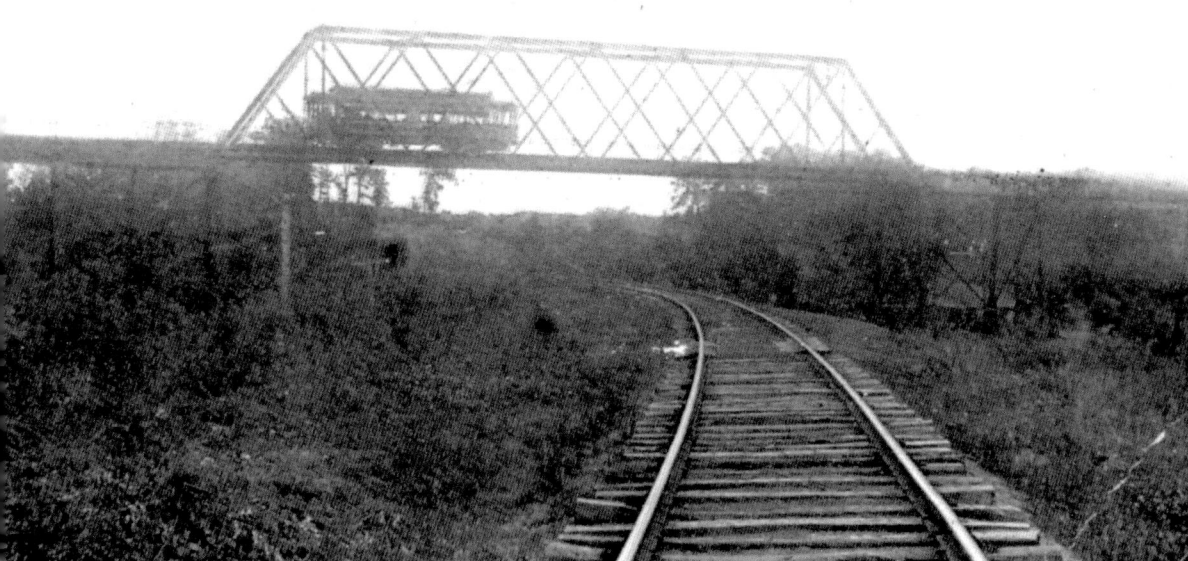

In this view, an electric car passes over the Wabash steam line tracks between Bluffs Junction and Edwardsville. In 1909, a train wreck occurred on the Wabash lines just west of Edwardsville. An engine and two cars were speeding around the curve at the Alton Road intersection when they crashed into four cars loaded with coal that had been left on the tracks. It was believed that the coal cars had somehow escaped during switching. (Courtesy of June Nealy.)

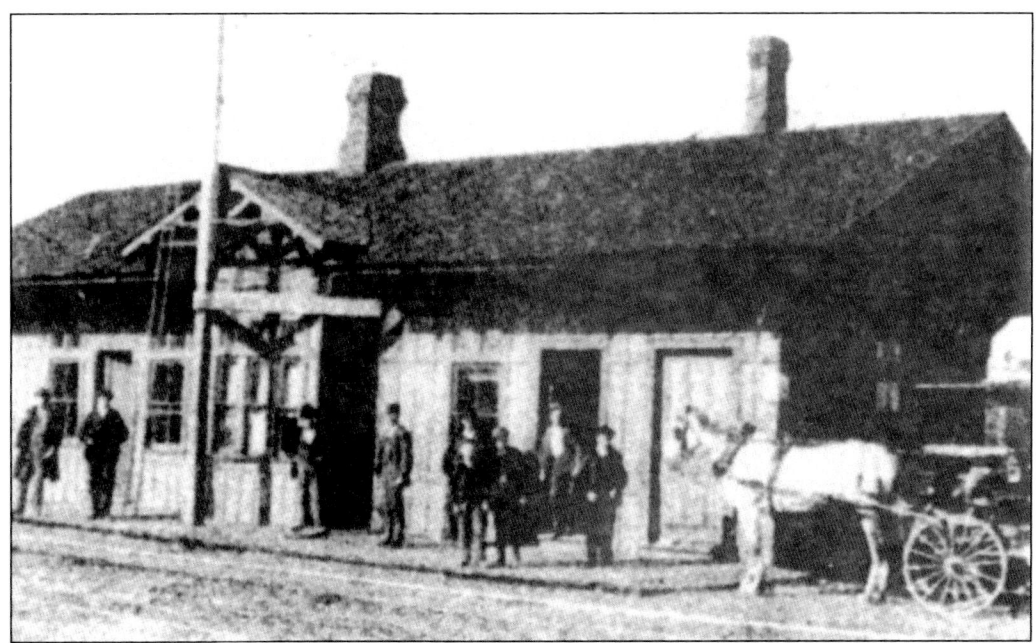

The Clover Leaf Depot was built in the 1880s across the tracks from where the N. O. Nelson Manufacturing Company would be built. The photograph above was taken around 1895, and the picture below was taken in the 1970s. In 1922, the Clover Leaf line was bought by the Nickel Plate line. In March 1929, a disastrous head-on collision between two freight trains of the Nickel Plate system occurred just three blocks from the siding where one train should have allowed the other to pass. Fourteen cars piled up and a fire broke out. An engineer, a fireman, and a brakeman, all from Charleston, were killed. Two others were injured. Torpedoes placed on the track were said to have exploded just before the crash, but they were believed to have been intended as a warning to workmen in the yards. (Courtesy of Michael A. Sporrer.)

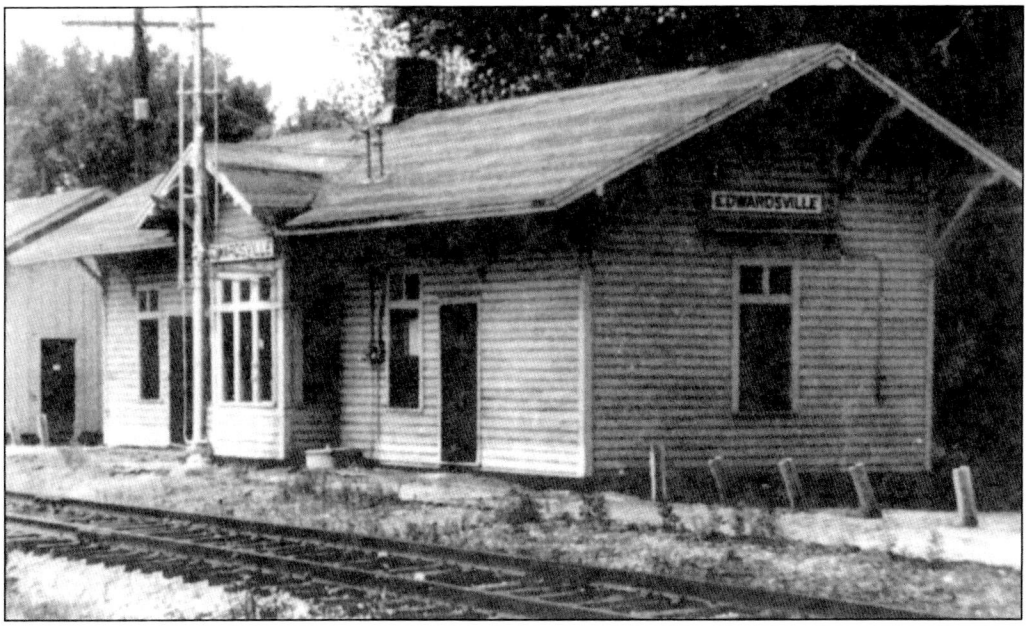

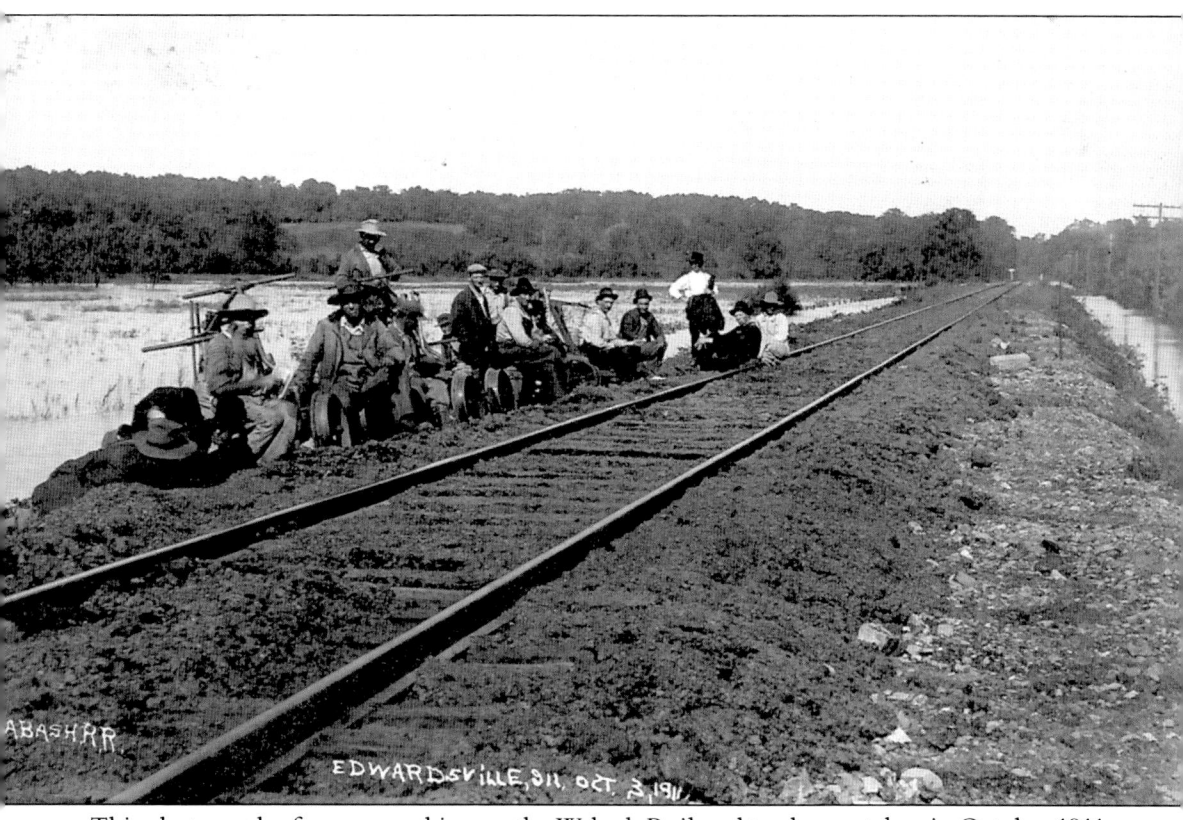
This photograph of a crew working on the Wabash Railroad tracks was taken in October 1911. At that time, the Wabash system extended about 34 miles through Madison County, from about the southwest corner of the county to near the northeast corner, skirting the north side of Edwardsville. (Courtesy of June Nealy.)

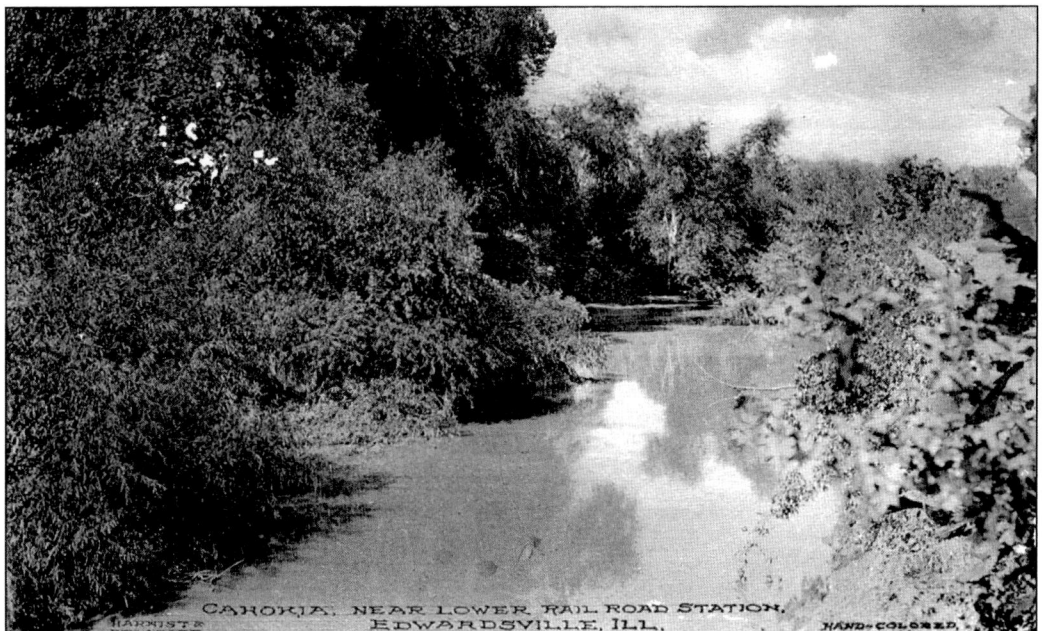

This view of Cahokia Creek was taken about 1900, before it was straightened in 1912. In 1915, Cahokia Creek flooded, washing out the concrete supports and the beams of an Illinois Terminal Railroad bridge. Cahokia Creek flows southwest through Madison County, to the west of Edwardsville, toward the Mississippi River. (Courtesy of June Nealy.)

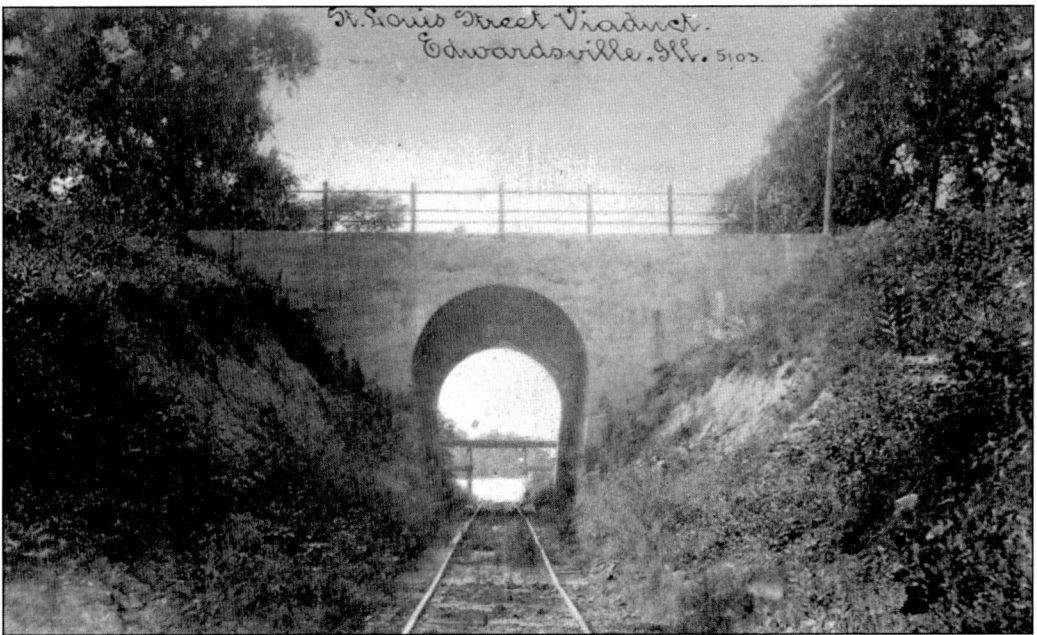

When this photograph was taken around 1910, railroad tracks ran through this viaduct under the west end of St. Louis Street. Today the tracks have been removed and homes have been built on the land sloping down on both sides from St. Louis Street, to Randle Street on the north side, and toward Minnesota Street on the south side. (Courtesy of June Nealy.)

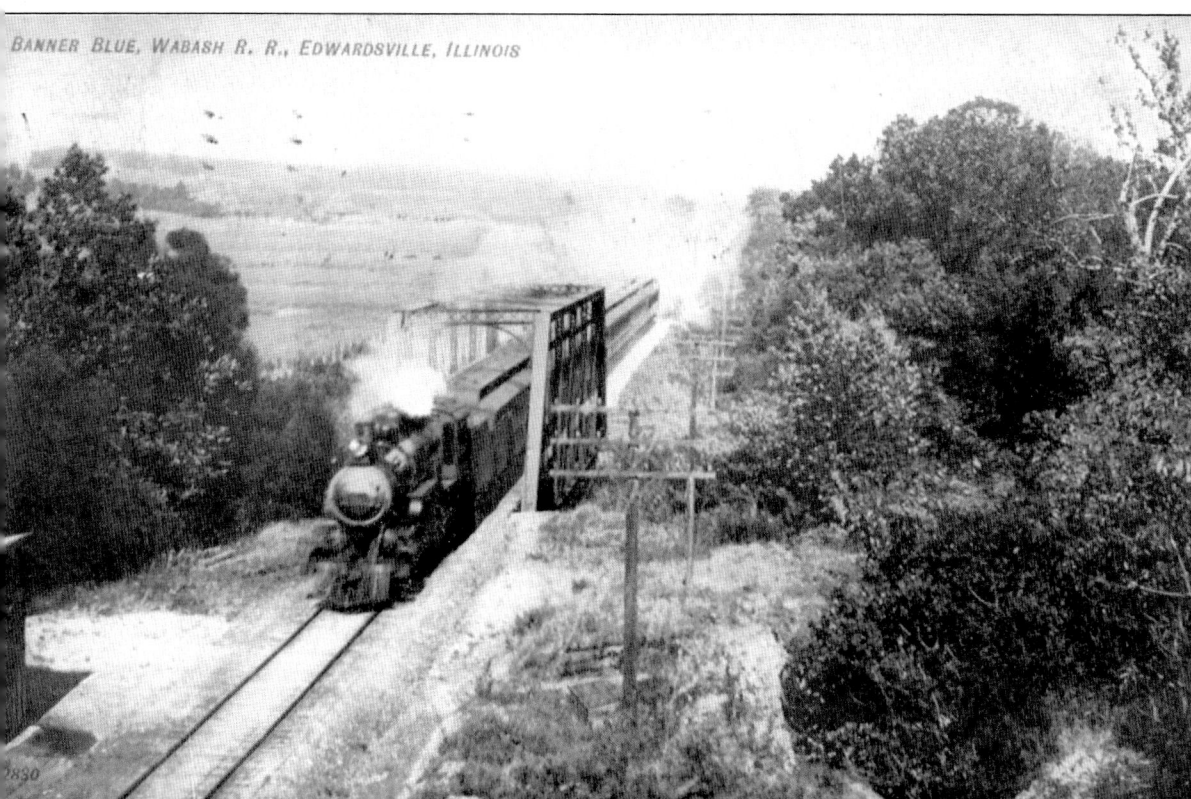

The *Banner Blue*, the *Blue Bird*, and the *Midnight* were streamliners introduced by the Wabash Railroad in the 1940s, running between St. Louis and Chicago. Their popularity held until Amtrak took over passenger service in 1971. The Wabash line experienced foreclosure and several reorganizations and was known by several names, including Wabash Railway and Wabash Railroad. (Courtesy of Michael A. Sporrer.)

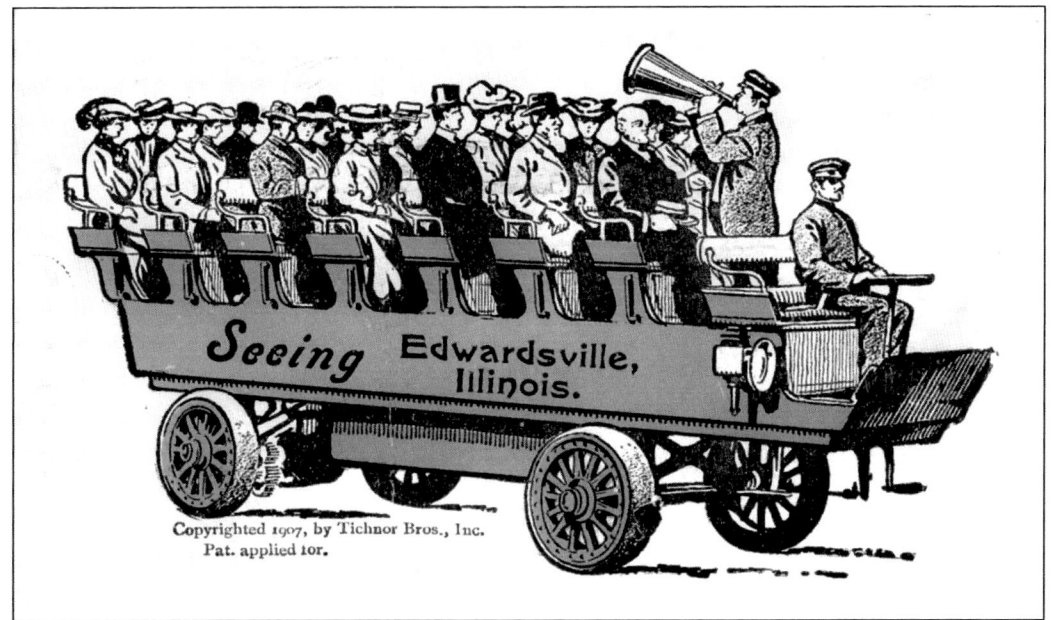

The exterior of this 1907 double postcard shows a drawing of a tourist vehicle, emphasizing the new importance of the automobile in society. The postcard was produced by Tichnor Brothers, a major postcard publishing and printing company in Massachusetts that produced cards nationally from 1912 until 1987, when the company was sold. (Courtesy of SJ Morrison.)

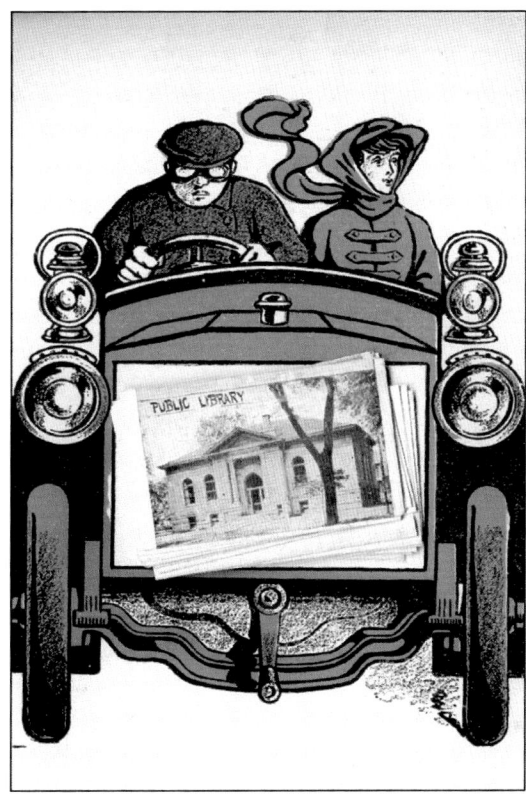

The interior of the above card, with more automobile artwork, also featured an accordion-pleated paper foldout with about a dozen images of local landmarks, including the courthouse, the Prickett residence, and Main Street. The first one is visible, showing the Edwardsville Public Library. These were miniatures of popular local postcard images. (Courtesy of SJ Morrison.)

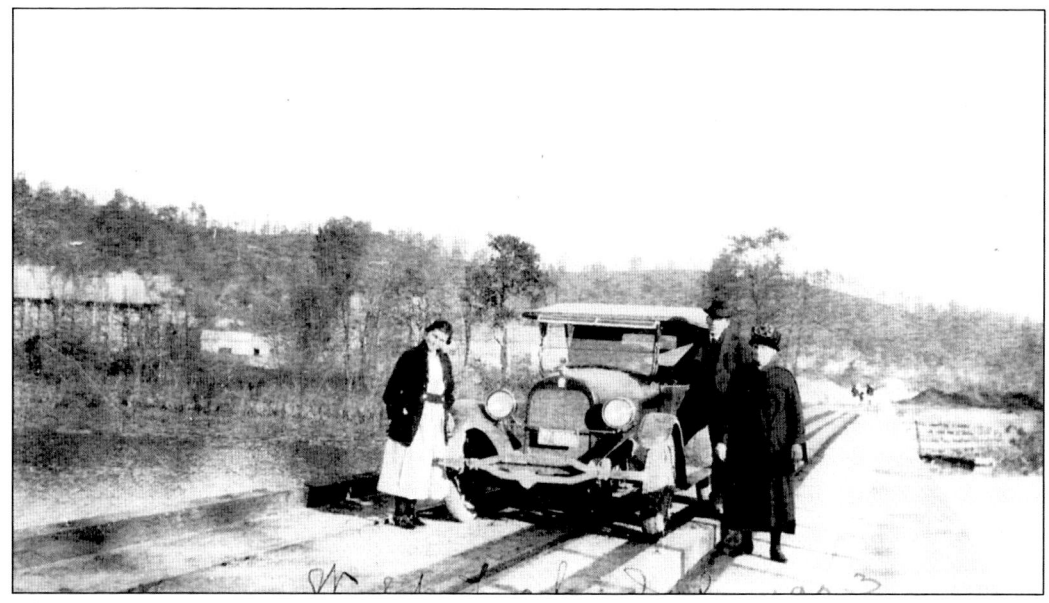

These motorists, two of them identified on the back of the postcard as "Billie Green and Ada," pause for a photograph on the bridge at Wolf's Lake. By 1923, when this photograph was taken, the automobile had firmly established itself across the United States and was often included in photographs. (Courtesy of June Nealy.)

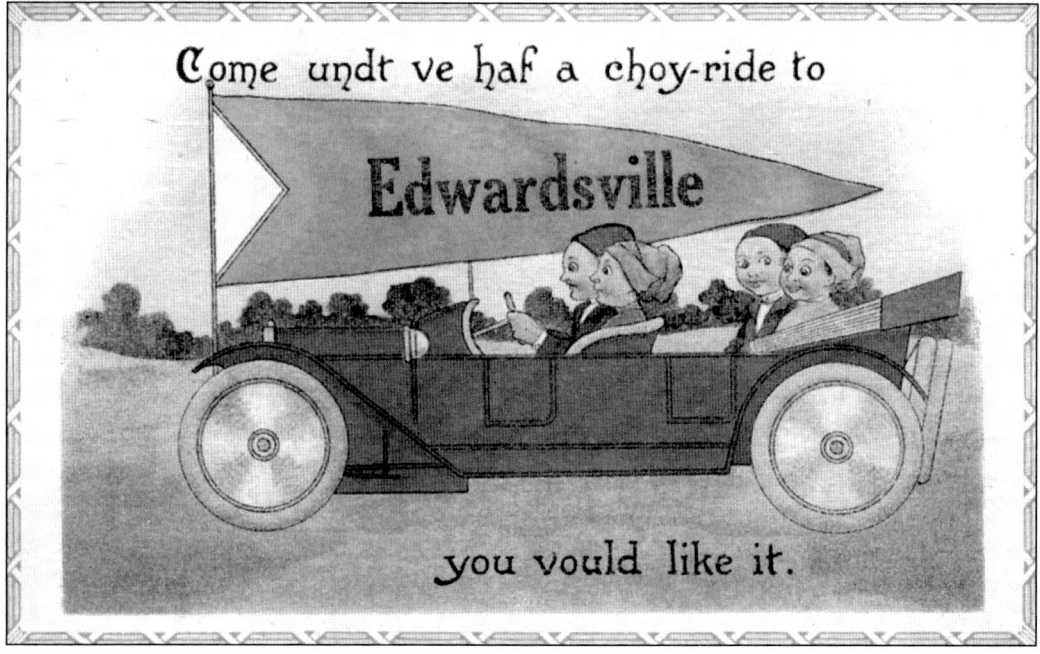

As postcard collecting grew into a wildly popular hobby, different types of postcards appeared, including comic, romantic, history, and fantasy topical cards. Although they were designed primarily with the postcard collector in mind as opposed to serving any particular purpose (such as a tourist view card or a holiday greeting card), they still often reflected the times, such as this comic automobile card, postmarked in 1914. (Courtesy of June Nealy.)

Nine
LIVING THE SOCIAL LIFE

Social life in Edwardsville during the late 1800s through early 1900s ranged from theater openings with ladies in ball gowns to band concerts in Edwardsville City Park, from fishing expeditions at Wolf's Lake to the Czech and German gymnastic societies, and from Sunday school picnics in the summer to sleigh rides in the winter. Messages written on postcards also mention dances, parties, plays, blackberry picking, and traveling.

Two theaters on Main Street provided entertainment, the Tuxhorn Opera House and the Wildey Theatre. The opera house was on the second floor of a building built by John S. Trares in 1884. The facility included 800 seats, dressing rooms, six sets of scenery, and a large stage. A second-floor walkway connected it to the St. James Hotel, which was convenient for hotel guests. In 1906, the Tuxhorn Opera House closed. The Wildey opened in 1909, and a woman wrote in a message to a friend in New York that "They took in over $1,100 at the opening play. Seats were from $3 up. It had poured down rain all day long. But cabs were used, for the theatre gowns were elaborate."

Balls, dances, and parties were plentiful, ranging from the exclusive with admission invitations and newspaper coverage, to the family gatherings of the working class. Numerous fraternal lodges were established and included Knights of Pythias, Catholic Knights of Illinois, True Redeemer Lodge, Illinois United Brothers of Friendship, Order of Pocahontas, Redmen, Grand Army of the Republic, Star Lodge, International Order of Odd Fellows, and Modern Woodmen, as well as Knights of Columbus and Masons, which are to this day still in existence in Edwardsville.

Music was important in social life. The many German immigrants in Edwardsville organized some of the first musical groups, such as the Maennerchor, a men's singing society. Adam and Catherina Schwarz arrived in Edwardsville in 1844, bringing with them a rosewood German accordion. Springing from their children and grandchildren were the Edwardsville Enterprise Band, established in 1885; the Independent Orchestra; and the Schwarz Sisters Orchestra, consisting of all nine daughters of Enterprise Band leader William C. Schwarz.

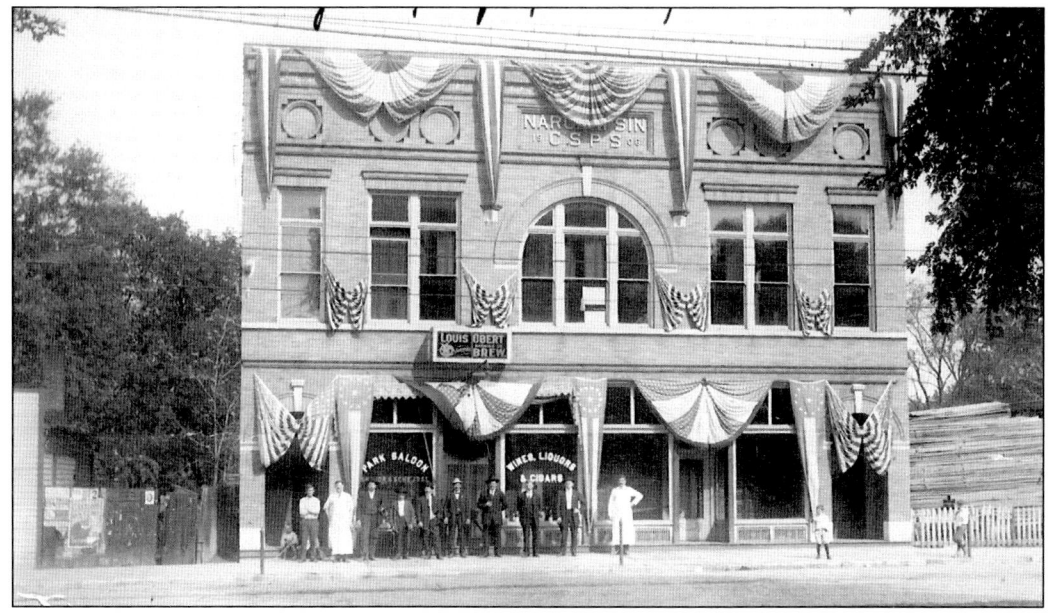

The Narodni Sin, which means National Hall in Czechoslovakian, was built on Vandalia Street in 1906 by Anton Hlad. The letters *CCPS* stand for Cecho Slovensky Podporujici Spolky, or Czechoslovak Protective Society. On the first floor of the building at the time this photograph was taken, probably 1912, was the Park Saloon, its signs offering "wines, liquors and cigars" and "Louis Obert Brew." (Courtesy of Neal Strebel.)

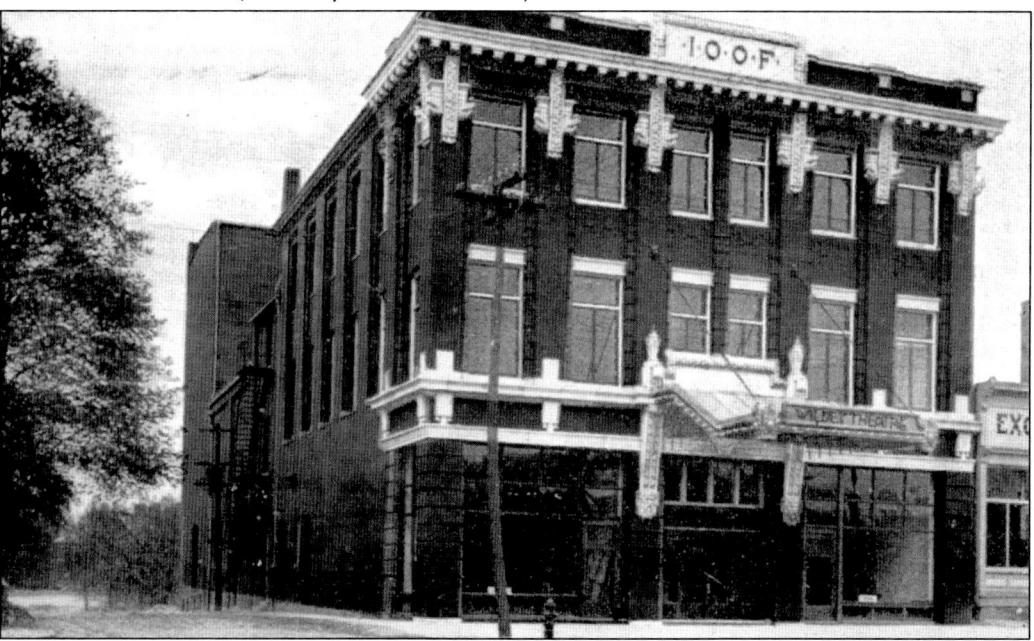

Wildey Theatre on Main Street was constructed as part of the International Order of Odd Fellows (IOOF) lodge in 1909 through an investment effort led by the local chapter. On the third floor was a meeting hall, on the second floor a small theater, and on the main floor a 1,150-seat theater with boxes, balconies, and equipment necessary for major productions. The building was named for Thomas Wildey, who founded the IOOF in 1819. (Courtesy of June Nealy.)

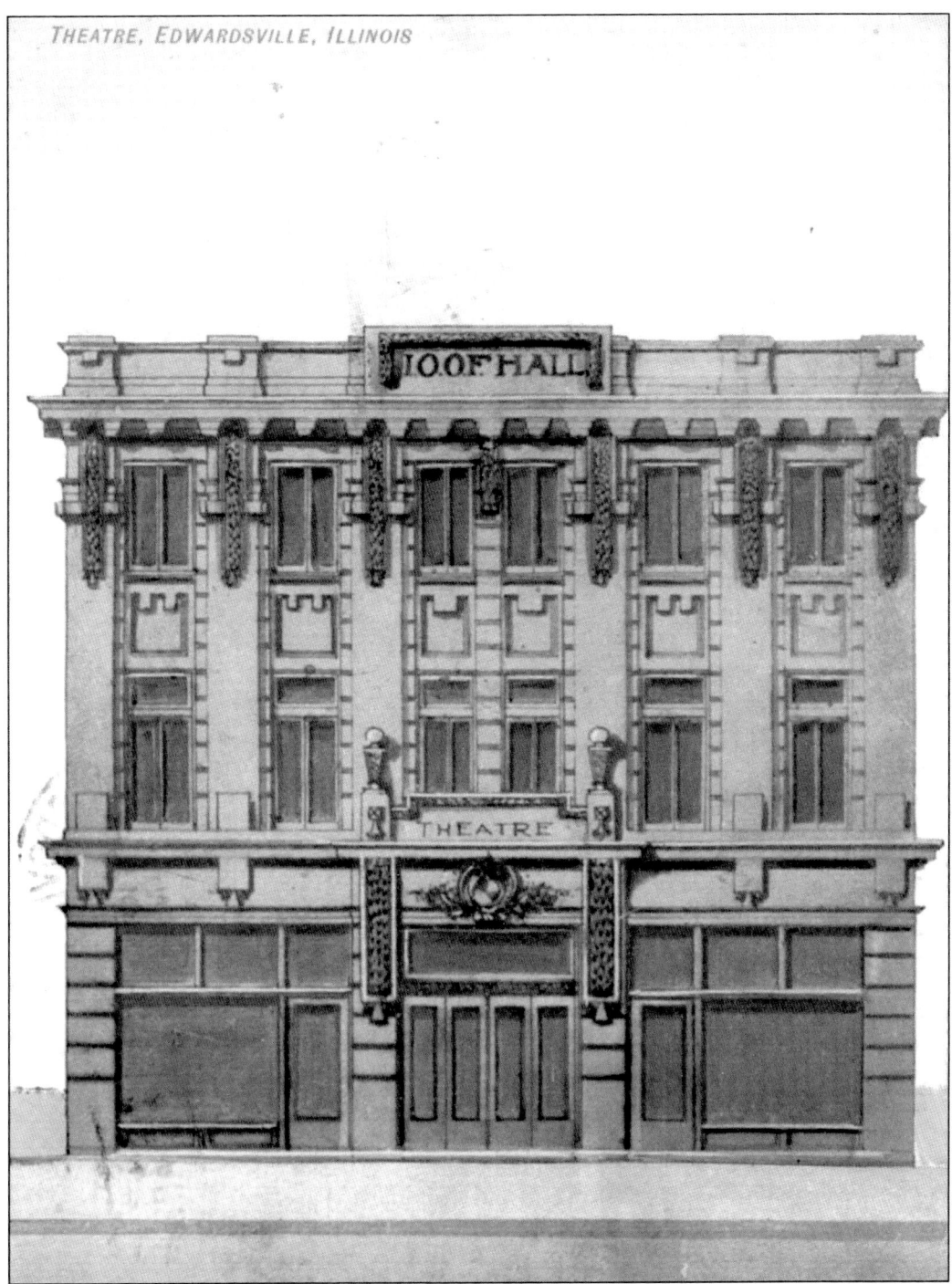

A veritable who's who of big-name entertainment played the Wildey, including W. C. Fields, Al Jolson, and Ginger Rogers. Later on, silent movies and then the talkies were shown. It operated as a movie theater until 1984, when it was closed. The masonry building cost around $30,000 to construct and was designed by architect G. H. Kennerly of St. Louis. Kennerly, along with a party of his friends, attended opening night. (Courtesy of June Nealy.)

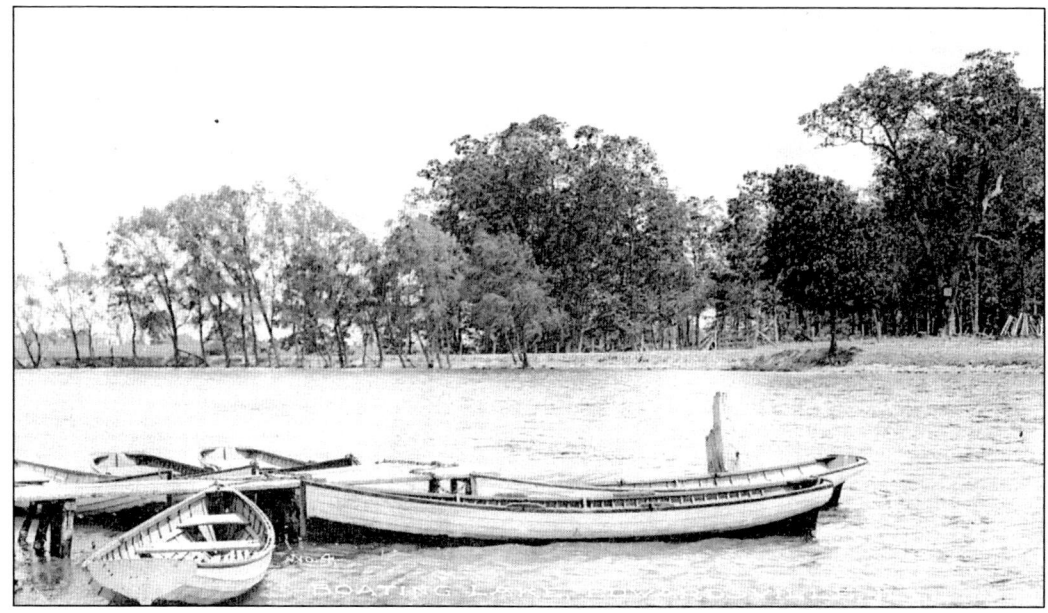

Wolf's Lake, also known as Wolf's Reservoir, was on the south side of Edwardsville between the Madison Coal Company and the National Mastic Roofing Company. It was popular for boating and known to be a good place for fishing. In 1909, a woman named Nonie wrote to a friend in St. Charles, Missouri, on the back of this postcard that "This is a fine place to go fishing—better than the Missouri." (Courtesy of June Nealy.)

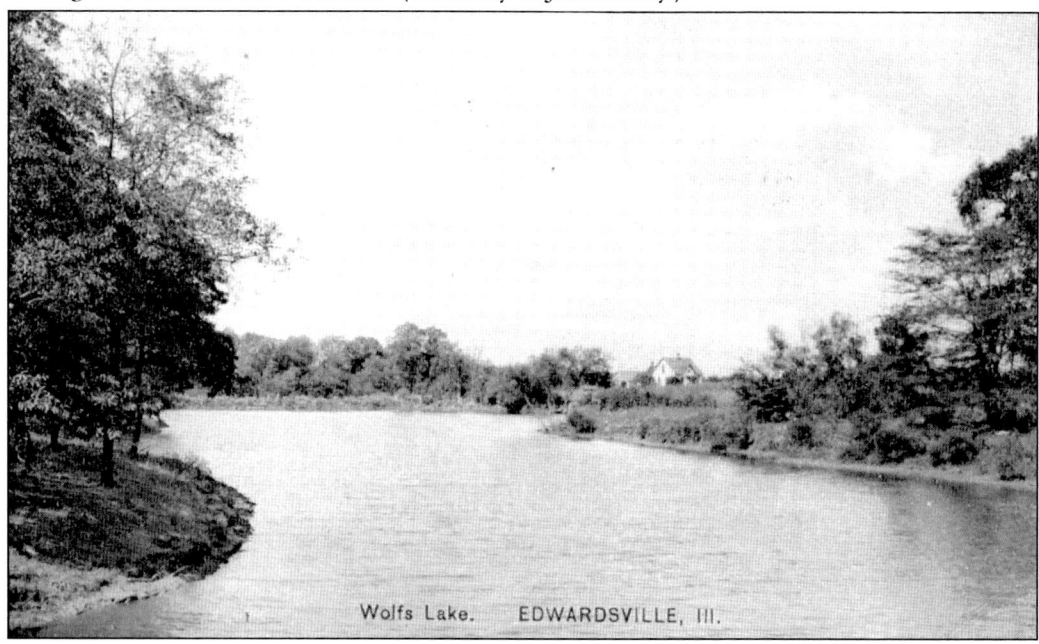

Wolf's Lake also supplied water for nearby industries. The Edwardsville location of Madison Coal Company was formerly Wolf Coal Mining Company. The Fix family moved to Edwardsville and purchased the Benjamin Stephenson house; Fix's daughter married Frederick A. Wolf, and they also moved to Edwardsville. The Wolf family acquired more land in the vicinity and in 1880 formed the Wolf Coal Mining Company. (Courtesy of June Nealy.)

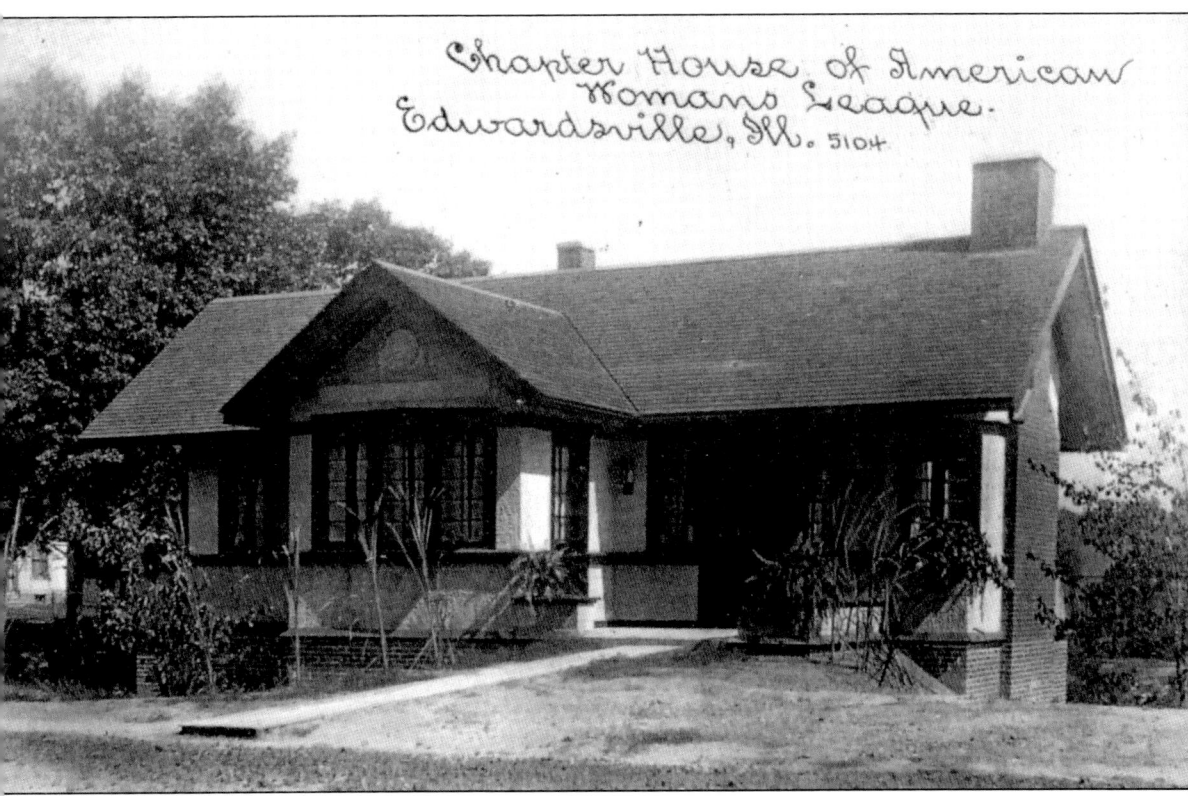

The chapter house of the American Woman's League on High Street was dedicated on July 20, 1909, the first chapter house built by the league. The name and the emblem, a wreath of acanthus leaves, are visible under the front eave. The Terry Chapter's officers were president Agnes McKee, first vice president Josephine Smith, second vice president Jessie Benedict, treasurer Ada Atchinson, and secretary Mrs. David Fiegenbaum. (Courtesy of June Nealy.)

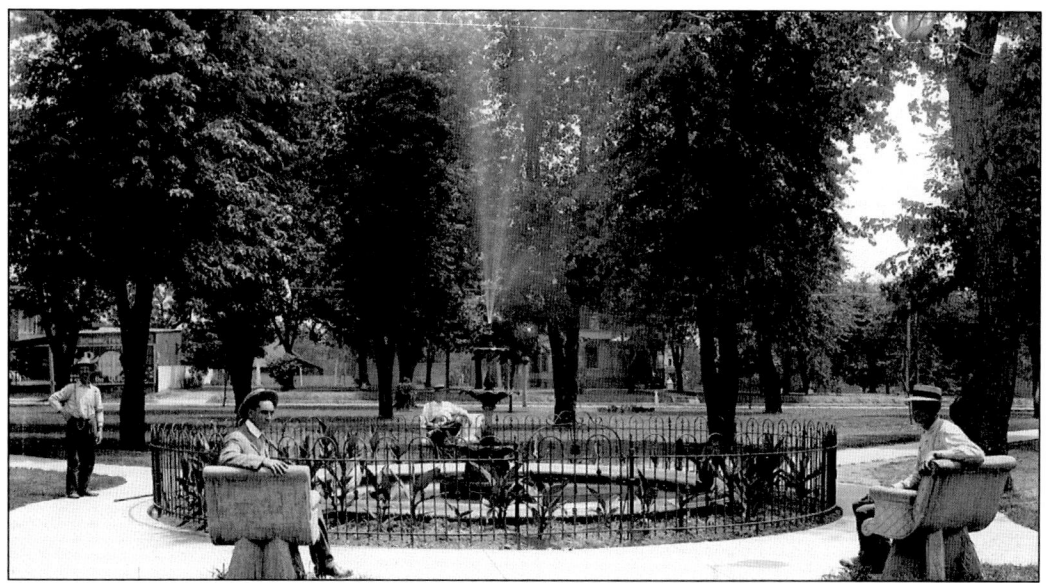

The fountain and benches in Edwardsville City Park in front of the Edwardsville Public Library surely provided many opportunities for social conversation and newspaper reading. Beginning in 1885, the Edwardsville Municipal Band played weekly concerts in City Park during the summer months. In 1899, local No. 98 of the American Federation of Musicians organized in Edwardsville, and since then, the band members have been unionized and paid. (Courtesy of Michael A. Sporrer.)

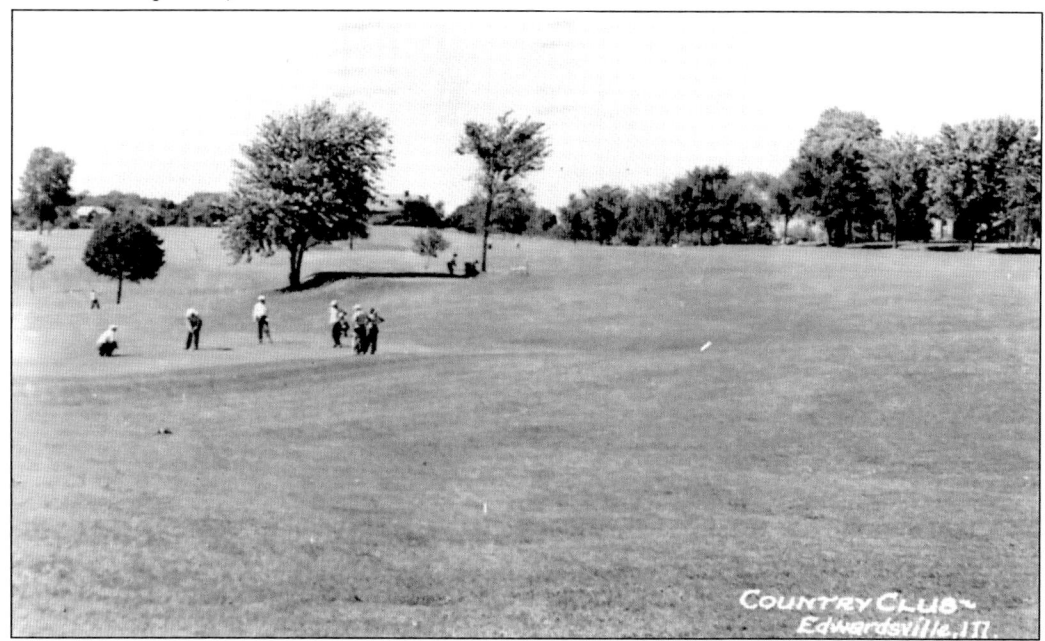

The E.G. Golf Club was established in 1922, with the first nine holes designed in 1924 by Larry Packard. In the 1950s, Packard and Brent Wadsworth worked together on designing the original back nine. Also during that decade, the name was changed to Sunset Hills Country Club. It is one of the oldest golf clubs in southern Illinois and considered still to be steeped in tradition. (Courtesy of Neal Strebel.)

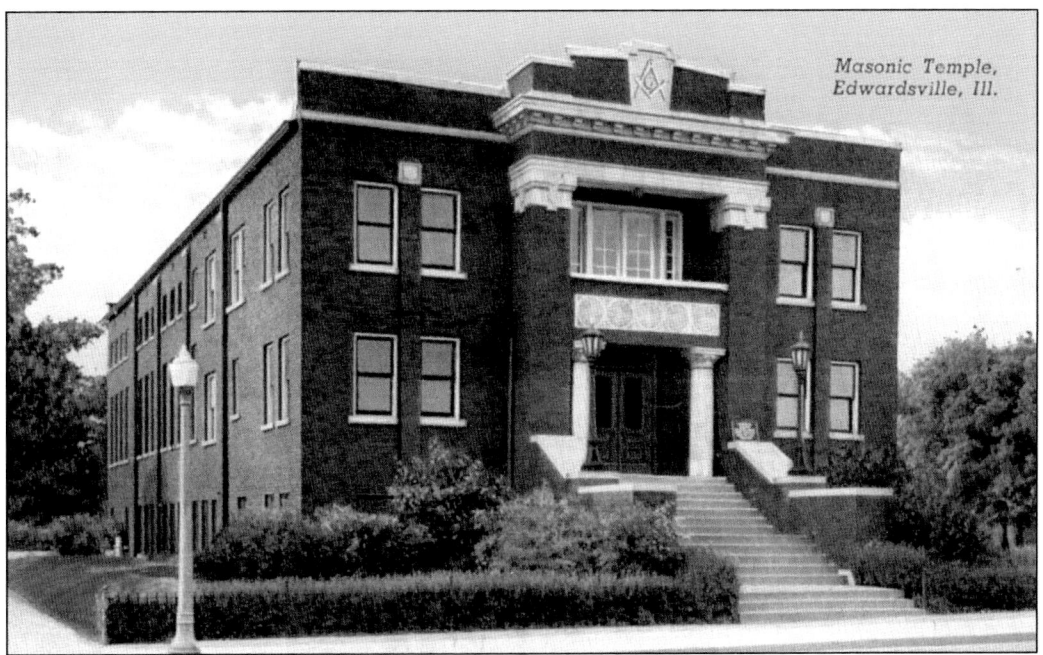

This Masonic temple building was constructed in 1927 on Hillsboro Avenue for Masonic Lodge No. 99, which had received its charter in 1851. There were about 300 members at the time of the building's construction. An earlier lodge, Libanus No. 29, met as early as 1819 in Edwardsville. (Courtesy of June Nealy.)

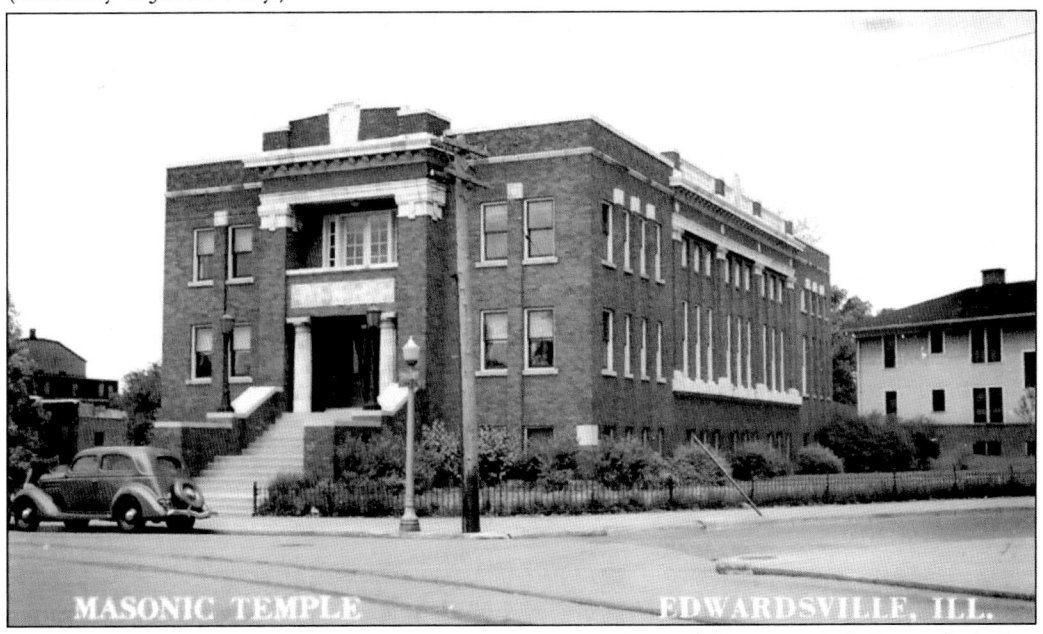

Many prominent Edwardsville men were founding members of the Masonic lodge at their first meeting in the hall of the Sons of Temperance on March 24, 1851, including banker John A. Prickett, William Glass, Matthew and David Gillespie, Dr. John Weir, H. K. Eaton, James S. Jett, and Thomas O. Springer, clerk of the circuit court and recorder of deeds. (Courtesy of June Nealy.)

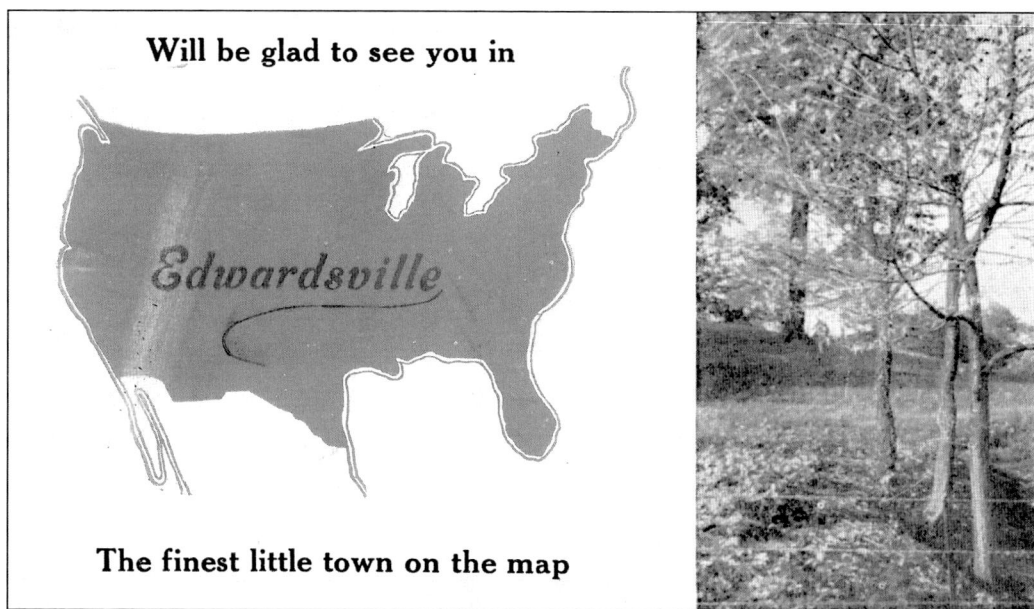

The postcard craze began in Europe in the 1870s and caught fire in the United States in the 1890s. Buying, writing, sending, and collecting postcards became the most popular collectible hobby in the world. In a postcard message, an Edwardsville woman boasted, "I got 105 cards in February and hope to get more in March." Around the dawn of the 20th century, the publishing of printed postcards was said to have doubled every six months. European card publishers began opening offices in the United States around 1907. Many postcards were produced in Germany, where the printing methods and artwork were very good. World War I diminished the supply of cards coming from Germany. Lower quality cards from England and the United States, the influenza epidemic, the telephone, and the movies all helped to bring an end to the golden age of postcards. (Courtesy of June Nealy.)

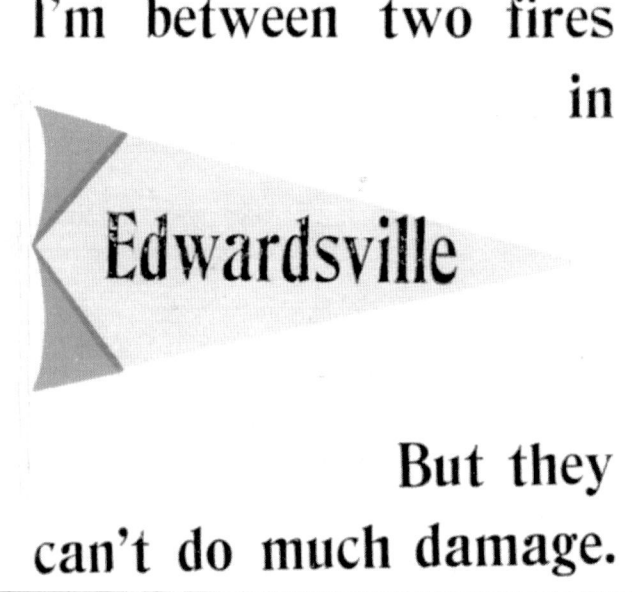 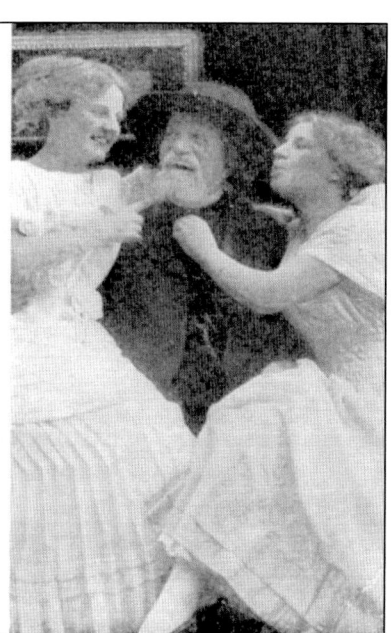

Ten

PARKS, MONUMENTS, AND THE MADISON COUNTY CENTENNIAL

The oldest park in Edwardsville is Lusk Park at 535 Randle Street. It is the site of the city's oldest cemetery and is also considered to be one of the oldest cemetery-parks in the state. It was acquired by the city in 1913 with cooperation by the Lusk family. In the 1930s, many improvements were made. Sod, shrubbery, and rock walks were added after a cleanup of the grounds. The city street department installed a concrete entrance from Randle Street, and an ornamental fence was added along that side. A six-ton "rust-colored boulder" was brought from Pere Marquette State Park and installed on a concrete base, for which Madison County Historical Society planned a commemorative plaque. With additional land donated by the Lusk family, Lusk Park covers 2.8 acres.

Hotz Park, at St. Louis and Randle Streets, has the honor of being the smallest park in the city at 0.2 acres. Named for Henry P. Hotz, who served as mayor from 1902 to 1912, the park is thought to be one of the smallest parks in the state and the nation. The May 18, 1914, issue of the *Intelligencer* stated that Mayor Hotz "put through many public improvements, including the wonderful triangular 'Hotz Park,' which you must not miss seeing if you visit elevated Edwardsville."

City Park is Edwardsville's most centrally located park and took on special significance in 1906 when the Edwardsville Public Library was constructed there, and in 1912, when the Madison County centennial monument was placed there. In 1911, the Illinois state legislature appropriated $5,000 toward the creation and installation of a Madison County centennial monument. At that time, planning for the centennial began in earnest, with civic leader Charles Boeschenstein serving as president of the Edwardsville Centennial Association. Numerous committees planned parades, decorations, exhibits, and dedications. Gov. Charles Deneen, an Edwardsville native, spoke at City Park to a huge crowd and presided over the unveiling of the centennial monument. Edwardsville had gone to great lengths to create a wildly successful celebration that would honor the past century of Madison County's history and of Edwardsville's history, which were inextricably tied.

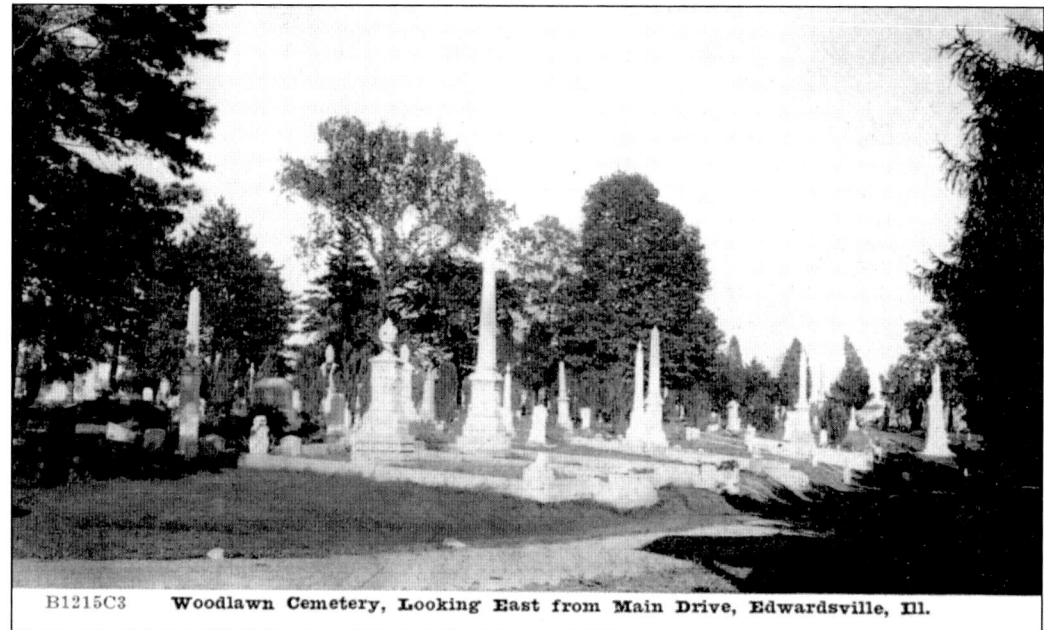

B1215C3 Woodlawn Cemetery, Looking East from Main Drive, Edwardsville, Ill.

Woodlawn Cemetery was established in 1871 near the west end of St. Louis Street, originally known as Fairgrounds Road. The first groundskeeper was John Amschler, hired in 1879. Amschler had served in the Union army during the Civil War. The original public cemetery was established on Randle Street on land donated by pioneer John Lusk. (Courtesy of June Nealy.)

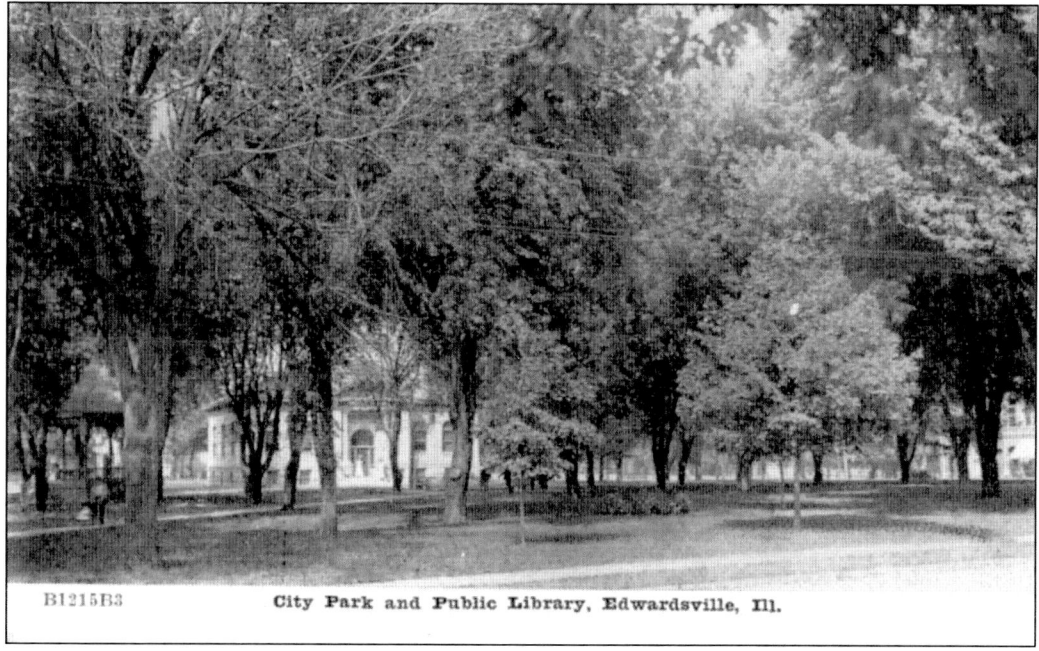

B1215B3 City Park and Public Library, Edwardsville, Ill.

Edwardsville City Park, shown here around 1909 after the public library was built, is bordered by Park, Kansas, Buchanan, and Vandalia Streets and covers 2.088 acres. The April 10, 1889, issue of the *Intelligencer* mentions improvements to the park, including new gravel walks and iron seats and concerts during good weather by the "Enterprise cornet band." (Courtesy of June Nealy.)

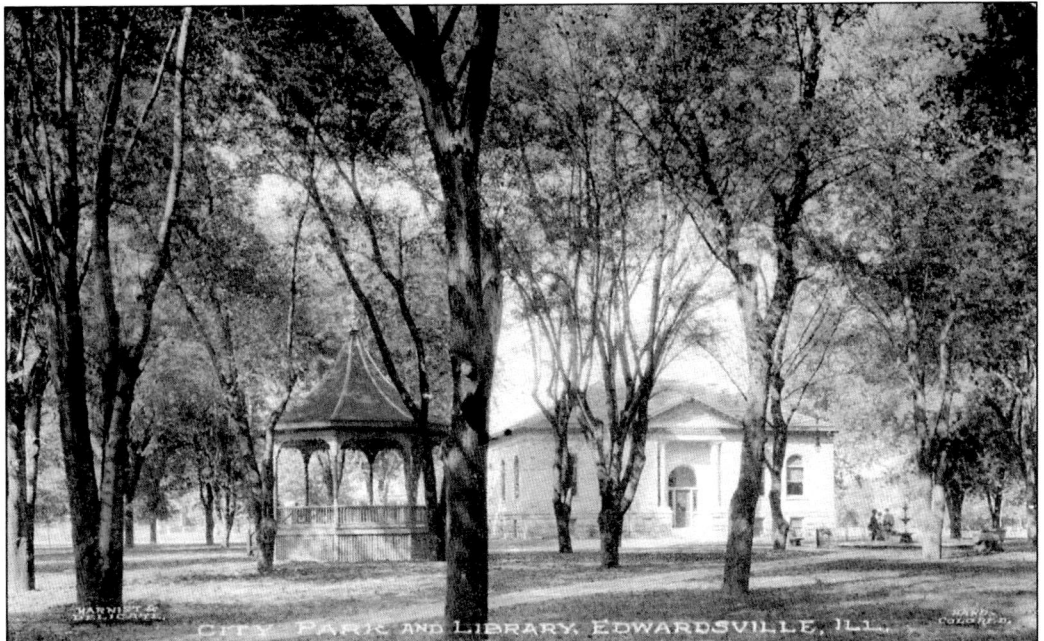

City Park has been the site of band concerts for well over 100 years. Weekly band concerts through summer months were begun in 1885. In 1899, local No. 98 of the American Federation of Musicians organized in Edwardsville, and ever since then, band members have also been union members and have been paid by the city for their services. (Courtesy of June Nealy.)

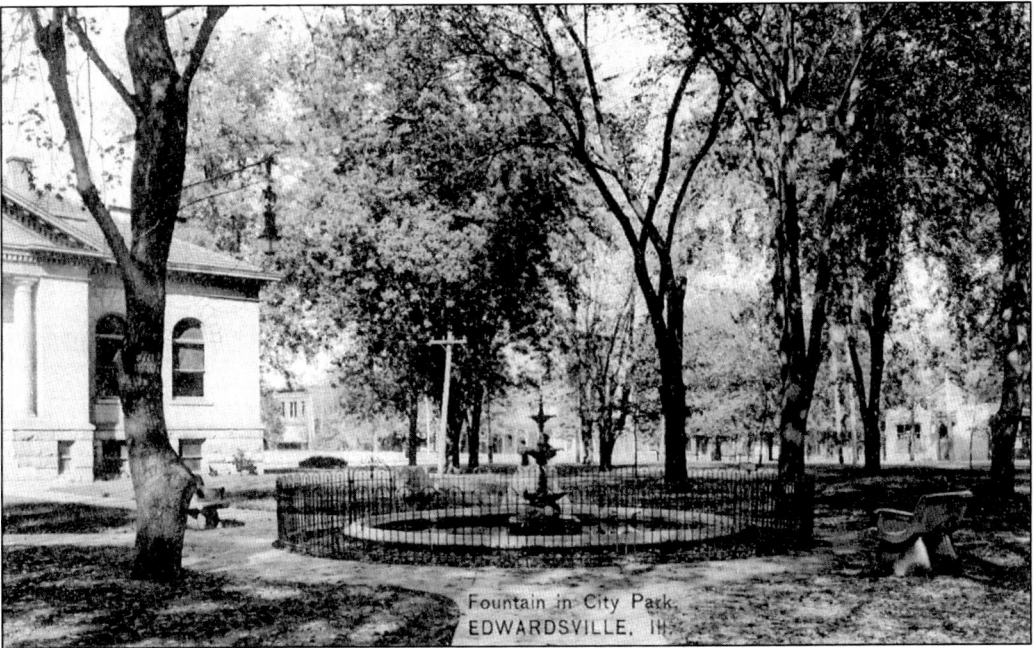

This lovely fountain became part of the landscaping, gracing the lawn in front of the public library on the Buchanan Street side until the Madison County centennial monument was placed there in 1912, leaving the circular fountain ring visible around the base of the new monument. (Courtesy of June Nealy.)

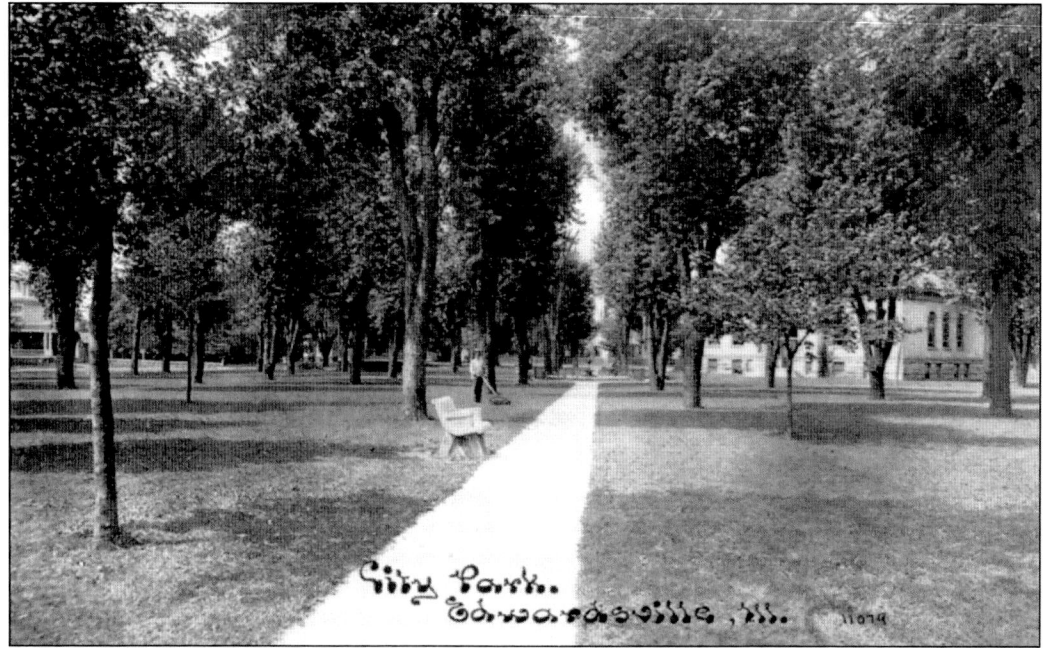

This view of a worker cutting the grass in the block-square, nearly three-acre Edwardsville City Park surrounding the library was taken soon after the dedication of the library in 1906. This path cut across the park from the corner of Buchanan and Park Streets to the intersection of Vandalia and Kansas Streets. (Courtesy of June Nealy.)

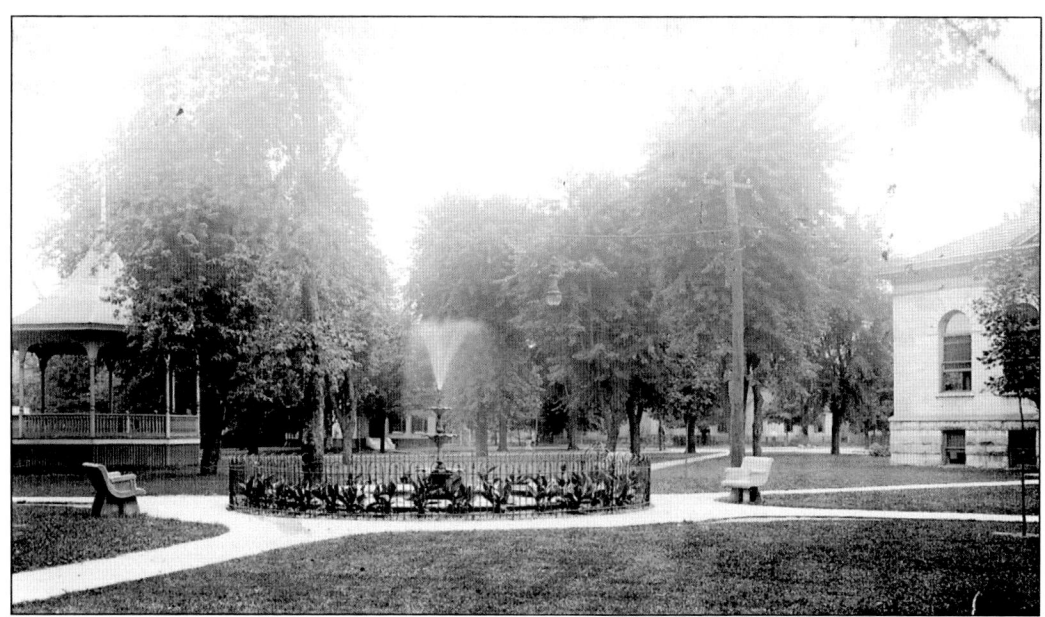

Noted St. Louis photographer H. H. Bregstone captured this view about 1910 of the completed Edwardsville Public Library, the bandstand, the fountain, the walks, and the well-kept landscaping of City Park. Park Street is in the background. (Courtesy of June Nealy.)

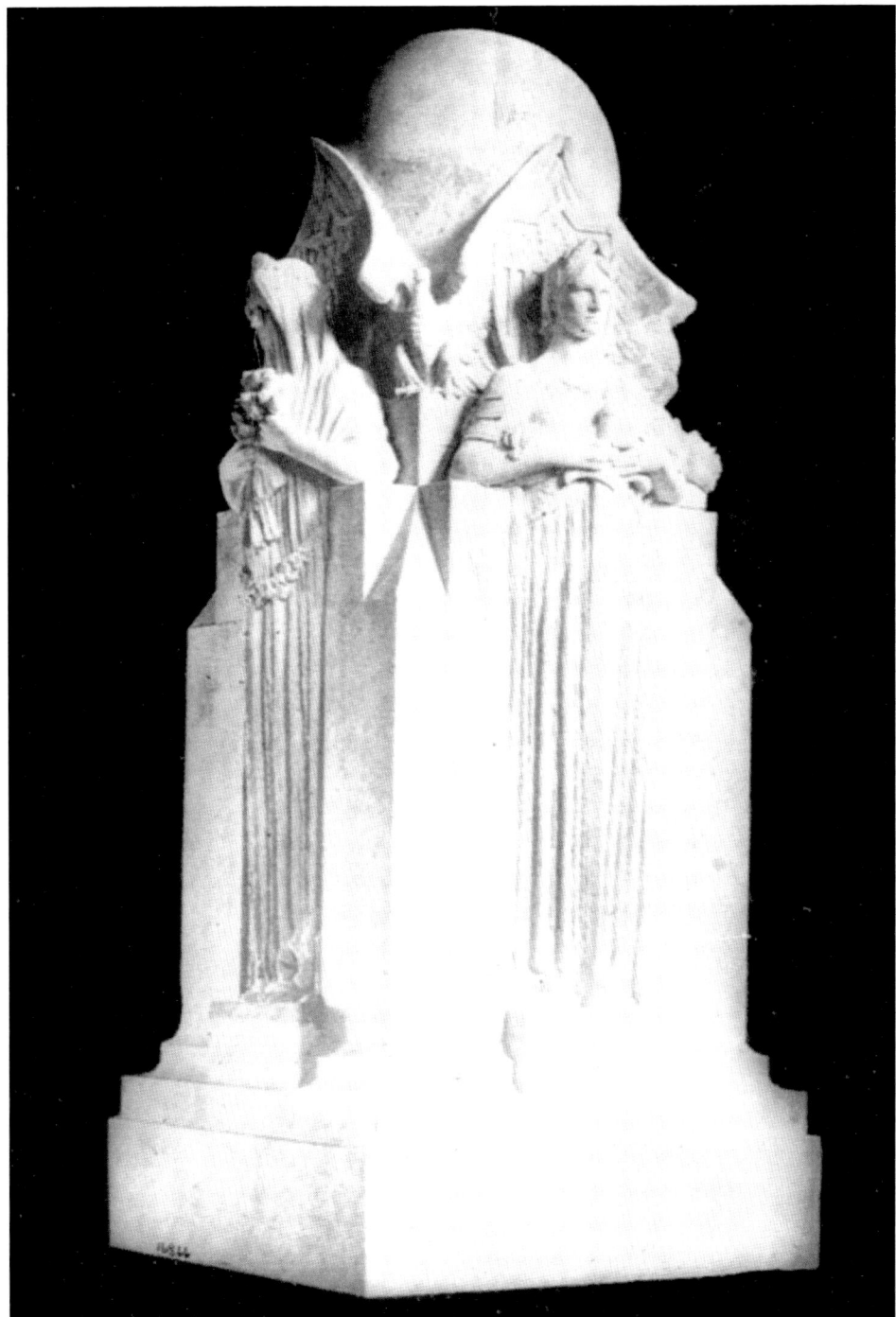

The Madison County centennial monument was commissioned as an outdoor sculpture to be placed in City Park in 1912 as a lasting reminder of the centennial. The monument was made of Georgian marble on a stone base and measures approximately 15 by 6 by 6 feet. The monument was footed on the basin of the old fountain; the ring of that fountain is still visible. (Courtesy of June Nealy.)

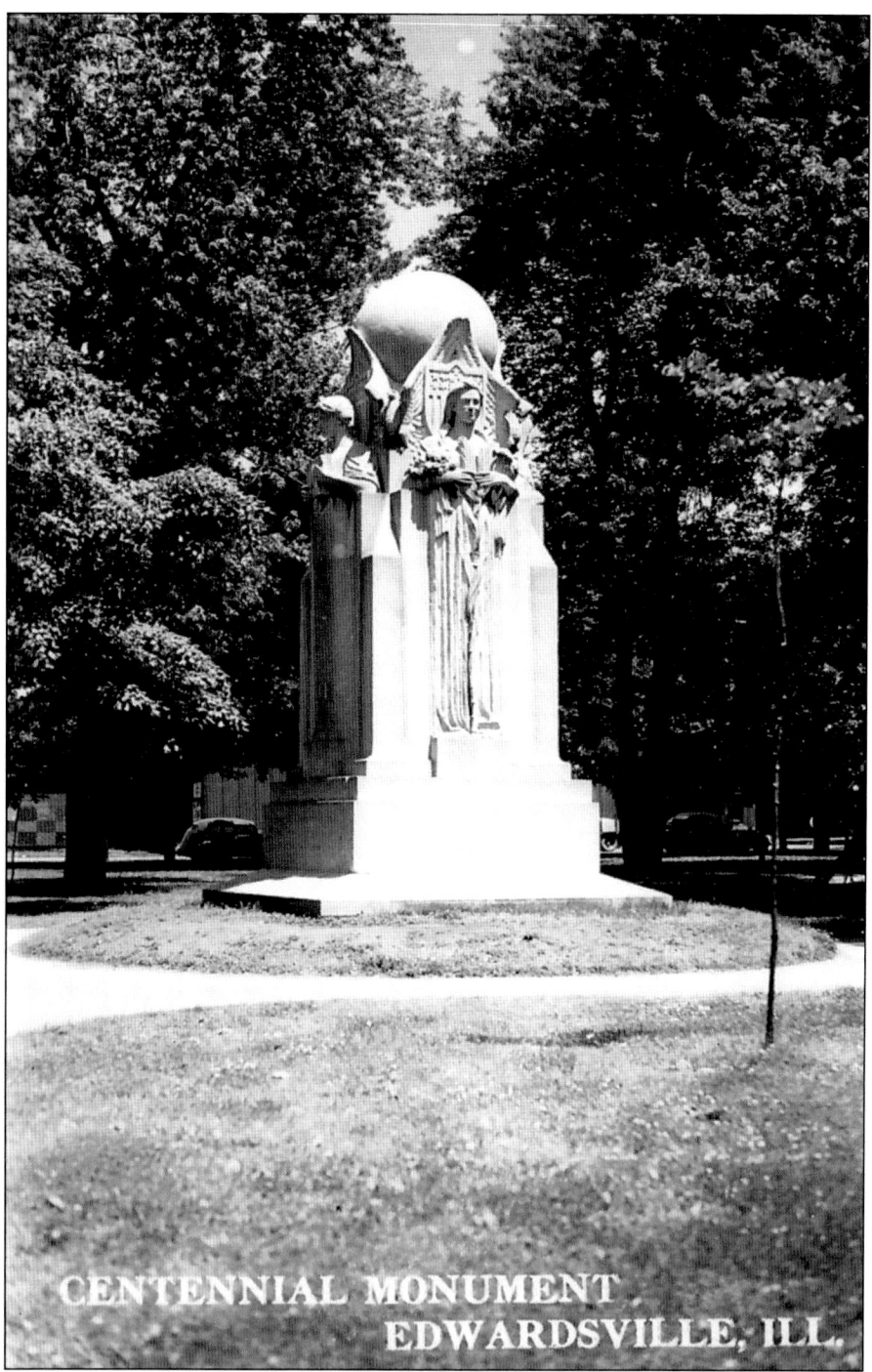

The inscription on the front of the monument reads, "In grateful memory of the early settlers who by courage industry and endurance transformed a wilderness into a land of order place and plenty." The inscription carved on the back reads, "Commemorating a century of achievement Madison County founded September 4, 1812 erected by the State of Illinois." (Courtesy of June Nealy.)

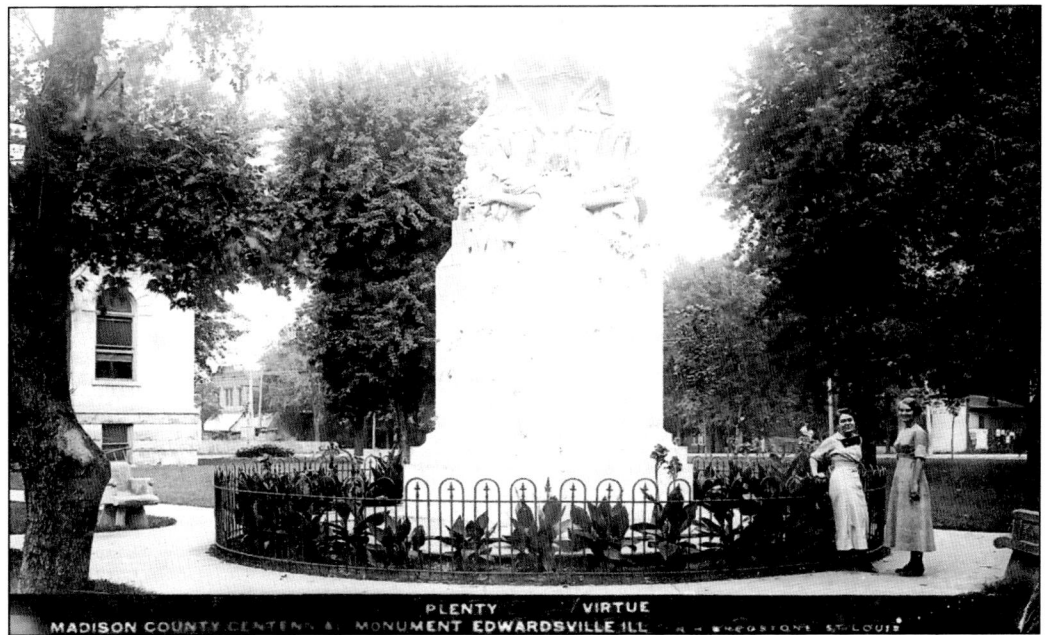

The sculpture depicts the four cardinal points of civilization and progress. The female figures represent Learning (book and pen), Justice (sword and tow pillars), Plenty (fruit and grain), and Virtue (veiled maiden). The four figures stand back to back, with a large globe engraved with the state of Illinois at the top in the center. (Courtesy of June Nealy.)

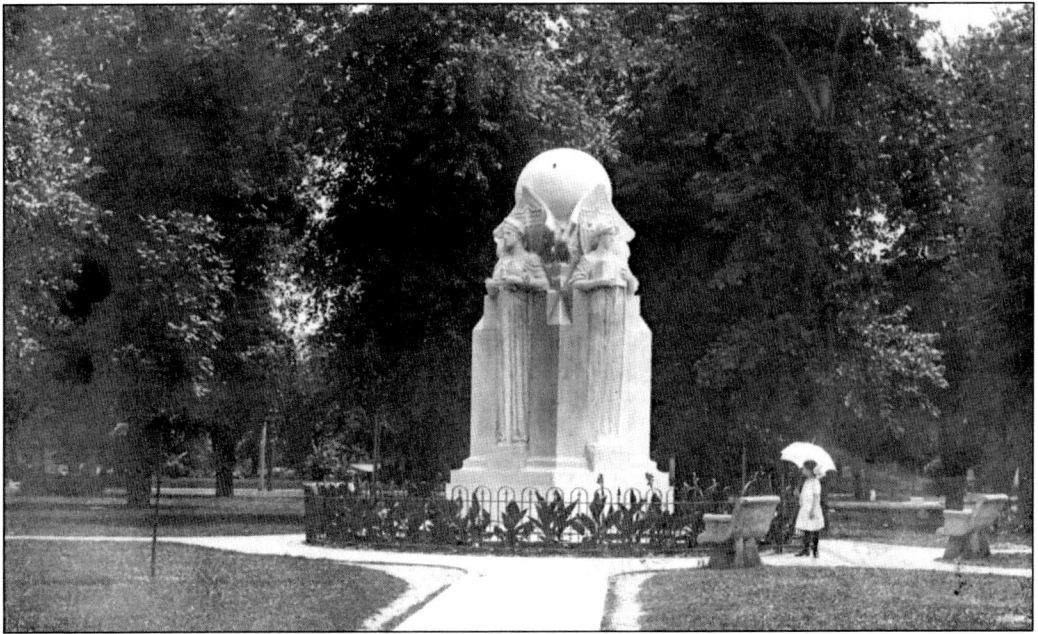

The monument was created by sculptor Charles J. Mulligan (1866–1916), who created a number of other sculptures in the Midwest: *Lincoln the Rail Splitter* at Garfield Park and *Lincoln the Orator* at Oak Woods Cemetery, both in Chicago; *Law and Knowledge* and *Justice and Power*, both at the Illinois Supreme Court Building in Springfield; and *Peace Monument* at the Adams County Courthouse in Decatur, Indiana. (Courtesy of June Nealy.)

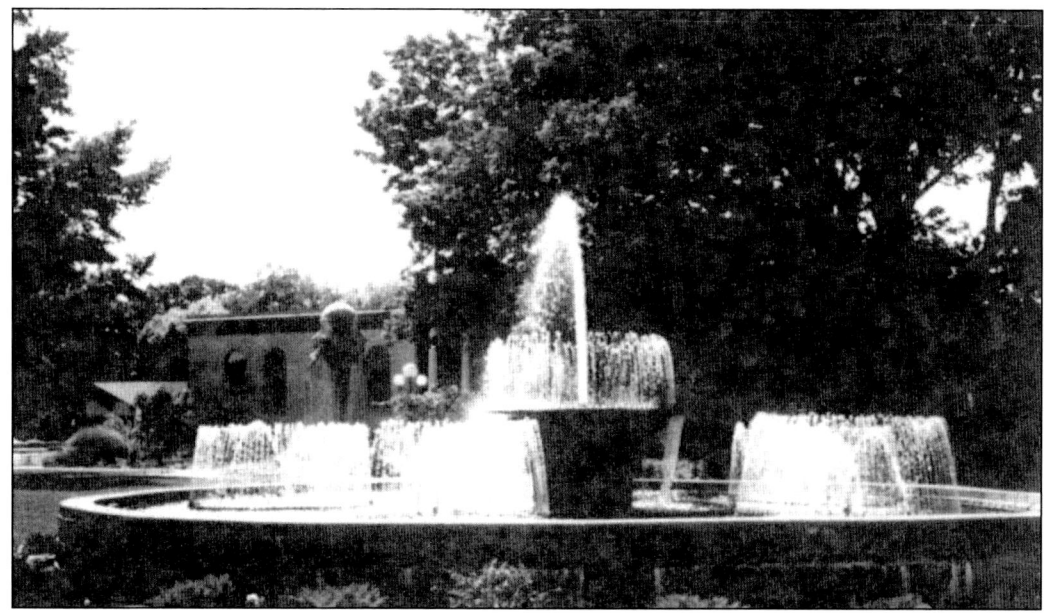

When the centennial monument was placed on the old fountain base in front of the Edwardsville Public Library, another fountain was soon created northeast of the old fountain location. The new fountain was donated by Mr. and Mrs. Richard Bearden. (Courtesy of Michael A. Sporrer.)

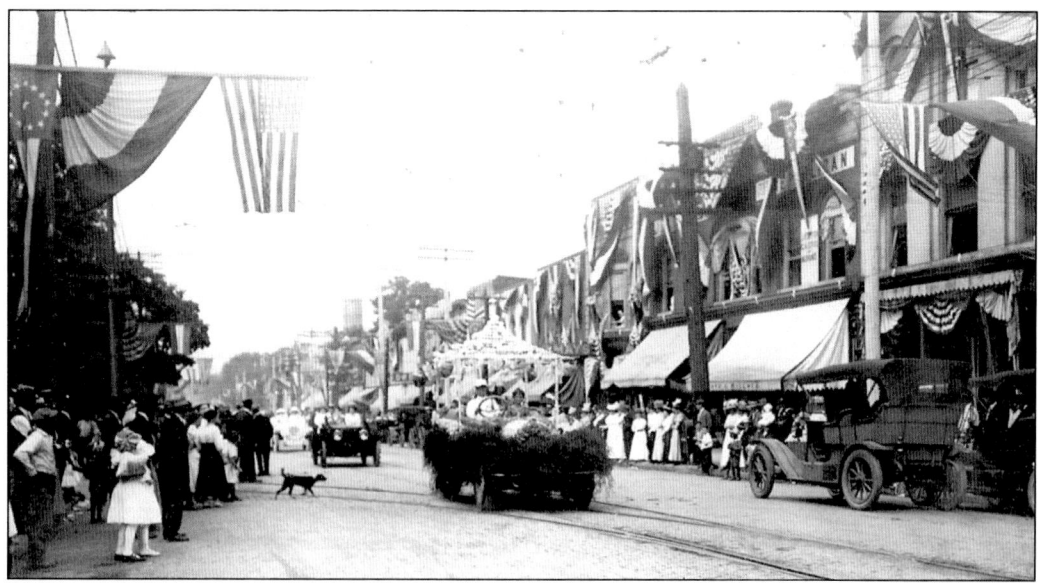

The Madison County centennial festivities began on September 14, 1912, and lasted for eight days. Factory whistles, bells, and 100 rounds shot from a cannon set up in Leclaire Park signaled the beginning of the festival. (Courtesy of Neal Strebel.)

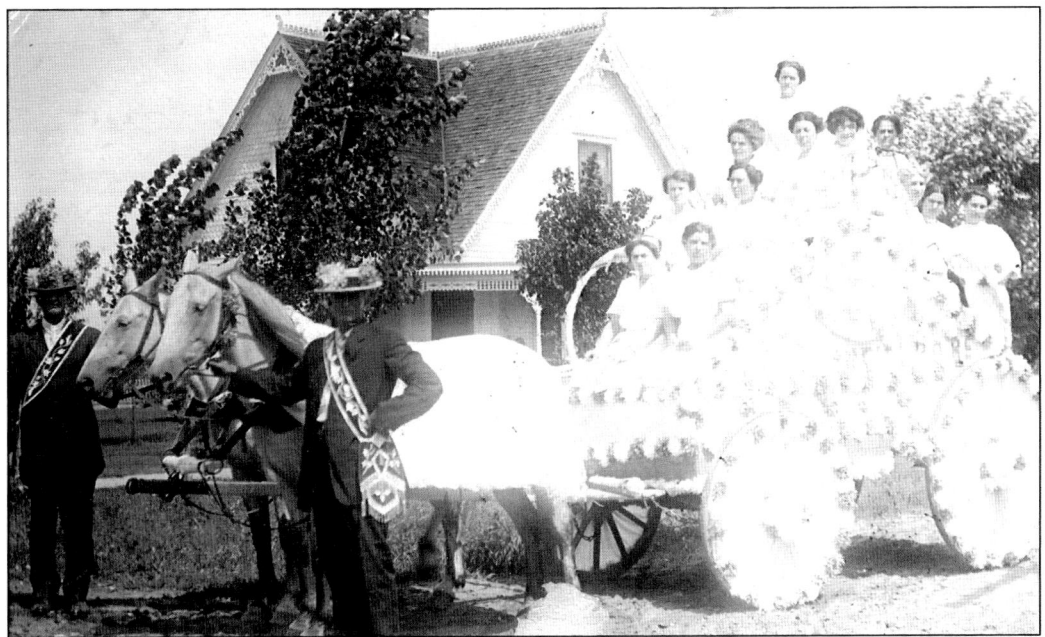

Besides the parades, special ceremonies were held at the Fort Russell site and at the building of Thomas Kirkpatrick, an early pioneer. In an open field nearby, airplanes landed and took off. A number of citizens bravely took flights that day, including the first Madison County female to fly in an airplane, Mary Lusk. (Courtesy of Neal Strebel.)

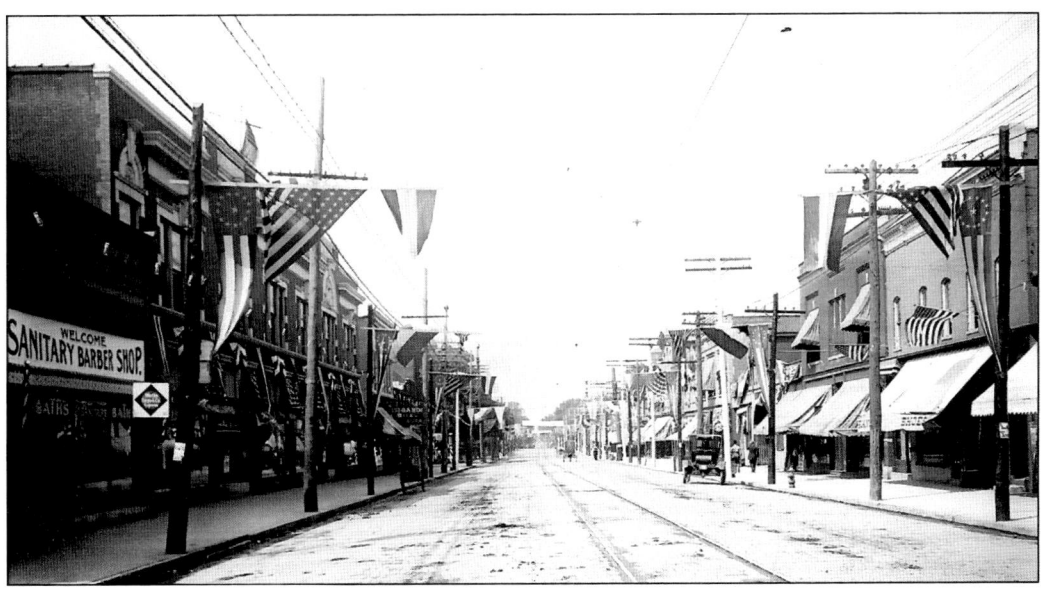

Main Street was decorated with 200,000 square yards of bunting and flags during centennial week. Numerous parades were held, family gatherings were planned, native sons and daughters returned home, and a historical exhibit of treasured family mementos was put on display in the school buildings on Kansas Street. (Courtesy of Neal Strebel.)

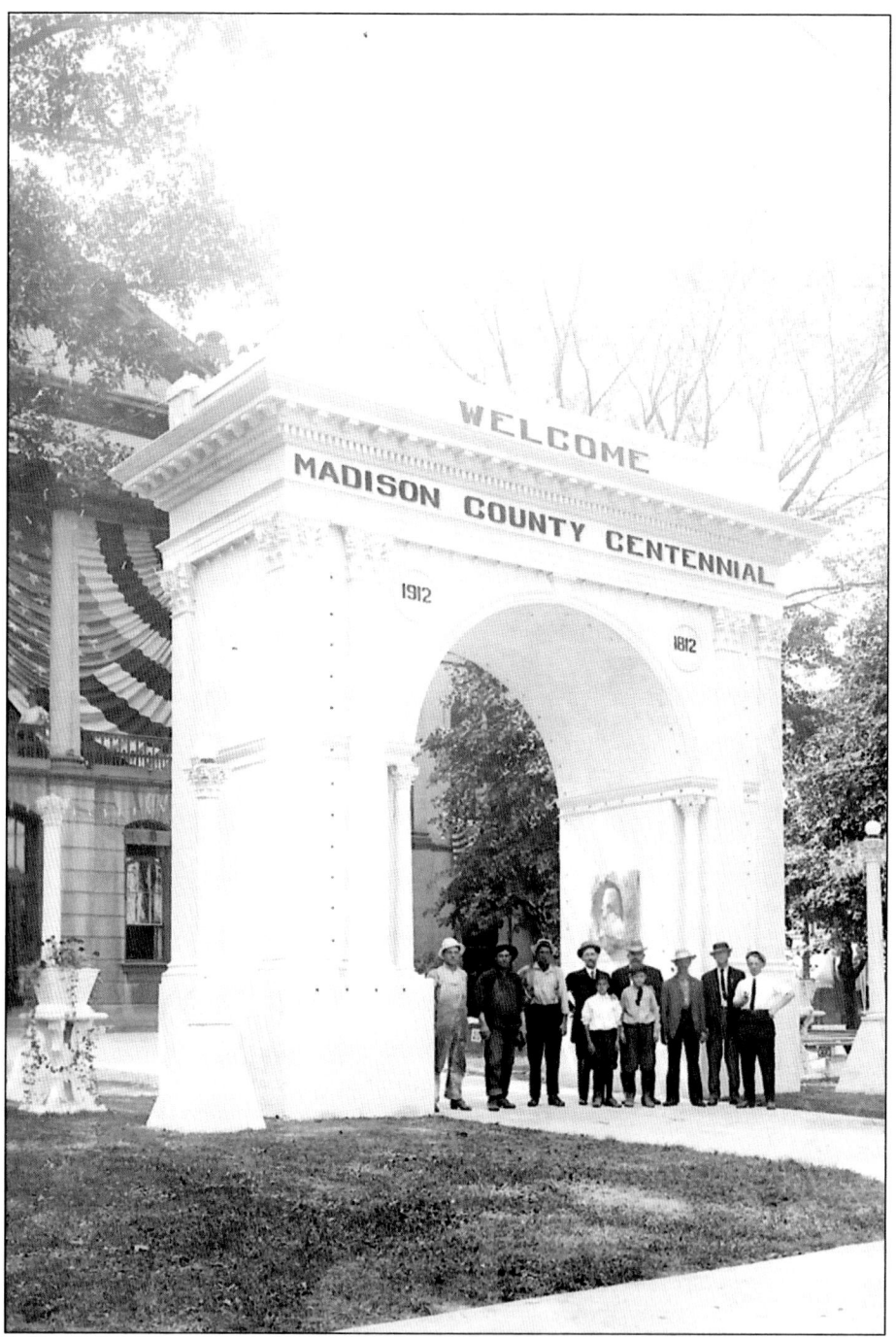

The Madison County centennial arch was designed by local architect M. B. Kane and was made of plaster of paris. Styled after a Parisian design and intended to recall the splendor of the 1904 Louisiana Purchase Exposition, it was erected in 1912 in front of the 1857 courthouse on North Main Street. In a weeklong celebration, Edwardsville citizens took a look back at Madison County's century of history and the nearly 100 years of progress of their own city. Undoubtedly, some wondered what the next 100 years would bring. (Courtesy of June Nealy.)

Bibliography

Blain, Robert R., editor. *A History of the Cooperative Village of Leclaire.* Edwardsville, Illinois: Leclaire Centennial Committee, 1997.

Brink, W. R. and Company. *History of Madison County, Illinois.* Edwardsville, Illinois: W. R. Brink and Company, 1882.

Davis, James E. *Frontier Illinois.* Bloomington and Indianapolis: Indiana University Press, 1998.

Flagg, James S. *Our 150 Years: Madison County Illinois 1812–1962.* Edwardsville, Illinois: East 10 Publishing Company Inc., 1962.

Hair, James T. *Gazetteer of Madison County.* Alton, Illinois: James T. Hair, 1866.

Historic Tour of Edwardsville: Pre Civil War Buildings and Sites of Interest. Edwardsville, Illinois: Edwardsville Economic Development Commission and Edwardsville Historic Preservation Commission, 1998.

Historic Tour of Leclaire Village: A National Historic District. Edwardsville, Illinois: Edwardsville Economic Development Commission and Edwardsville Historic Preservation Commission, 1998.

Historic Tour of St. Louis Street: A National Historic District. Edwardsville, Illinois: Edwardsville Historic Preservation Commission.

Morrison, SJ. *A Centennial History: Trinity Lutheran Church, Edwardsville, Illinois.* Edwardsville, Illinois, 2001.

Nore, Ellen, and Dick Norrish. *Edwardsville: An Illustrated History.* St. Louis: G. Bradley Publishing, 1996.

Portrait and Biographical Record of Madison County, Illinois. Chicago: Biographical Publishing Company, 1891.

Ress, David. *Governor Edward Coles and the Vote to Forbid Slavery in Illinois, 1823-1824.* Jefferson, North Carolina: McFarland and Company, Inc., 2006.

Williams, Nola Jones. *Lincoln School Memories: A History of Blacks in Edwardsville Illinois.* Privately published, 1986.

Youngs, J. William T. *American Realities: Historical Episodes, Volume II From Reconstruction to the Present.* Fourth edition. New York: Longman, 1997.

Discover Thousands of Local History Books Featuring Millions of Vintage Images

Arcadia Publishing, the leading local history publisher in the United States, is committed to making history accessible and meaningful through publishing books that celebrate and preserve the heritage of America's people and places.

Find more books like this at
www.arcadiapublishing.com

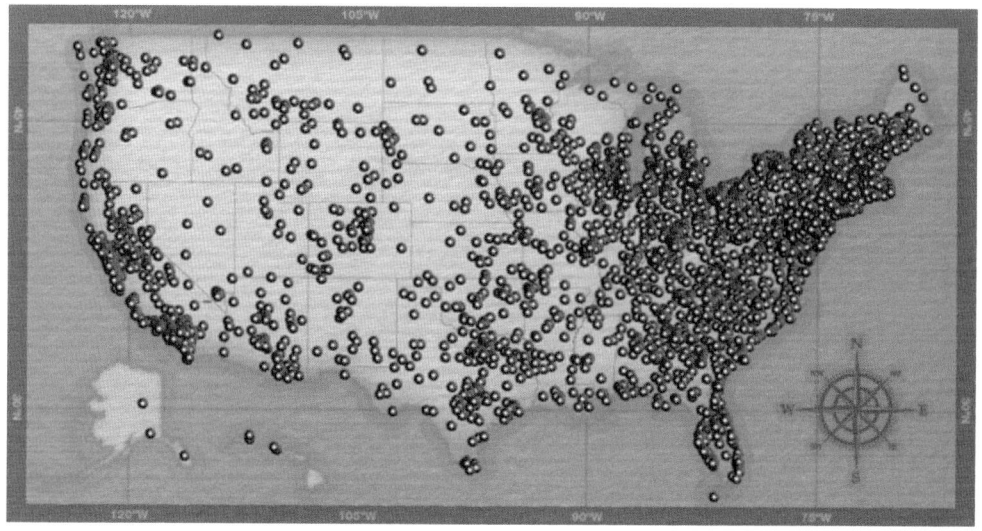

Search for your hometown history, your old stomping grounds, and even your favorite sports team.

Consistent with our mission to preserve history on a local level, this book was printed in South Carolina on American-made paper and manufactured entirely in the United States. Products carrying the accredited Forest Stewardship Council (FSC) label are printed on 100 percent FSC-certified paper.

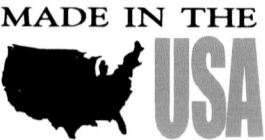

MADE IN THE USA